GOING PUBLIC

Everything You Need to Know to Take Your Company Public, Including Internet Direct Public Offerings

JAMES B. ARKEBAUER
with RON SCHULTZ

Dearborn
Financial Publishing, Inc.®

This publication is designed to provide accurate and authoritative information in regard to the subject matter covered. It is sold with the understanding that the publisher is not engaged in rendering legal, accounting, or other professional service. If legal advice or other expert assistance is required, the services of a competent professional person should be sought.

Acquisitions Editor: Danielle Egan-Miller
Managing Editor: Jack Kiburz
Interior Design: Lucy Jenkins
Cover Design: Scott Rattray, Rattray Design

© 1998 by James B. Arkebauer

Published by Dearborn Financial Publishing, Inc.®

Printed in the United States of America

98 99 00   10 9 8 7 6 5 4 3 2 1

Library of Congress Cataloging-in-Publication Data

Arkebauer, James B., 1939–
    Going public : everything you need to know to take your company
public, including Internet direct public offerings / James B.
Arkebauer, Ronald M. Schultz
        p.   cm.
    Rev. ed. of: The entrepreneur's guide to going public.   Dover, N.H.:
Upstart, 1994.
    Includes index.
    ISBN 0-7931-2835-8 (pbk.)
    1. Going public (Securities)—United States.   2. Going public
(Securities)—Law and legislation—United States.   3. Corporations—
United States—Finance.   I. Schultz, Ronald M., 1951–   II. Arkebauer,
James B., 1939–   The entrepreneur's guide to going public.
HG4028.S7A75   1998
658.15′224—dc21   97-48651
                                                                    CIP

Contents

Preface   xi

Acknowledgments   xiii

Introduction   xv
What's the IPO Outlook?   xv
Who Are the IPO Players?   xvi
Is My Company Ready?   xviii

PART ONE
Overview of the Process

1. The Advantages and Disadvantages of Going Public   **3**
Advantages for the Company   4
Advantages for the Founders   6
Benefits for Employees   7
The Securities Exchanges   7
The Disadvantages of the Public Marketplace   9
Frequently Asked Questions   15

2. Alternatives to Going Public   **16**
Private Financing   17
Debt Financing   17
Subordinated Debt   18
Sources of Debt Financing   19
Other Options   22
Frequently Asked Questions   25

3. The Cost of Doing Business   26
Underwriter Costs   27
Professional Costs   29
Additional Up-Front Costs   31
Hidden and Future Costs   33
Frequently Asked Questions   34

4. Timing   35
Time Planning   38
A Two-Step Process   38
Timetable   39
Frequently Asked Questions   39

5. The Business Plan   42
The Next Step   44
Business Plan Structure   45
Preprivate Financing   47
Special Executive Summary   47
Follow-Up   48
Frequently Asked Questions   48

PART TWO
Assembling the IPO Team

6. The Management Team   51
Frequently Asked Questions   56

7. The Board of Directors   57
Good and Bad Boards   57
An Informed Board Is a Helpful Board   59
What to Expect from a Board of Directors and What Not   59
Makeup of the Board   61
Board of Advisers (Advisory Committee)   63
For Directors Only   63
Officers' and Directors' Questionnaire   64
Frequently Asked Questions   64

8. Consultants and Advisers   65
Consultants   65
Advisers   68
Planning Ahead   70
Frequently Asked Questions   71

9. Accountants   **72**
A Brief History Lesson   72
Selecting Accountants   74
Preparation   75
Auditing   76
Familiarity Is a Must   77
GAAP Must Be Observed   78
Time Costs Money   79
Auditors Are Accountable   80
Frequently Asked Questions   80

10. Attorneys   **82**
Letting Go   82
The Difference between Large and Small Law Firms   83
Getting Along   84
Questions to Ask   84
Billings and Fees   85
Legal Responsibilities   87
The Multiple Counsel Approach   87
Frequently Asked Questions   88

11. Financial Printers   **89**
Costs   90
Qualifying the Financial Printer   91
Ancillary Services   91
Frequently Asked Questions   92

12. Financial Public Relations   **93**
The Public Relations Mystique   93
Four Steps to Effective Corporate Financial PR   94
The Public Relations Difference   95
The Rewards of Financial PR   96
Making a Commitment   97
Choose a Professional   98
Start Early, Stay Late   98
Where Do You Find Them?   99
Evaluating the Financial PR Firm   99
Frequently Asked Questions   101

13. Transfer Agents   **103**
Frequently Asked Questions   105

PART THREE
Before the Offering

14. Incorporating the Public Company   **109**
State Laws   109
Articles of Incorporation   110
Frequently Asked Questions   117

15. Stock Control   **118**
Percentages Do Not Necessarily Mean Control   119
Frequently Asked Questions   120

16. Valuation and Pricing   **122**
Preliminary Considerations   122
Alternatives   124
Selling Shareholders   124
Valuation versus Pricing   125
Price-Earnings Ratio   126
Pricing   127
Frequently Asked Questions   129

17. The SEC   **130**
Investigation and Enforcement   131
Information Availability   132
Frequently Asked Questions   132

18. Federal Securities Legislation   **134**
History   134
The Securities Act of 1933   135
The Securities Exchange Act of 1934   136
Other Significant Legislation   137
Frequently Asked Questions   138

**19. Regulation D and Alternative Methods of
Private Financing**   **139**
Preprivate   140
Private   141
Regulation D (Reg D)   142
Alternative Methods of Private Financing   149
SCOR and ULOR and U-7   154
Avoiding Integration   155
Frequently Asked Questions   155

20. Due Diligence   **157**
Legal Responsibility   157
Corporate Cleanup   159
Accounting Due Diligence   161
Dual Responsibility   162
Frequently Asked Questions   162

21. Underwriters   **163**
Types of Underwriters   164
Types of Underwritings   166
Finders   168
Shopping   169
Underwriter Selection   170
The Underwriter's Dilemma   172
Underwriting Agreement   178
Frequently Asked Questions   181

22. Self-Underwriting   **183**
The Big Fallacy   183
The Carrot   184
Market Makers   184
"Blue-Skying"   185
Pros and Cons   185
Frequently Asked Questions   186

PART FOUR
The Public Offering Process

23. The Registration Statement   **189**
The Regulations   190
Filing Process   192
The Registration Statement Part I (the Prospectus)   193
The Registration Statement Part II   204
Misstatements   204
Officers' and Directors' Questionnaire   205
Overview of the Process   205
Frequently Asked Questions   206

24. Filing and Review   **208**
Prefiling Conferences   208
Filing Technicalities   209
Initial Filing   210
Comment/Deficiency Letter   211

Types of Reviews   213
Amendments   213
Preliminary Prospectus (Red Herring)   215
Stop Order   216
Stickers   217
Acceleration Letter   218
State Filings (Blue-Sky Laws)   218
NASD Review   221
Frequently Asked Questions   222

25. Selling the Issue   **223**
Barred Publicity during Registration   224
Allowed Publicity during Registration   225
Brokers' Due Diligence Meetings   226
Tombstones   230
Escrow   231
Closing   231
Frequently Asked Questions   234

26. Listings   **236**
The New York Stock Exchange   236
The American Stock Exchange   237
The Regional Exchanges   238
The Over-the-Counter Market   238
Public Listings   243
Broker-Dealers and Wholesale Market Makers   243
Frequently Asked Questions   244

PART FIVE
Completing the Public Offering

27. Aftermarket Trading   **249**
Overallotment   250
Market Makers   252
Analysts   255
Frequently Asked Questions   258

28. Continual Reporting   **259**
Form SR: Application of Proceeds   260
Form 8-K: Current Reports   261
Forms 10-K and 10-KSB: Annual Report   262
Forms 10-Q and 10-QSB: Quarterly Report   263
The Annual Report   265

FCPA: The Foreign Corrupt Practices Act   268
Form 3   269
Form 4   270
Insider Reporting and Trading Restrictions   270
Schedules   271
Other Forms and Schedules   273
Frequently Asked Questions   274

29. SEC Rule 144   **276**
One-Year Period and Two-Year Period   276
Affiliates   278
Other Considerations   278
Frequently Asked Questions   279

30. The Financial Press   **280**
Frequently Asked Questions   282

31. Shells and Pools   **283**
Public Shells   283
Advantages and Disadvantages of Shells   286
More Questions to Ask   287
Finding a Shell   289
Acquiring a Shell   289
Spin-off Shells   290
Blind Pools   290
Frequently Asked Questions   294

PART SIX
Internet Direct Public Offerings

32. Internet Direct Public Offerings   **297**
Overview   297
Advantages of Internet DPOs   299
Primary Differences with IPOs   300
Company Suitability for a DPO   301
Frequently Asked Questions   302

33. Introduction to the Regulation of DPOs   **303**
The SEC   303
Basic Registration of Securities   303
Small-Business Forms   304
What the SEC Says   306
Vehicle Choices   307
Frequently Asked Questions   308

34. Filing the DPO   **309**
Regulation A: A Quick Overview   309
Specifics of Reg A and Its *Fine Print*   310
More *Fine Print*   313
SCOR: A Quick Overview   314
Regulation D-504   316
Intrastate—or Rule 147   317
Closing Thoughts   318
Frequently Asked Questions   318

35. Trading DPO Stocks   **319**
Order-Matching Services   320
Electronic Matching Services   321
The Pacific Exchange   321
A Final Comment on DPO Trading   325
Frequently Asked Questions   325

36. IPO and DPO Investor Tips   **327**
Investing Questions   330
A Quick Trip through a Prospectus   333
Wrap-Up   338

Glossary   341
Index   349
About the Author   361

Preface

I've dealt with the process of taking companies public for 20 years. I've worked with entrepreneurs and their support professionals to assist them in going public. After a while I began to see the frustration of the people involved. It is, after all, difficult to comprehend all the various aspects and complexities of the process. This is especially true of entrepreneurs who are pressed for time and often don't know the correct questions to ask.

I have been frustrated in the past with many business authors who have had little practical, first-hand experience. Some authors have taken their own company public, practiced in one of the professional positions, or come from academia. But they often have a narrow point of view and a very specialized perspective. In my case, I have gained an intimate knowledge of the over-the-counter (OTC) market as a player, broker, trader, corporate finance officer, and syndicator. I also have been a public company founder, officer, president, and director, and have invested in hundreds of companies, both public and private. I took my first company public in 1970 and have been involved in more than 50 initial public offerings (IPOs) in one capacity or another. With two decades of hands-on experience, I feel I have gained a thorough knowledge of IPO business cycles and government actions and reactions. This includes an understanding of the internal politics and how the various players who are central to the process interrelate.

Being involved in a publicly held business is an entrepreneur's ultimate dream. Taking a company public is the major reward. It brings glamour and prestige, and is one of the acknowledgments of success in business, but taking a company public is a complex process. It involves many different business disciplines and can be mysterious and confusing even for those who have been through it several times. It's not surprising that entrepreneurs and their management teams are intimidated. Consequently, they seek helpful information from attorneys, accountants, public relations executives, and other support professionals.

Many of these professionals will acknowledge, however, that they don't have a complete understanding of the complementary disciplines, or in many cases a full grasp of the total process. Some may have only a cursory knowledge of many of the subjects, others an in-depth knowledge of some of the subjects. What they share is a common need to gain a greater understanding of the overall process or to gain additional insight in specific areas.

Accountants may be knowledgeable about the financial aspects of the process but recognize they may be weak in the legal areas. A stock broker may want more information on aspects of the securities exchanges; a company president may wish to better understand the investor relations area; a venture capitalist may want more information on the role of financial printing; or a banker may wish to gain knowledge on how to structure a deal.

The major need of the prospective chief executive officer (CEO) of a public company and those on the IPO team is a fuller understanding of a complicated subject. This book is a complete guide for taking a company public. It explores all aspects of this process and examines what a successful offering requires, what roles come into play, and more.

There is another area in which this book will be very helpful: academia. For the business school teacher who is instructing current entrepreneurs, entrepreneurs-to-be, or MBA students, this book becomes the definitive bible as the text for course instruction or for use as a supplemental text. It covers the going-public process from beginning to completion.

With this third edition, I've added a new section on the subject of Internet direct public offerings (DPOs). The reader will find that it explains the basics of the process and presents an overview of the applicable rules and regulations. DPOs have gained new popularity because of the Internet's ability to distribute information to a broad audience at very little cost. This capability has also presented a challenge to those involved in the highly regulated world of securities offerings, resulting in constantly changing rules and regulations that make it difficult to present all the variables in a single book. Consequently, readers will find an Internet site devoted to assist them in their quest for the latest information at: http://www.venturea.com/dpo.

I've tried to capture the experience of taking a company public and pass it on to you as knowledge. My entrepreneurial wish for you is that *Going Public* will help you gain the experience and capture the dream.

Acknowledgments

The dedication is to my father, who wasn't an entrepreneur but who set an example for the kind of dedication necessary to foster the entrepreneurial spirit. From the family unit one builds the framework for future successes and failures. I appreciate many unnamed individuals who fed me the experience of business, sometimes with eyedroppers, other times by dump truck.

Taking a company public is a team effort as is writing a book. The public company entrepreneur needs an effective team as much as an author. My entrepreneurial team goes back 25 years or more.

I'm indebted to the thousands of people whose business plans and entrepreneurial dreams I have shared. I'm also indebted to the hundreds of public company executives I've worked with and the hundreds of support professionals they have engaged. From them I continue to learn.

In addition, I am thankful to Harper Business, who was the original publisher, as well as to Jeff Herman, who was my agent. Spencer Smith, former president of Upstart Publishing, was responsible for the second edition. My original coauthor, Ron Schultz, played a major role in bringing the first edition to final acceptable form. I would be remiss not to thank two outstanding entrepreneurs who provided original inspiration and have provided additional ongoing encouragement: Maita Lester and Cheryl Chatfield.

Special acknowledgment goes to Danielle Egan-Miller, acquisitions editor at Dearborn Financial Publishing, who spearheaded the effort to incorporate the DPO section of this new edition. I thank her for insight and support.

Introduction

What's the IPO Outlook?

America's success as a world leader in so many areas comes in large part on our country's being built on the foundation of a free enterprise system. This freedom to attempt entrepreneurship, to fail and attempt again and again is also reflected in the initial public offering (IPO) markets. Simply, what goes up comes down, and what comes down (at least in financial markets) goes back up again. The interesting thing about this scenario as it concerns IPOs is that when the market demand drops, it has always come back stronger than ever before. I have a theory: similar to the readjustment we have witnessed over the last several decades of the increasingly higher levels of the stock markets in general, the IPO indexes also continue to rise to new levels. I don't see the trend changing, with the exception of the inevitable blips, through the turn of the century.

Throughout the 1980s until the market crash of 1987, both the numbers of new issues and the total dollar amounts kept rising from the levels in the 1970s. Even with the 1987 crash, the numbers in the late 1980s rebounded and were greater than the numbers in the early 1980s. The 1990s have seen these numbers soar over any past highs.

So what's the point? *Our economy always has money for good deals.*

If you're committed to building an excellent enterprise, you'll be able to attract financing. If part of your financing plans call for IPO dollars or even using an IPO as an exit, you can count on your strategy being valid—assuming you meet the normal qualifications and assuming you are willing to adapt to current marketplace trends.

Under the presumption that our interest rates will remain in the single digits, you can virtually count on the fact that the IPO market will continue to soar. In fact, the longer interest rates maintain the low levels of the 1990s, the greater the pent-up demand for the larger returns traditionally promised by IPOs. Many investors tend to place part of their investment dollars in what are considered more speculative investments, and the longer they are receiving returns that barely keep up with inflation in their general investments, the more they are inclined to increase the speculative portion of their portfolios.

This point is reinforced if one looks at the traditional venture capital community—that is, the professionally managed funds that are subscribed to by institutional investors such as pension funds and insurance companies. After withdrawing from venture capital investment in the late 1980s, these funds have returned with investments in the billions of dollars—all in an attempt to seek higher overall portfolio returns. And remember, venture capital uses the IPO markets to cash out of their entrepreneurial investments.

Investments in the emerging growth companies typically encompassed by IPOs are fascinating to investors. It appears to me that we are developing a backlog of dollars that will go into these companies well into the turn of the century. Plan on it, and start your planning by considering several subjects that need to be addressed right up front before getting into the nitty-gritty of taking a company public. First, how do I go about identifying the players I can talk to about taking a company public? Second, how do I determine if my company is suitable for becoming a publicly traded company? Both of these are great questions that I get asked frequently. Unfortunately, neither of them can be given succinct answers. I can, however, offer you some helpful guidelines.

Who Are the IPO Players?

Networking is a major key to success in going public. Ask peers, accountants, attorneys, your butcher, baker, and candlestick maker what they know about going public. You'll be surprised how many people know someone who knows something or somebody that knows *all* about going public—or how many can identify that funny acronym IPO.

One of the best sources of information are those who have taken their company public or those who are in the upper management of a company that has gone public, preferably someone who has accomplished the task in the last several years. But don't make the mistake of talking or developing a relationship with just one individual. The going-public process is so complex, so specialized to each situation that every individual comes away from an IPO project with some heavily skewed opinions. You are making a significant worklife decision in taking on a public offering and you should not make it in a vacuum or by depending on a single viewpoint.

The process of gaining an education should not be "short-timed." You should give yourself ample time to question, absorb, and requestion various aspects as they pertain to your particular situation. You need a diversity of opinions about a lot of different areas. This book will help by presenting a comprehensive overview, but it can't help you sort out all the peculiarities about your particular industry or company's position.

If you don't examine the key points and strategies before getting into the thick of things, I'll guarantee you'll regret it. Once into the process, events start moving so fast with so many daily decisions to make that you can easily make some wrong choices. Few of these will be deal threatening, but a lot of little mistakes that could have been prevented with more "think-time" can add up to haunt you later.

Obviously, one of the best sources of help is a peer who has been through the process. Take him or her out to lunch, golf, or tennis; go out of your way to develop a rapport. Establish an understanding with this person so you can continue to come back and gain the benefit of his or her experience by soliciting this person's opinions as you travel down the IPO road. It's been my experience that individuals who have accomplished a successful offering are more than willing to share their insights. They remember how much they would have liked to have had someone to ask "dumb questions" to. They'll help; just ask.

If you have stockbroker friends, especially those with regional firms, talk to them confidentially about your plans. Ask if they could arrange a meeting for you with the head of their respective corporate finance departments. Department heads are usually willing to talk with a prospective underwriting client. They will gladly share their opinions about the current market atmosphere, their interest in looking at your deal, and their recommendations of other parties you might talk with, including their favorite legal and accounting contacts.

But be cautious. Don't wait until you're about ready to take the plunge. I feel that a one-year to two-year lead is not the least bit inappropriate. As you get into the broader points, you may find that you have to do some corporate cleanup or restructuring—like shedding a division or department, or acquiring a compatible subsidiary. If this proves to be the case, you will want sufficient time to accomplish these prepublic tasks in a timely and cost-effective manner.

Bottom line—networking. Do this with stockbrokers, investment bankers, consultants, attorneys, accountants, friends, and peers. It might sound trite but the practice of not leaving a stone unturned still applies.

Is My Company Ready?

I've seen the extremes of company readiness from the starry-eyed inventor to the company with $100 million a year in revenues. Fortunately, most of the time the prospective "IPOer" is a little more grounded. Inventors realize that their product should probably be at least past the prototype stage, although I've seen IPOs completed on new companies without prototypes (the deals died), and I've encountered $100 million companies that haven't yet been approached by an aggressive investment banker—albeit a rare exception.

Again, the word *networking* comes to the front when you are seeking opinions about the viability of your own IPO. Securities and Exchange Commission (SEC) accountants and lawyers have a good sense of both the marketplace and the prerequisites for eligibility and reception to IPOs in general. I can state unequivocally that if you do not have an attorney or accountant, you are not ready to consider going public. Your business structure just isn't sophisticated enough to merit a public offering. There are a couple of other broad qualifiers that you can count on.

With a few exceptions, today's underwriters—those stock brokerage houses that take companies public—will consider any deals that allow you to qualify for a National Association of Securities Dealers Automated Quotations (Nasdaq) listing with the proceeds received from your offering. The minimal requirement for trading on the Nasdaq—the over-the-counter market—is that a company have a minimum of $4 million in net tangible assets.

Another qualifier is loosely defined as "sex appeal." Companies with sex appeal have a better chance of securing an IPO than those with little sex appeal. So what is sex appeal? It's difficult to give a precise definition, but some examples will help. In the late 1970s and early 1980s, any company that had the words *gas* and *oil* or *energy* in it had sex appeal; ditto, *solar* or *computer.* By the late 1980s, if *LBO* or *biotech* was inferred in talking about a company, there was sex appeal. In the mid 1990s, the sex appeal word was *Internet.*

The IPO markets run in waves, waves of fashionable investment. I'll discuss this further in Chapter 4 on timing. If you're in a hot "business news" market area, suffice it to say your company has sex appeal. If the financial magazines and newspapers have a continual stream of stories about your industry, consider yourself blessed and don't waste any time checking out your IPO potential. The markets are also fickle; they can change the interpretation of sex appeal about as fast as the evening news changes its lead story.

And what about nonsexy companies? How about all of the mundane companies that simply fight it out for an increase in market share of normal everyday products or services? Or companies that make good profits by manufacturing our daily essentials? Maybe you have a nice service business that you know can be even more successful if you can just expand your territory.

A lot of so-called mundane offerings are brought to market every year. Just as investors come in all shapes and sizes, so do underwriters and their preferences for the types of deals they do. With the advent of the Internet, the direct public offering promises even more potential for entrepreneurs with mundane offerings as well as a new method to take your company public independently (see Part Six).

Again, broaden your networking contacts. The daily practitioners of the IPO game will gladly help you interpret the market outlook, identify the players, and assess your potential. It's in their best interest—they are the ones who are always seeking a new pair of entrepreneur's pockets to get into. They'd love to have a chance at yours.

Overview of the Process

1

The Advantages and Disadvantages of Going Public

Going public—two simple words on which hang the dreams, aspirations, and inspiration of many practicing and visionary entrepreneurs. These words represent respect in the business community, and, equally important, they can mean great financial reward. These two words can open the door and expand an entrepreneur's company by using other people's money. Going public allows the company's owners to revel in the precious benefits gained for owners and investors alike. Can this be reality? The answer is unequivocally yes.

As our society continues its evolution from an industrial/manufacturing foundation to a service/information base, we are finding that the decade of the 1990s and beyond are producing an increasing number of entrepreneurial stars. These enterprising company owners are becoming richer faster and take more people with them than ever before. Why? Because as our society has become more global and consequently more complex, we have also become more aware of the problems raised by this increasing diversity. The challenges we will be facing are great. Once again the doors of opportunity are open to those industrious individuals ready to jump in with an appropriate and timely solution. However, the spark that brings these primed issues to flame is capital, and going public is the flint on which capital reserves are struck.

Basically, going public is the process by which a business owned by one or several individuals is converted into a business owned by many. It involves the offering of part ownership of the company to the public through the sale of equity or debt securities. The purpose of this book, then, is to examine in detail how successful entrepreneurs build the various teams necessary to accomplish this profitable objective. The following chapters will lay bare the regulatory constraints applied by federal and state governments, and expound on the gathering and coordination of the management teams, consultants, accountants, lawyers, underwriters, printers, and public relations experts necessary to breathe life into an initial public offering (IPO) and bring the entrepreneur's dream to reality.

The road to public riches is not without pratfalls and pitfalls. The task can be arduous. But I hope this book will help the potential "publicteer" proceed with eyes open so that he or she may actually reap the capital fruits that lie ahead.

Advantages for the Company

Why set out upon a road beset with danger? In 1985, Dr. John E. Young of the University of Colorado conducted a study of 562 companies that went public between September 1980 and March 1984. Although this was more than ten years ago, the study reconfirmed past studies and continues to track current informal studies. Young found that the majority of CEOs cited two fundamental reasons for going public. The first was to raise capital as a source for *ongoing financing*.

Capital is the "wealth used in trade." It is the money invested in a company that allows it to

- fund start-up operations;
- purchase equipment necessary for production;
- increase inventories of both raw and finished goods;
- support growing receivables;
- expand ongoing operations;
- support the company's administration;
- further research;
- develop the next generation of product;
- retire prior debt; and
- increase market share.

Contained within every one of these capital purposes is the primary objective for raising capital—to support and sustain the growth of the company. For a regional company that may be going national, the additional capital that can be raised through an IPO is often a way to attract an acquisition or to form mergers.

By way of an IPO, the entrepreneur converts a portion of the ownership of the company into shares of stock and allows investors to purchase that percentage, thereby sharing the business with the public. The investors hope their added investment will enhance the company's possibility for successful growth and thus increase the value of their share of the company. This is the second fundamental advantage Young noted for taking a company public: *stock value appreciation.* The potential monetary reward that an original investor—whether family member, friend, venture capitalist, or, of course, corporate founder—can realize from the leveraged selling of a company's stock makes all other financial leverages seem like pocket change. Few legal investments can beat the reward to be gained by an original investor from a successful IPO.

For most people, recapitalization and stock value appreciation would seem reason enough to fight the dragons on the road to going public, but a company can gain other advantages. A public company has a broader equity base, thus increasing its opportunities for obtaining financing for future efforts. Increasing the bottom-line net worth of a company as well as its debt-to-equity ratio enables it to borrow at lower interest rates from traditional institutions. If the company's stock performs well after the IPO, it may also obtain further equity capital without having to give up as great a percentage of the company as it did in the initial offering.

Another advantage of going public is the improvement in corporate image. A public company receives more media attention in the financial community than does a private firm, and publicity can strengthen competitive position in the marketplace. Favorable trade press attention can attract both new business and new interest in the company. Dun & Bradstreet, Moody's, Standard & Poor's, and many other financial information publishers issue special notices on new public companies and follow their progress. The more public exposure a company receives, the greater its chances for success.

The media, however, are not the only carriers of good news. It is not uncommon for customers, suppliers, and business associates to purchase stock shares in an IPO. This increased involvement in the company and its products or services often results in preferential treatment ranging from better terms on contracts to increased reliability of delivery schedules.

Because the financial activities of a public company are required to be regularly reported, management has an opportunity to obtain a higher degree of public confidence. Its books are open to the world, which often allows greater borrowing flexibility in both straight and convertible debt. Companies can structure deals to fit the dynamics of the current financial marketplace. The added credibility of this open-book policy broadens financial avenues such as bonds, debentures, and preferred stock.

Public companies often enjoy an added prestige in the political arena. Shareholders from different areas of the country can influence legislation that might affect the company. This is true on all levels of the political scene, whether in local city councils, state legislatures, or on Capitol Hill.

Advantages for the Founders

Beyond the gain to the company coffers, the single greatest financial advantage of going public falls to the founders of the company. All the spoils don't go to the CEO but are distributed to passive founding investors in addition to officers and members of the management team who have remained active in the company's daily activities. Their nonmarketable stock investments in their once privately held firm are converted into a marketable stock in a public company. Shares once valued at a dollar or less may be issued in an IPO at $10 or more per share. Simple math will reveal that a founder's original $10,000 investment is now worth upward of $1 million. One need think only of the initial investment of Apple Computer's Steven Jobs or Microsoft's William Gates and their worth today to illustrate the potential: the percentage of return on a founding investment versus the net worth value of the company can be phenomenal. Typically, a stock sells at 10 to 12 times its earnings, known as the price-earnings, or PE, ratio. In a small IPO, this ratio may be as high as 30 to 40 times the company's annual earnings.

An IPO also provides founding insiders with the opportunity to diversify their personal investment portfolios. It's common practice for the officers of a private company with a significant track record to have a good part of their personal wealth tied up in their company. An IPO allows these officers to liquefy some of their investment. In many cases, officers have made loans to the company, advanced money, or even postponed payment of their salaries. With the proceeds from an IPO, these debts can be cleared up as can bank loans to the company secured by officers' signatures or property.

One advantage of going public that a founding officer would probably like to delay as long as possible is minimizing estate tax problems: the payment of taxes on the estate of company principal would not have to come from company funds as might be necessary in a privately held firm. The establishment of stock value in a public market simplifies appraisals for inheritance taxes.

As should be increasingly evident, going public offers a wealth of enticements for the founding officers. And to better deal with this new wealth, the liquidity of public stock allows control over the timing of capital gains. As a final bonus, should a founding shareholder wish to secure a personal loan from a financial institution—say to buy that small 20-room cottage on five wooded acres—marketable stocks offer a more acceptable form of collateral.

Benefits for Employees

Founding officers are not the only beneficiaries when a company goes public. There are also added benefits for management and other employees working for a public company. Few medium-size or small companies can hope to compete with large companies in salary offers. In a public company, stock options can be an attractive employment inducement, a form of payment that's a plus for both the company and the management executive. Cash salaries come directly from the company's earnings, whereas stock options are paid for by the increased value of the stock itself. A stock option can also be a blessing for the executive dealing with the Internal Revenue Service. In many cases, higher salaries result in higher tax brackets, but a stock option permits a portion of compensation to be taxed as longer-term capital gains.

Working for a small public company, management can directly contribute to the profit margins and stock market value of the company. Not only does this provide a certain ego satisfaction, but it can prove profitable for the manager as the stock rises in value.

Stock option plans and employee stock option plans are both excellent incentives for quality performance even beyond recruiting good employees. Employee-shareholders can follow their investment in their company in newspapers and financial publications. And if employees have had an opportunity to acquire stock before an initial public offering, they will also be able to experience the large financial multiples. The immediate price appreciation of their stock not only creates a pride of accomplishment and long-term loyalty but also makes for wealthier and happier employees.

The Securities Exchanges

The places where these dreams become reality are the stock exchanges, for a company can return its profits to its shareholders not only through periodic dividends but also through stock value appreciation: The owner of the stock can sell it for a profit if someone believes that the stock is worth more than the selling price, that its price-earnings ratio is undervalued, or that it will rise further.

The primary marketplaces for these stock transactions are the New York Stock Exchange (NYSE), the American Stock Exchange (AMEX), and the over-the-counter market (OTC). The NYSE and the AMEX have always been considered the "big boys" on the Street.

Times have changed however. The OTC, now better known as the Nasdaq (which stands for National Association of Securities Dealers Automated Quotations), is the stock trading system most used for taking companies public. It is the world's oldest and largest marketplace for stock transactions. Brought here by European merchants, this negotiated trade market has traditionally been the home for newer and smaller public companies. The name *over-the-counter* came about when banks, as a supplement to their other services, literally sold securities over their counters; these were purely negotiated sales as opposed to the auction house sales of the NYSE and AMEX. Over the years, the bankers were replaced by broker-dealers, who coalesced into a network for buying, selling, and providing quotations on stock prices, an informal network that evolved into today's more formalized OTC market.

All U.S. markets, whether the OTC, AMEX, or NYSE, are regulated by both the federal Securities and Exchange Commission (SEC) and state laws. Founded by the Securities Exchange Act of 1934, the SEC enforces the Securities Act of 1933 that was passed by Congress to protect investors in public offerings from unscrupulous dealing. The act requires disclosure statements by public companies and provides criminal and civil penalties for inadequate or inaccurate disclosure of material facts. We will discuss these acts and their regulations in greater detail in Chapter 18.

It was the enactment of the 1933 and 1934 acts that made the IPO process as cumbersome and costly as it has become. Each state additionally regulates the sale of securities. These regulations, called blue-sky laws, were created for much the same reasons as the federal securities acts: to protect gullible investors from promoters offering them the sky, the stars, and the rest of the firmament. As we will see, these laws and regulations require a great deal of time, money, attention, and accountability. And though in the long run the advantages of taking a company public outweigh the disadvantages presented by the process, the disadvantages should nonetheless be looked at as well.

The Disadvantages of the Public Marketplace

The entrepreneur can easily get carried away by the looming potential of huge benefits that can be gained from going public. That's just part of the story. So lest you, the reader, imagine going public as simply sitting back and waiting for the money to flow in, it behooves us to make a fuller disclosure here. Knowing both the positive and negative sides of the process will better prepare the individual or group contemplating such an important move.

If caution is not observed, the negatives could very well outweigh the positives. It would be folly for the entrepreneur to think a positive attitude will suffice to win the battle. Rather, one must be prepared for the negatives and pitfalls that keep cropping up at every turn. More often than not, one will meet with the misgivings of family and friends over the intention of sharing a company with the public as well as the mountains of paperwork and the seemingly endless outlay of money. Patience, persistence, and perseverance are very necessary for the entrepreneur seeking to go public! For there are a multitude of rules to contend with along with mind-boggling regulations and constraints that the entrepreneur must observe before he can finally grab the golden ring.

The primary disadvantages of going public can be grouped under three categories:

1. Disclosure/accountability
2. Control or loss of control
3. Expenses

Most companies would prefer to keep their business and financial activities to themselves and on principle consider it a disadvantage if they must expose the details of their operations. But the SEC requires that all operations of a public company be public. Inevitably, management suffers some loss of control. Simply filing the forms and paying the fees required of a company going public are costly. In the beginning there's a lot of money going out and not much coming back. There is also no guarantee the company will ever actually become public.

Disclosure

From an operational standpoint, the company must disclose its marketing methods and indicate the areas to which they apply, including mail orders, direct sales, representatives, retail outlets, and distributors. In most cases, a company must supply data on how its market areas are defined, its number of salespeople, sales by areas, and sales of specific product lines. Although it may seem like a tremendous loss of confidentiality, most competitors, employees, unions, and suppliers, as well as customers, have little interest in expending the time or effort required to seek out this information.

Many entrepreneurs consider this type of operational information about sales and marketing sacrosanct. But rarely have these financial and statistical disclosures had any detrimental effect on a company's operations. Usually, the price a company charges for its product or service, the cost of materials, and employee compensation are governed by market forces and not compromised by financial disclosures.

For all intents and purposes, the main reason for these disclosures is to assure that management complies with its fiduciary responsibilities to the company shareholders. In a private company the money at risk belongs to the owners, but in a public company the money invested and at risk is accountable to its public shareholders. This is also why annual and quarterly reports are required. There's no way around it. A company going public must disclose such hard financial facts as sales, profit margins, competitive positions, and remuneration of officers and directors.

Accountability

Accountability is a form of confession by the company going public. There can be no secrets from the government or the general public for such a company. It must account for its modus operandi and reveal its inside transactions, which are usually transactions of monetary value between the company and its officers or directors. They include such things as the common ownership of a supplier or a common facilities relationship. If an officer or director, for example, is also an owner or shareholder in a firm that supplies, or purchases from, the company, those transactions must be reported. It is not unusual or unlawful for the company to lease or sublease office or facility space from an officer or director, but the cost to the company should be no higher, and preferably lower, than prevailing market rates. These transactions are termed *non-arm's-length arrangements* and require no formal outside appraisal. Similar principles apply to items like patents, which are often owned by an officer and licensed to the company; in such cases it is not unusual to have royalty or fee payments revert to the officer.

This accountability disclosure will continue every quarter for the life of the company. Consequently, management needs to carefully review all insider dealings on a continuing basis. A telling example was contained in the prospectus for one IPO that disclosed the president of the company had purchased a swimming pool from the company before the public offering. The pool had previously been listed as an asset under the heading of "employee recreational facility." More likely than not, the fact that the pool was located in the president's backyard was a determining factor in the decision to purchase it.

Insider reporting requirements, covered more fully in Chapter 28, concern inside trading. Companies must divulge the names of all officers, directors, and other persons who may be privy to inside information about their company's operations. The company must account for changes in management, any surge in profits, a proposed sale of the company, or any other factor that could affect the price of the company's stock. The term *insider* applies irrespective of an individual's status as a significant shareholder. Such insiders are required to file regular and special reports with the SEC on their stock positions and trading activity in the company's stock. Principals of a company, in particular, must disclose their purchase or sale of company stock. If they fail to do so, they can be subject to stiff penalties for what the SEC considers a misuse of their position and authority.

Even the most innocent sale of stock by a principal could be misconstrued by analysts if the reason for it is not reported. For instance, the president of a company may need to sell stock in the company to pay for a family member's surgery. It must be reported or it could appear to the casual observer that the president is doing something underhanded and could eventually cause a whole series of unintended disadvantages for the company, including mistrust.

Accountability disclosure can also affect daily decisions by management. Companies have a tendency to shy away from instituting long-term or short-term goals that may be of overall benefit to the company but adversely affect the price of its stock. CEOs are constantly being pressured, both internally and externally, to maintain high growth rates. Because financial results must be reported quarterly, the displeasure of brokers and shareholders quickly becomes obvious should sales or earnings fail to meet expectations or projections.

Most companies have no trouble with their accountability reports to the SEC. The difficulties arise when a CEO must deal on a daily basis with shareholders, brokers, or others with a vested interest whose money is riding on the company's progress; they want to know what the company is doing for them. Naturally, investors and market makers want information to be promising, or these shareholders and brokers who influence investments in the company could become disenchanted with the company's performance and sell their shares. Unfortunately for management, this is not a group that can be ignored.

Another disadvantage arising from accountability is the process involved in obtaining shareholder approval. Many standards and procedures must be followed; for instance, there are regulations covering the length of time between notification and a shareholders meeting. There's even a regulation covering the size of type in which the proxy is printed. A more serious disadvantage in owning stock in a public company, especially large stock positions, is the invasion of privacy for estate valuation. In a private company the value is rarely a matter of public record. In a public company the published daily stock price provides a definite benchmark for the IRS. Of course, it's very possible that the company may be worth more than the stock price indicates.

Control or Loss of Control

As with disclosure/accountability, disadvantages arising from losing some control of a company are bound to affect management's operating style.

After an IPO the primary shareholders will own a smaller percentage of the stock than before. There are a few exceptions—the issuance of nonvoting stock or debentures for example—but in general management must accept the fact that some control of voting stock will be lost in going public. As a rule, a public company can anticipate a loss of absolute (51 percent plus) voting control. Even if more than 51 percent is retained by management after the initial public offering, subsequent offerings and acquisitions could further dilute control.

A significant loss of control involves timing. Timing often controls the destiny of a company. Invariably, CEOs lose some control over the time spent on day-to-day activities as well as over the timing of company decisions and moves for the benefit of the company, the financial community, and the shareholders. Dealing with the financial community whenever the company's stock price falls is not an easy task, but management can't control changes in the company's stock price resulting from general or industry trends. Thus, it is important when contemplating acquisitions (especially when company stock is involved) that sound corporate judgment and the timing of the deal be carefully considered. Prolonged negotiations with the company to be acquired can prove devastating by diluting the public company's stock. Here's why. Usually, the amount of stock to be issued to the acquired company is negotiated at a fixed dollar or asset value of the acquired company. In the interim, if the public company's stock declines, it will have to come up with more of its shares to meet the agreed purchase price. Buyers beware!

IPOs are the most vulnerable when it comes to timing. Public interest at the time of an IPO can mean success or failure, and the public is as fickle as it's reputed to be. Consider the following:

- 1969 saw over 1,000 new offerings for a total of $2.6 billion. (Stocks were doing well that year.)
- 1975 saw only six new offerings for just $34 million. (It was a time of recession.)
- 1983 saw 888 new offerings for $12 billion. (The computer boom created a glamourous stock market.)
- 1986 saw 719 new offerings for over $22 billion. (The biotechnology boom was riding high, and such stocks were much sought after.)
- 1988 saw the market drop over 500 points in one day. (It proved devastating to new issues.)
- 1992 saw almost 400 IPOs for almost $24 billion, and in 1996 the total amount of dollars raised was just short of $40 billion for 868 companies. (The Internet was hot.)

The number of IPOs and amounts of money raised are always affected by national and worldwide economic trends. Interest in IPOs changes with interest rates, inflationary or recession trends, general stock market conditions, and perceived "hot industry" movements.

During the time an IPO is in the works, management is particularly vulnerable. If the bottom falls out of the market, it may not be possible to complete the IPO. The same holds true if the aftermarket is inactive and trading thin. If the fickle buying public doesn't take to a new issue, its days could be numbered and management has little or no control over the outcome.

The lack of control in operating a public company can seem overwhelming. But even if management decides it's had it with being a public company, there's little it can do. It could make an effort at getting the company acquired with the provision that the management stay in place. Or it could try to go private again, a move that requires considerable cash and lots of agony and patience. Or it could merge with another company, an alternative that could end up being the most troublesome of all because of the difficulties in coping with two management teams.

The problem of control also arises in connection with insider stock purchases. SEC Rule 144 establishes holding periods, in effect saying that for two years after it comes into their possession, insiders cannot sell company stock they have received, been given, or bought. Other SEC regulations limit the amount and the timing of personal stock sales, discussed in greater detail in Chapters 28 and 29.

Board meetings are subject to certain requirements. The informal control normally exercised in private companies is not considered sufficient for a public company. Public company operating procedures require more frequent, more substantive, and more formal board of directors meetings. SEC guidelines require careful preparation of all items offered for board resolution. (More about boards of directors later.)

Expenses

We have already stated that the cost of going public is high. Be aware, too, that once a private company becomes a public company, the costs don't stop. SEC regulations continue forever. The average layperson may think this a disadvantage, but the sophisticated entrepreneur looks upon it as the cost of doing business.

The CEO or the accountant of an IPO who writes the checks, however, will probably react unfavorably to the number of checks that must be written and the amounts that must be paid to accomplish the IPO. Worse yet, a company that has been in business prior to an IPO will have to detail its financial history for two to five years depending on how the company registers.

It may cost more initially but save money in the long run to enlist the aid of accountants and attorneys who are specialists in SEC and public company requirements. Their fees usually correspond to their expertise. But they can save your having to do things over. Other requirements, such as printing, underwriting, commissions, registration and transfer fees, and corporate promotional expenses are necessary evils you really shouldn't try to shortcut.

It is also advisable to secure the help of a professional financial public relations firm to handle communications with shareholders and the financial community. These are expenses many private companies consider unnecessary, but matters are different for a public company. Public relations is your direct line to the people your company needs to reach to survive. (The importance of financial public relations will be discussed more fully in Chapter 12.)

All levels of upper management are affected by the demands of a public company's operations. Much of this time is directed toward complying with SEC and public company reporting requirements that would not be required in a privately held company. Management must constantly itemize its duties in detail. Time is money. Going public gets to be very expensive.

FREQUENTLY ASKED QUESTIONS

Do the advantages outweigh the disadvantages?

Bottom line, when all is said and done, the large majority of CEOs say yes. Besides the increase in their personal fortunes, they receive the money needed to assist their company's growth.

Will I lose control of my company?

Usually no. In fact, as you will read in Chapter 15, most management teams gain a larger amount of control. They just have to manage better to meet the expectations of the public shareholders.

Doesn't it cost an awful lot to go public?

Yes, especially out-of-pocket up front. However, the additional equity from an IPO enhances a company's net worth. If the management team does a good job in operating the company, being public makes it a lot easier to get more money to support more growth.

Do I have to make public all my proprietary information?

Not at all. The SEC regulations don't require a company to disclose proprietary knowledge. This is especially true when applied to internal or product and production processes.

2

Alternatives to Going Public

Growing companies are constantly searching for new capital either through debt or equity, though it's not always easy to come by. But for the entrepreneur, raising money is a way of life. Going public is one way to secure needed capital. It can relieve the pressure, and it can also turn out to be the pot of gold at the end of the rainbow. The problem: it takes money to make money. The process of going public often requires a lot of money up front to cover the cost of services and fees, and fees, and fees. But look at it this way: If it were all easy to come by, there would be nothing special about entrepreneurs.

Some entrepreneurs consider going public no different from other alternatives to raising money. What's more, they have proven it time after time. But the process does require time—and it costs money. The first thing to be done is to put together a business plan to use as a fundraising tool. Second is the actual raising of the financing. Each alternative to raising money requires a different approach to the business plan. It happens fast in the movies and on television, but, generally speaking, it is never quick, it is never simple. In fact, it is usually quite painful and exasperating. Entrepreneurs often find themselves chasing down blind alleys.

What all entrepreneurs soon discover they must reckon with in pursuit of the elusive dollar are high interest costs, dilution of equity ownership, potential restrictions on daily operating flexibility, and even constraints on future growth.

Private Financing

For some entrepreneurs the best way to accomplish private equity financing has been through the use of Regulation D, which is a limited offer and sale of securities without registration under the Securities Act of 1933. (Chapter 18 is devoted to that subject.) The most common form for raising private capital, however, is to borrow it for either the short or long term. Short-term debt is traditionally used for working capital and some equipment purchases. But most often new businesses require long-term debt or permanent equity capital to support major expansion and anticipated rapid growth. The advantages of borrowing are that it is a relatively simple process to arrange. It does not take a great deal of time and does not dilute equity ownership. The disadvantages are that it is a high-risk strategy as far as the company's growth is concerned in that incurring debt subjects the company to a firm obligation. A downturn in business or an increase in interest rates could result in the inability to service the debt payments.

If borrowing is the answer, the question is, from whom? The following pages will address the various types of financing and other potential borrowing sources as well as identifying other possible capital sources.

Debt Financing

Pure debt (loan/borrowing) financing can take several forms. It is available from such varied sources as banks, finance companies, or leasing companies and is considered to be an increased risk for the company as borrowed funds require repayment. However, loans do increase the borrower's return on equity (leverage). Costs to be considered in using debt financing are not only interest, which can be high, but also indirect costs that can be associated with some forms of debt, such as compensating checking account balances, for which the borrower is required by the lender (bank) to maintain a stated minimum balance in a non-interest-bearing checking account. This could mean that if the borrower received a $100,000 loan from the bank, the bank would insist that the borrower keep a minimum of $10,000 in the checking account with the stipulation that the account cannot go below $10,000. The borrower would be required to pay interest on that $10,000 even though it can't be touched—a common business practice. In addition, the lender may impose strict loan covenants in the form of performance ratios that must be maintained. That means, in effect, that the company's net worth versus assets cannot fall below a certain level, the company's inventory must remain at a certain level, receivables cannot go over a certain level, and payables cannot exceed a certain level. If any of these situations occur while the loan is in effect, the loan or portions of it can be called due.

Since the late 1970s, the cost of borrowing money by new companies has seen wide fluctuations. Interest costs on unsecured loans have gone as high as, or higher than, 25 percent. What's more, some long-term loans carry "equity kickers" in the form of stock warrants or rights to purchase stock. (This has become common practice with venture leasing companies and many private debt sources.) An equity kicker is a deal made with the company by the lenders, who are betting that the company will become successful because it is new and considered high-risk. If that happens and the company goes public, the lenders want the company to give them a warrant that allows them to buy x number of shares of the company's stock at today's price as compensation for lending the company money.

It may smell like usury, but savvy entrepreneurs know what the costs of borrowing money to fund a business often are. Unfortunately, prime rates of 10 percent plus—the cost for short-term borrowing from finance companies—can spell death for a small enterprise. The only hope is to try to obtain longer-term debt that could serve as junior, or secondary, to a bank loan.

Subordinated Debt

An alternative to bank borrowing is the placement of subordinated convertible debt debentures with private lenders that are venture capital firms and also referred to as Small Business Investment Companies (SBICs discussed later in this chapter). Most subordinated debt is unsecured and, consequently, junior (secondary) to bank loans. For example, Company A has a $500,000 bank loan from a venture capital firm that is secured by inventory and receivables. Company A wants to borrow another $500,000 from a bank to put in a new production line and buy more equipment. The equipment will ordinarily be enough to secure the new loan. However, if Company A goes bankrupt, the bank has first claim against the assets, and the venture capital firm must take a secondary position against the assets. It is second in line for payment after the bank. That's what makes the venture capital firm "subordinated." But assuming that the loan helped Company A reach its goals, the convertibility clause allows the venture capital firm to convert the subordinated debt debentures to stock at an agreed-upon date at prices to be determined at the time of the loan or on the date of conversion. In essence, the loan is subordinated but it is also convertible to stock.

Putting together subordinated debt placements takes experienced legal and accounting advice. In addition, careful consideration must be given to the long-term effects of equity dilution as it's possible that subordinated convertible debt holders could team up with other minority shareholders and, by their conversion rights, gain effective control of the company even though this is not very likely.

Sources of Debt Financing

Commercial Banks

Banks are traditional lenders for secured short-term or medium-term loans. These loans are usually revolving lines of credit to finance inventory buildup and are quite often seasonal or lent against a particular contract. Banks will also make mortgage loans on a longer-term basis against buildings, real property, and equipment, but they don't ordinarily provide unsecured loans or lend to start-up companies. Their modus operandi is consistent with other banks:

Commercial Banks

Costs	Floating rates to 5 points above prime
Maturity	30-day to 90-day notes; credit lines to 3 years; long-term mortgages to 7 years
Proceeds	Working capital; inventory; receivables; machinery
Collateral	Unsecured; secured against specific assets; personal guarantees
Advantages	Usually lower costs than other lending organizations; many branches
Disadvantages	Prefer established business; require personal guarantees and/or collateral

Commercial Finance Companies

Finance companies provide asset-based lending, most commonly against receivables and occasionally against inventory. Their rates are usually higher than those of banks, and they usually require a regular monthly reconciliation of their collateral (receivables/inventory):

Finance Companies

Cost	Floating rates to 7 points above prime
Maturity	Depends on loan size; usually less than 1 to 8 years
Proceeds	Working capital; acquisitions; machinery; equipment; real estate
Collateral	First liens on assets; personal guarantees

Leasing Companies

Leasing companies tend to offer the entrepreneur more flexibility than banks. The company may lease an asset (equipment), or it may buy it, sell it to the leasing company, and then lease it back (leaseback). Leases can often be made for longer time periods and set up with varying payment plans. Payments can be scheduled monthly, quarterly, semiannually, and, in some cases, annually. Depending on tax advantages, the lease contract may also contain balloon payments.

Leasing Companies

Costs	Prime plus 6 to 8 points
Maturity	Negotiable: operating leases as short as six months; financing leases for useful life of the asset
Proceeds	Machinery; equipment; real estate; acquisitions
Advantages	Easy deals; 100 percent financing; lessor carries risk
Disadvantages	High cost; no ownership benefits

Saving and Loan Associations (S&Ls)

Even with many well-publicized problems in the past, S&Ls are still a viable lending source. S&Ls are more inclined to finance against real property.

Savings and Loans

Cost	Competitive with banks; fixed or variable rate tied to prime rate
Maturity	Long term to 15 years; occasionally lines of credit
Proceeds	Real estate; some working capital; equipment
Collateral	Always secured; personal guarantees
Advantages	Attractive rates; experienced real estate lenders
Disadvantages	High minimum loan amounts; restrictive covenants

Small Business Administration (SBA)

The SBA is a lender of last resort. A company must be turned down by other lenders to qualify for an SBA loan. In most cases, the SBA will provide guarantees securing loans up to $500,000. It has a number of different loan programs with various qualifiers. Rates are reasonable, but programs are subject to government funding availability, have a lot of restrictive covenants, and require a lot of paper processing.

Small Business Administration

Costs	Floating and fixed rates; tied to prime
Maturity	7 to 25 years
Proceeds	Working capital; machinery; equipment; real estate (only when other financing is denied)
Collateral	Secured by liens; personal guarantees
Advantages	Last-resort lender; low cost considering risk; does not finance some types of assets; has many new programs
Disadvantages	Liens; personal guarantees

Industrial Revenue Bonds

Industrial revenue bonds are not for start-up or early stage companies with the exception of those companies that have substantial equity financing. They are mostly issued to finance large real estate projects or companies with large equipment requirements. Also, in most cases the issuing agency holds title to the property and leases it back to the company.

Industrial Revenue Bonds

Costs	Floating or fixed rates at 70 percent to 85 percent of prime at tax-exempt status
Maturity	Usually 5 to 15 or more years
Proceeds	Real estate; equipment; machinery; acquisitions
Collateral	Secured by the fixed assets
Advantages	Low rates; good maturities
Disadvantages	Depends on market availability; strict government rules; high closing costs, especially legal

Life Insurance Companies and Pension Funds

This type of financing is specifically for established companies with substantial equity financing. In addition, it is obtainable for large investment projects that frequently run into the millions of dollars.

Life Insurance and Pension Funds

Costs	Fixed rates tied to long-term markets
Maturity	5 to 25 or 30 years
Proceeds	Real estate; machinery; equipment
Collateral	Secured assets; debentures
Advantages	Interest rates; long-term maturity
Disadvantages	High minimum amounts; restrictive loan agreements

Leveraged Buyouts (LBOs)

A leveraged buyout (LBO) is a form of financing that has been around for decades, but it became glamorized in the 1980s. It simply amounts to borrowing against the assets of a company and then using the cash flow realized from the company's continuing operations to pay off the debt. Buyers frequently sell off some of the assets to reduce the debt and, as part of their operating procedure, drastically cut operating costs to increase the cash flow. Sources of financing for LBOs are commercial banks, asset-based lenders, industrial bonds, and private investment pools. LBOs usually get their initial funding from investment banks.

Other Options

We have just presented a number of ways to go for debt financing. But the entrepreneur should know that there are alternatives to public offerings and semiprivate offerings for equity financing. Many professionally managed firms, composed of sophisticated investors whose sole business is venture capital funding are out there, but it takes a capable, well-informed management team to access this kind of money. Some alternate areas for equity financing that are worth considering are discussed below.

Professional Venture Capital

Professional management companies that manage high-risk funding provide venture capital, which is supplied by such institutions as insurance companies, pension funds, and some limited partnerships.

Professional Venture Capital

Amount Available	Usually $500,000 and up; occasionally for start-ups
Structure	Convertible preferred stock
Cost	Generally a minimum 30 percent per annum compounded return
Proceeds	For very high growth to sales of $50 million
Advantages	Large amount of capital available
Disadvantages	Must have high growth potential

Research and Development Partnerships

Before the tax code changes of 1986, R&D partnerships were a major funding source for small companies. Some forms of these partnerships are still available; real estate partnerships, for example, are still being formed. Some astute entrepreneurs are also involved with real estate partnerships tied in with historic building renovation. They form an R&D partnership to buy a building that will be used to house their business. Because the financing for the building came from outside the company, it further leverages the money raised in going public. Entrepreneurs who find this method applicable for their purposes should discuss this type of funding source with their CPA.

Small Business Investment Companies (SBICs)

The Small Business Administration (SBA) licenses and provides leveraged financing to SBICs, which in turn provide various forms of venture capital to entrepreneurial enterprises, usually in the form of convertible/subordinated debt.

Small Business Investment Companies

Amount Available	$100,000 to $1 million
Structure	Convertible debt; debt with warrants
Cost	Reasonable interest; dividends; equity
Proceeds	Working capital; acquisitions; LBOs

Advantages	Subordinated capital; 5-year debt; fixed interest
Disadvantages	Equity dilution; must prove fast growth

Minority Enterprise Small Business Investment Companies (MESBICs) are identical to SBICs except for the fact that they are designed for, and only available to, minority-owned businesses.

Small Business Innovation Research Grants (SBIR Grants)

Several grant programs are funded and administered by various federal agencies. The grants (first stage up to $50,000, second stage to $500,000) are primarily available for new product development. The product, if successfully developed, belongs to the company, but the stipulation is that the government has an option to purchase the technology. These grants are also offered to individuals as well as companies.

Small Business Innovation Research Grants

Amount Available	First stage to $50,000; second stage to $500,000
Structure	Grant by federal agency
Cost	Documented proposal must be submitted
Proceeds	Seed capital for research and development of product
Advantages	Low cost; no equity to give away
Disadvantages	Limited capital commitment

A point of information: numerous grants are available from the federal government, foundations, and private sources, and not exclusively for research and development. It is estimated that the total grants from all sources amount to $100 billion annually. A directory listing most of the grants that are available in the United States is published by the Office of Management and Budget.

Finally, one additional means of finding capital that is frequently overlooked by entrepreneurs is a combination of financing. Considering all the possible sources that are available, using a combination of multiple sources of capital may be just the answer to building a business that is successful and profitable. All it takes is a little resourcefulness.

FREQUENTLY ASKED QUESTIONS

Is there any one big financing secret?

There sure is and it's often overlooked. Successful entrepreneurs use combinations of financing. They identify both debt and equity sources and then combine them for the best results.

How do I determine what type of financing I should use, debt or equity?

That is what speadsheets are used for. If you don't know how to work them up with your computer, ask your CPA or a good numbers-cruncher for help. Good business planning will show you if you should do your financing with debt or equity.

Don't the various government programs take a lot of time and effort?

It is all relative. The government has really streamlined a lot of the process. Contact the ones that seem appropriate for you and you'll probably be surprised at how fast they can help.

Are these the only alternatives for financing?

There are a lot more. Pay close attention to Chapter 19 and be sure to review the section on Internet direct public offerings.

3

The Cost of Doing Business

No doubt about it—the rewards and benefits that are possible from going public can be incredible. On the other side of the ledger, to the uninitiated the costs involved to get through the process may seem even more incredible.

Don't let the fear of those costs deter you. As I repeat throughout this book, it is important to approach these expenses as simply the cost of doing business. The book generally addresses the entrepreneur seeking to realize $4 million to $15 million through an IPO. A very small percentage of this size IPO is done on a best-effort basis, that is, the underwriting broker has no obligation in the event the shares are not sold. If the underwriter can't sell the company stock, the underwriter returns the shares. The large majority of this size IPO are done on a firm commitment basis, that is, the underwriter basically assures the company it will buy the stock in anticipation of reselling it to the general public. In either case, whatever costs accrue during the process remain the responsibility of the entrepreneur whether the IPO is sold or not. It is therefore incumbent upon the CEO or the management group that must make the ultimate decision to proceed with the offering to be prepared to spend some money. Regardless of the cost, a well-versed entrepreneur knows that more money can come through an IPO than through any other method of equity financing. All things considered, it takes money to make money.

The same basic costs and percentages apply to IPOs up to approximately $8 million. Generally speaking, selling commissions and underwriter percentages decrease above that amount. Professional and promotional costs for offerings exceeding $6 million to $8 million are considerably higher, however, as they usually require the services of highly skilled national, or even international, professional and support firms.

There are no hard and fast numbers. Total costs and expenses for smaller IPOs can reach 24 to 39 percent of the offering or total monies raised. This is not considered excessive by experts in the business. For example, a survey conducted on 478 smaller IPOs in the late 1980s showed that general expenses, which included underwriters, attorneys, accountants, printers, and miscellaneous fees, ranged from 6.4 percent to 41.4 percent.

Costs can vary considerably. In an attempt to be more explicit, I'll consider the following areas individually:

- Underwriter costs
- Professional costs
- Up-front costs
- Hidden and future costs

Underwriter Costs

Commissions

The largest single cost item in a public offering is the underwriter's share or commission, also referred to as the underwriter's discount. Basically, it's the underwriter's take for raising the money and amounts to a percentage of each share of stock sold. The generally accepted percentage for an IPO is up to 10 percent. In theory, the figure is negotiable; in fact, the underwriter pretty much dictates the amount.

The following questions are used to determine negotiating commissions:

- How large is the offering—how many shares are to be sold?
- What efforts will be required to sell the stock and will the underwriter handle the whole package or will it be spread around?
- What is the type or quality of the offering and will it be an easy or a hard sale?
- How complex is the offering?
- How is the company valued?
- What are the commissions for similar offerings and how comparable is this one?
- What is the sex appeal of the company? Does the company offer the public something of substance, thus making it a more attractive buy?

- What is the current market environment—a good time to offer this stock? Is the economy right for it?

If the underwriter does the deal in-house, that is, if the stock is sold by brokers who work for the underwriter, the underwriter keeps the full commission. The in-house split is usually 30 percent and 70 percent, meaning that the house keeps 30 percent of the commission and the individual broker receives 70 percent. Brokers like new issues because this 70 percent payout exceeds their typical 30 to 50 percent share.

In most cases the underwriter will syndicate an IPO, offering part of the underwriting to other brokerage houses and keeping only a portion in-house. When this is done, the lead, or original, underwriter "reallows" 70 percent of the commission, which means the underwriter retains 30 percent for expenses. The syndicate members, in turn, will pay 60 percent of the commission to their brokers, who actually sell the IPO and keep a 10 percent override for themselves.

Nonaccountable Expense Allowance

The nonaccountable expense allowance is a fee charged to the company by the underwriter that is called nonaccountable because it can't be construed as an integral part of the offering. It was instituted as a means of reimbursing the underwriter for so-called out-of-pocket expenses that include such things as postage, phone costs, printing, entertainment, marketing expenses, and even legal expenses—for example, hiring a lawyer to review the work of the IPO company's lawyer. Although the fees are called nonaccountable, the National Association of Securities Dealers (NASD) requires the underwriter to account for them. The underwriter's legal counsel usually prepares a boilerplate report, which the issuing company accepts as a matter of course.

Underwriters use some of their nonaccountable expense money to offset part of the promotional costs of an IPO. These include payment of a portion of the "tombstones"—ads that appear in financial papers, such as *The Wall Street Journal* and *Barron's,* or the financial section of local newspapers. The ads say in effect that here is an approved offering by an appropriate agency as evidenced by the announcement.

Another important nonaccountable expense is for due diligence—the obligation on the part of the underwriter to inform the brokerage community about the validity of the issue. It amounts to an investigation of the client, with findings relayed to brokerage houses by formal or informal meetings.

(Tombstones and due diligence will be covered in more detail in Chapters 21 and 28.)

The nonaccountable expense allowance fee generally ranges from 1 to 3 percent of the total monies raised in a public offering. On IPOs up to $8 million, the accepted formula is about 3 percent, or $240,000. It has been standard practice for the company to pay one-third of the fee, or $80,000, at the time of signing a letter of intent, which simply means an intent to go through with the offering. The balance—$160,000—is usually paid upon completion of the offering. It is also generally accepted that the down payment on the nonaccountable expense allowance is nonrefundable.

It's worth stressing that once a letter of intent is signed with an underwriter and a down payment is made on the nonaccountable allowance, the company will probably never see that money again even if the IPO is later canceled. There have also been reports of an underwriter making a deal with another brokerage house to take over the letter of intent with neither completing the offering. (Chapter 21 on underwriters will deal with this issue in greater detail.)

Professional Costs

Legal Fees

Legal expenses are usually the second largest expense after underwriting commissions. On an IPO of up to $8 million, legal costs can vary between $30,000 and $175,000 depending on the complexity of the issues that must be dealt with. Legal issues include the history of the company (how far back it goes), whether other stocks from other companies are involved, whether the company operates in different states or foreign countries, whether patents must be accounted for, and how the company will be structured—the new officers involved, ownership, and so on.

Start-up companies, companies with no prior history, are clearly the easiest to set up. Although very few have been done since the late 1980s, the attorney for a start-up company, as a rule, has to file only for incorporation prestructured for public company operation. Follow-up involves no more than preparing a registration statement and filing the actual IPO. Even so, this legal cost can amount to anywhere from $20,000 to $75,000.

Included among legal expenses of an existing company is corporate cleanup. This involves a review of the minutes of directors and shareholders meetings. Lawyers must also review all formal agreements and contracts between the company and other interested parties, contracts that can cover anything from leases for copy machines to customer purchase orders. The process of tidying up corporate loose ends can result in renegotiating contracts, which of course means more legal work. Corporate cleanup can be time consuming if the company has been in existence for a number of years and has a long operating history, but it must be completed prior to any offering. What's more, in all probability the company will have to revise its articles of incorporation and bylaws. And should the company opt to create an employee stock option plan (ESOP) or an incentive stock option plan (ISOP), there will be still more legal fees.

Actually, there aren't too many shortcuts when it comes to legal fees in an IPO. Depending on negotiations with the underwriter, the offering company may occasionally even pay all or part of the fees of the underwriter's counsel. Those fees might be for a review of the company attorney's work, the cost of filing with NASD, and complying with state blue-sky regulations. Blue-sky regulations refer to the requirements most states have that all of the relevant information regarding the activities of the company be fully divulged.

In most cases much of the required information is readily available if an existing company has maintained legal counsel on an ongoing basis, thus minimizing the legal fees at the time of going public. (More about legal fees in Chapters 9 and 20.)

Accounting for Accounting

As with attorney fees, accounting fees can vary considerably. They're usually at a minimum for a start-up company with no history to justify. The initial costs would include establishment of an accounting system and the audit that must be done immediately before filing an IPO.

The accountant, or accounting firm, reviews and verifies the data in the registration statement and prepares the "comfort" letter. This letter goes over the accountant's responsibilities and says, in effect, that the audit accounting firm is satisfied with the method used to report the company's financial statement.

If the registration process becomes complex, the accountant may find it necessary to prepare a stub statement, or interim audit, usually followed by another letter of comfort confirming that everything remains as reported. A ballpark figure on the cost for a simple start-up IPO could run approximately $5,000 to $15,000.

Accounting costs for existing companies will, of course, be higher. SEC regulations require an audit covering, at a minimum, the two years preceding the filing for an IPO. Because the necessary information should have been compiled in the normal course of business, the accountant then only has to review the audit procedures for compliance with SEC accounting rules. The information is not always complete, however, and the accountant may have to perform a new audit, which could increase accounting costs by $20,000 to $60,000.

If an existing company had no audit performed during the two years prior to filing for an IPO or did not have its inventory audited, the audit accountant's job becomes a monumental project for it must then include such items as major write-downs and all figures that could seem to be significant in the transaction must be disclosed. Such information can look dubious, and it is up to the accountant to reduce its apparent significance. The work is time consuming, and the costs rise accordingly: an initial audit of this type could range from $20,000 to $100,000. In sum, depending on the complications that arise, the accounting fees, which must be disclosed in the IPO prospectus, can range from $10,000 to $100,000 or more.

Because the right kinds of numbers make an IPO look attractive to the financial community as well as to individual investors, it's common for accountants to be key members of the IPO's management team.

Investment Bankers and Consultants

Investment bankers and consultants are the people who keep an IPO on course. For a management group considering going public, these are the experts who can exert influence, who know the problems, and who can help to bring the process to fruition. Investment bankers usually work for fees or for fees plus a piece of the action, which could include stock or options. Their participation and fees must also be disclosed in the registration statement. (I'll discuss investment banking in greater detail in Chapter 21.)

Additional Up-Front Costs

We have covered the primary up-front costs a company will face in the process of an IPO, but they seem never to stop. In addition to stamps, paper, phone calls, special forms, entertainment, and office equipment, up-front costs include registration fees and printing.

Printing

Printing costs include the typesetting as well as the printing of the initial registration statement and prospectus for submission to the SEC, NASD, and individual state securities commissions. These documents must conform to detailed regulations covering type style and size, so it behooves the company to work with a printer that regularly prints these publications. Most companies and their legal counsel have word processors, computers, or other office equipment compatible with the printer's, and these can prove to be cost savers because changes are often required after a registration statement or other document has been printed. Any change, whether a typo, an error, or a change in information requires reprinting to comply with the regulations.

The first thing to be printed is usually the registration statement. Only a small quantity will be required—25 or fewer. Following that printing, the company will publish a preliminary offering, or what is called a "red herring." A red herring is an advance version of the offering that is distinguished by red print on the cover, where it very plainly states that it is a preliminary document. This is followed by the definitive prospectus, which contains the complete information about the offering. Both may include color photos and graphics. The quantity depends on the requirements of the underwriters, the size of the selling syndicate (a group of brokers, sales people, and/or investors that facilitate fundraising for the IPO), and the ultimate distribution of the stock.

An additional cost is for printing the actual stock certificates. The old custom of engraving beautiful, intricate designs has given way to modern techniques. Financial printers today keep books of stock designs on which a company has only to stick its logo. It does the job, and does it cheaply.

Printing costs can range from $10,000 to $100,000, but the norm is usually between $20,000 and $60,000. (See Chapter 11 for further discussion.)

Registration Fees

When it comes to registering an offering, it seems that every regulatory body in existence has its hand out. For individual states, the costs vary from token fees of perhaps $10 to many thousands—whatever the traffic will bear. Some states create their own individual filing forms, preventing you from filing duplicates of one form. Just coping with the various forms can drive an attorney to distraction, and it drives up legal costs as well. Adding insult to injury, few states will accept private company checks to cover the fee payment; they require certified checks.

Here is a list of the major regulatory and related bodies and their fees:

- Securities and Exchange Commission (SEC). When the registration statement is filed with the SEC, fees must be paid at the rate of $\frac{1}{29}$ of 1 percent of the maximum dollar amount of the securities being registered.
- National Association of Securities Dealers (NASD). Upon filing, $500 plus .01 percent of the offering's maximum dollar amount (maximum of $30,500).
- Blue-sky regulations. These state filing fees vary from $10 to $1,000 to a percentage or a combination of fee and percentage. (See Chapter 24 for details.)
- National Association of Securities Dealers Automated Quotations (Nasdaq). For companies that will be trading on the Nasdaq (initial minimum of $4 million in net tangible assets), the initial entry fee is $5,000. A yearly maintenance fee for continued listing, which is mandatory, is assessed on the company's total assets ($250 to $2,500).
- Miscellaneous listings. These are fees for listing the company in financial rating books such as Moody's, Standard & Poor's, and various other magazines, newspapers, and financial publications.
- Transfer agent. This person or service perfects the transaction of closing the sale. When the order comes in for shares, the transfer agent is responsible for issuing them. Very few public companies are equipped to act as their own stock transfer agent, so engage a computerized professional to serve in that capacity. (See Chapter 13.) Initial setup fees range from approximately $1,000 to $10,000. Quarterly maintenance fees depend on stock trading activity and the extent of the company's use of services.

Hidden and Future Costs

During the lengthy process of going public, additional and unanticipated costs will crop up. These hidden and future costs might include extra transportation costs to and from consultants, attorneys, accountants, and underwriters; lunches and entertainment; and revising and copying documents. Postage can mount up as can long-distance phone calls, faxes, and messenger deliveries. Other significant expenses can arise in coordinating legal counsel, accountants, underwriters, and printers located in different cities.

An important item is promotion: Many thousands of dollars can be required to make the brokerage community and the investing public aware of the company—through meetings arranged by underwriters and brokerage houses, samples of products or services, brochures, and audiovisual aids. (This area is covered in detail in Chapter 25.)

Another cost worth mentioning, though one rarely considered in today's financial community, is directors' and officers' liability insurance. Not only is it difficult to obtain, but the costs are prohibitive even though it is desirable, especially for a small company that could use it.

Although CEOs and management teams have considerable control over the amount and extent of some of these hidden and future costs, the costs invariably exceed what is anticipated—or rather what is not anticipated.

FREQUENTLY ASKED QUESTIONS

So what's the underwriter's total take?

Seldom less than 8 percent (commission of 6 percent plus another 2 percent in fees) and frequently up to 13 percent (commission of 10 percent plus 3 percent in fees).

How much CEO time is part of the cost?

Thirty hours a week for six months is not unusual for the CEO plus the time and effort of other executives and support people.

Can't I get some of these support costs to bet on the success of the IPO?

Commission payments always depend on the success of the IPO. However, a lot of the other support costs have to be paid as they are incurred. More information on costs and their payment terms are contained in following chapters.

Does it really take so much money to get money?

Unfortunately, yes. If it were easy and cheap, everyone would do it. Good deals can attract the up-front money for a promised piece of the action.

4

Timing

No matter how ready your company is, no matter how much in love you are with the product or service you're willing to share with the public, if the market is in the doldrums, if the economy is bad, if the world situation is far from rosy . . . stop a moment and ask yourself, is the world really ready to beat a path to your door regardless of market conditions? Even if your answer is a resounding yes, hold off if you can until the market and economy say go.

The timing of an IPO—that is, the time an IPO is placed on the market—should be well calculated. All too often a company is in position to go public, but for any number of reasons market conditions may not be receptive at that particular time. Proceeding with it as planned could easily jeopardize a good IPO.

Every market analyst and expert will tell you that even though your company is chafing at the bit to go public even if the market isn't gung ho at the time—wait! Market makers, analysts, and economists have learned from hard experience over the last couple of decades that the market has been prone to take sudden reversals and leave underwriters and companies high and dry. So it's worth playing it safe, and let the conditions of the time dictate whether you should proceed with your offering.

It may seem that I protest too much. But by doing so, I may help you, the entrepreneur, keep intact your dream of going public and subsequently making those marketplace millions. It's important to remember the old adage, "There's a time and place for everything." When the timing *is* right, the company contemplating an IPO had better have all its necessary requirements, pieces, and players in place. It should also be prepared to jump in as soon as the situation changes from bad times to good times and the IPO market starts to take off. The underwriters must also be ready to put the IPO out quickly to take advantage of a booming market as the value of an IPO stock may shoot up dramatically.

From the company's standpoint, a full commitment is necessary by all involved to be able to forge ahead without hesitation. The CEO and management team can focus this commitment by answering certain pertinent questions. Following is a checklist of questions that you may find helpful:

- Is management ready?
- Are the team players identified and in place pending additional financing?
- Are their credentials prepared and satisfactory?
- Are they prepared for the loss of privacy inherent in going public?
- Are they up to facing outside investor pressure in the decision-making process?
- Is planning in place?
- Has strategic planning been developed to implement both short-term and long-term goals?
- Do these plans include such important areas as people, products, production, marketing, and finance?
- Have R&D areas been identified?
- Have second-generation (follow-up) products or services been determined?
- Can all public reporting requirements, especially in the financial area, be met with timeliness?
- Is the company ready?
- Is the product or service ready to go?
- Has the product or service been tested?
- Will the second year as a public company show significant growth?

If you answered all the above questions with a *yes,* your IPO is ready to go. You owe it to your company to keep a sharp eye on the market for an opening. When the market window is open—in other words, when investors' money starts pouring into the market—you'll find prepared companies flocking through.

"When the going gets good, the good go public." So, observe the Boy Scout credo and "Be prepared." Savvy entrepreneurs can have a field day once the market opens up. Valuations tend to skyrocket, and IPOs can go public at 30 to 40 times earnings (or projected earnings). Those are numbers that dreams are made of. At such times IPOs proliferate, and entrepreneurs and underwriters race to get in before the market window closes. Some make it . . . some don't.

I made much ado about cautioning you not to bring out an IPO until the time is right. In reality, that's good advice. But if you missed the big surge and the market starts turning down, don't lose hope. A company can still gain entry. There are other ways to go in a slow IPO market. The company could seek other capital sources at reasonable costs that will not damage the IPO stock value, such as debt financing, subordinated debt, or convertible debt. These are the cheapest, most popular debts and the safest way for the company to survive until the market opens up again. (I examine these choices more closely in Chapter 19.)

The CEO of an IPO, of course, hopes to catch a rising stock market and take advantage of good timing. Bear in mind, however, that the market is fickle. Remember that. Its timing is difficult to judge. Its fickleness is hard to grasp. A company's successful entry in the market depends on many uncontrollable factors. It depends on current and future international trends. It depends on private and government economic forecasts, on current and projected interest rates, on domestic and foreign political developments, and on rates of inflation. It also depends on whether the company is engaged in a hot industry—one that's in favor at the moment. Emotion always rules the stock market, be it bullish or bearish. A triumphant entry depends, too, on whether the IPO market is oversaturated with new offerings.

Seldom are all the factors for assessing the right timing for both the company and the market positive. But when they are, the result is a "hot stock."

To create activity on a potentially hot stock, underwriters will often purposely price the stock at 10 to 15 percent under its true value. For example, they will bring out a $20 stock at $17—thus giving it an opportunity to go up immediately to create interest. This practice may mean a quick profit for the underwriter, but it occasionally proves devastating for management because it's almost impossible for management to produce results in the short period of time needed by the investment community to justify the artificial price of the stock. The problem is that management can't put the new money to work fast enough to support its goals. Therefore the rise isn't sustained, and the stock price drops.

The big trouble with hot issues is that greed can override the whole market system. People play the market but the company can't really take advantage of it. By the time a stock settles down to a proper value, the "quick buck" players are usually out of it. Now management is forced to spend a lot of time dealing with the investment community, trying to convince it of the company's exciting potential, taking away from the time that is needed to manage the company and attain its set goals. This hot situation doesn't happen too often, and some companies would welcome the opportunity to be in such a predicament. More often than not, entrepreneurs bringing an IPO to market spend their time trying to convince the proper parties that this is a good time to bring this particular company public.

It should be obvious by now that the time needed to realize an IPO from inception to fruition is crucial to its success. Now let's explore more closely some of the details that affect that timing.

Time Planning

You have made the decision to go public. How quickly can you get the show on the road? Expect it to take some time—4 to 12 months—to comply with the requirements of the host of public and private regulatory agencies on the local, state, and national level. You'll be dealing with accountants, attorneys, and other professionals whose goals, you may think, are to do nothing but make your life miserable.

The time when you go public also depends on how much preplanning you've done. A few IPOs are just rank start-ups. The key management people may be committed to the deal but the whole team may not be. And although some sources of funding are identified, they may not be committed. It's even possible the company is not yet ready to operate. That doesn't mean the deal isn't viable. Usually, by the time the deal is ready to go, everything and everyone will be in place.

Most companies contemplating an IPO are already operational. For these companies, going public may be like starting over from square one because, in all probability, they will need to revamp their corporate structure. Their articles, bylaws, and accounting system may need to be revised, and they may lack a positive cash flow and find difficulty coming up with the monies needed to offset the initial offering costs.

A Two-Step Process

The process involved in taking a company public has two parts. First is the preparation for registration, and second is the registration itself. The time involved in the preparation for registration is within management's control. The second part of this process comes after the company has submitted its registration statement to the SEC. It becomes a waiting game that depends on the workload and timing of that regulatory body. It's important for the entrepreneur to realize that the first few months of the calendar year is a traditionally busy period for the SEC. If a company submits its statement at that time, the response will not be quick for that's usually the time the SEC reviews proxy statements for the annual meetings of existing companics. The best time to submit the registration statement to the SEC is during the second quarter. As a rule, once the first letter of comment about the registration has been received, its submission goes to the top of the pile and receives priority over new submissions.

Timetable

In the outline that follows we have grouped details for your use as a checklist and guide to the key steps of a public offering (Figure 4.1). This guide can be used for start-up as well as operational companies. Each company will, of course, have to adjust the process to fit its individual circumstances. For easier understanding, it has been divided into two parts—the steps involved (areas) and a timetable outline.

FREQUENTLY ASKED QUESTIONS

Because the market is really hot right now, can I go public in just three or four months?

If you have done a lot of planning, you can. Most underwriters, however, have their calendars filled up in hot markets, many up to a year in advance.

How fast does the market environment change?

The 1988 Black Monday market fall canceled all new offerings in one day. In good markets, the changes that close down the openings usually take a few months. Good markets usually develop over a period of six months or so.

Should I prepare no matter what the current market environment?

Talk with your attorney or IPO consultant. A lot of preparation can be accomplished and continually updated as you watch market changes. If you're sure you want to go public, the effort is well worthwhile.

FIGURE 4.1   Key Steps to a Public Offering

Estimated Time (in Weeks)

	Minimum	Average	Maximum
1. Business Plans	0	2	6
a. Corporate master plan			
b. Underwriter/legal/accounting plan			
c. Condensed plan (executive summary)			
d. Identify preprivate financing			
2. Identification of Associates	1	2	4
a. Retain attorneys			
b. Identify accountants			
c. Identify underwriters			
d. Establish preprivate financing			
3. Forming the Corporation	1	2	4
a. File incorporation			
b. Structure public offering			
(1) Identify founders			
(a) Percent founders			
(b) Percent preprivate			
(c) Percent private			
(d) Percent dilution			
c. Negotiate underwriter's letter of intent			
d. Retain accountants			
e. Negotiate outside agreements (patents, sales, licenses, consultants, royalties)			
4. Private Placement Prepreparation	2	3	4
a. Approval of private placement documents			
(1) Corporation			
(2) Underwriter			
(3) State			
5. Raising Private Funds	3	6	10
a. Establish escrow account			
b. Solicit private monies			

    c.   Prepreparation of public registration

    d.   Break private escrow

6. Audit and Registration Preparation   2   3   4

    a.   Complete initial audit

    b.   Retain printer

    c.   Retain transfer agent

    d.   Approval of SEC registration statement

        (1) Accountant

        (2) Corporation

        (3) Underwriter

7. Filings   6   9   12

    a.   Submit registration to SEC

    b.   File with blue-sky states

    c.   Clear with NASD

    d.   Initial comment letter from SEC

    e.   Print red herring

        (1) Send syndication indication request

        (2) Distribute red herring

    f.   Second letter of comment and reply

    g.   Third letter (if needed)

    h.   SEC acceleration request (if needed)

8. Raising public financing   4   8   12

    a.   Arrange due diligence schedule

    b.   Sign underwriter's agreement

    c.   Establish public escrow

    d.   Print prospectus

    e.   File with Nasdaq

    f.   Establish syndicate

    g.   Distribute prospectus

    h.   Conduct due diligence meetings

    i.   Place tombstones

    j.   Complete public offering

        (1) Legal and accounting opinions

        (2) Closing papers

            Total Weeks   19   35   56

            Total Months   5   9   13

9. Postcompletion

    a.   Break escrow

        (1) Corporation, attorneys, accountants, bank, transfer agent, respective counsel

    b.   Establish market makers/quotation

        (1) Pink Sheets

        (2) Nasdaq

    c.   Establish trading

    d.   File 8-K

5

The Business Plan

Professional investors will rarely consider a proposal for an IPO by a private or public company unless the proposal is first presented in the form of a cohesive, well-written business plan. Only after evaluating the feasibility of this business plan will they invest the first dollar.

A business plan is a written presentation that carefully explains the business, its management team, its products or services, and its goals together with strategies for reaching the goals. The entrepreneur or whoever writes the business plan will, in all probability, find it a painstaking process. But keep in mind, this is the selling tool, and it requires careful consideration of the multiple facets of a start-up or business expansion. It can't be written as an afterthought, and it should not be taken lightly. Check with any underwriter or professional investor anywhere in the country, and you'll hear horror stories about ill-conceived, poorly written, or sloppily put-together business plans. As great as the company's potential may be, it's usually doomed to rejection before it can even get a foot in the door if it has a poorly conceived business plan.

A business plan has two basic purposes. One is to present the company in an engaging way with interesting information on how the business will be run for the next three to five years, or possibly longer. The other, of course, is to raise the money to do so. There's no business without the bucks. The entrepreneur must put all the "hows" and needs together in one neat package. The human and physical resources must effectively interrelate with the marketing, operational, and financial strategies of the company. Unless an entrepreneur has magical powers of persuasion, this is not the time to try to fake it.

The business plan should be considered a vital sales tool for approaching any financial sources, investors, or lenders. They'll want to know that the plan has been carefully thought out by the management team. They'll want to be convinced that the team has the skills and expertise needed to effectively manage the company and is prepared to seize opportunities and solve all problems that arise. That's why the business plan must be well prepared, professional in tone, and persuasive in conveying the company's potential.

I can't stress too strongly that a good business plan is the cornerstone of successful financing. If you want their money, you've got to give them a good reason to buy. The business plan is where you lay out the reasons. It doesn't have to be unduly lengthy or complicated. But it must be informative and relevant. It needs to maintain logic and order, and show the company to be effectively positioned as a good investment.

More important, the business plan should be specifically directed to the funding source and satisfy its particular concerns. For example, you would orient and write the plan differently for presentation to a banker than for a venture capitalist, an underwriter, or a private investor. The venture capitalist would want to know what risks are involved, whereas the banker cares more about how good the security is. These concerns must be individually addressed. There are no hard-and-fast rules for preparing a business plan. The key word is *ingenuity*. Strive for inventiveness. Strive to be interesting.

Here are some general guidelines covering the nine basic elements of a business plan that should be helpful in writing it no matter whom it's directed toward:

1. Make it easy to read. There is so much competition for investment dollars today that if you want to get the jump on the next person, your plan will have to be well formatted and easily understood. Your introductory statement summarizing your operation is one of the most important sections—it must capture investors' attention and motivate them to read the balance of the plan. If they need a dictionary at their side to read it, they'll stop.
2. Your approach should be market driven—not product driven. If you want those magic doors to open you must understand that investors are primarily interested in how the product or service will react in the market. They want to see your research demonstrating how the customer will benefit before buying into your plan.
3. Evaluate the competition. Start by evaluating your product according to cost or time savings and revenue generation. Also show your

projections for sales growth. And show how your product or service is superior to others and how you intend to exploit the competitive advantage.

4. Present your distribution plan. Be specific about how the company will sell and distribute its product or service. Describe the method and what it will cost to get the product into customers' hands.

5. Exploit your company's uniqueness. Explain what will give your company a competitive edge in the marketplace—special attributes like patents, trade secrets, or copyrights.

6. Emphasize management strength. Show proof that the company is comprised of highly qualified people who can cover all the bases. Indicate the incentives that will keep them together and how they, the directors, and the advisers possess the necessary credibility.

7. Present attractive projections. Paint a realistic picture of where your company is going from here. Be detailed and keep it credible. Good validated forecasts are impressive.

8. Zero in on possible funding sources. As mentioned earlier, it's different strokes for different folks. Design versions of the plan to fit the idiosyncrasies of each source you plan to approach. A banker's interest lies in stability, security, and sound returns, whereas a venture capitalist is more interested in "early stage" funding with its higher risk and higher returns. Both will want to know how much equity their investment will buy and how the proceeds will be spent.

9. Close with a bang. Drive across the fact that you're offering a great deal. Be definite about how investors will get their money back and when. Specify the return: state how the investor will receive a 30 or 50 percent compounded annual return or whatever you're offering.

The Next Step

You're not finished yet. After you've drafted your business plan, solicit feedback. Ask a cross section of people in your business, whose judgment you trust, to review it. Don't fall in love with your words. Make the revisions that are necessary, then prepare a good oral presentation. In fact, you should have ready a 2-minute and a 5-minute oral attention grabber. Follow up with a detailed 15- to 30-minute presentation modeled on your written plan.

A word of caution: When preparing your financial projections, avoid the shortcut of relying on available computerized information—those preset formats in which you plug in figures and percentages. Individualize your financial projections. Think them out carefully. No two businesses are alike. And keep in mind that a new or start-up company won't fit the industry norm.

Your projections should include the financial obligations of bringing out your product: enlisting new management people and workers; taking on more space or manufacturing capacity; purchasing support materials; and even the time it will take to receive your accounts receivables.

Expect to spend two or three months to write a business plan and many more hours to prepare the presentation. Remember, your words not only have to paint a pretty picture, they must be persuasive as well.

It's of little use to approach the writing of a business plan as if it were a necessary evil. Rather, look at it as a helpful tool that can be used to exploit the advantages of a product or service. There are many specifics that should be included in a successful business plan. The following outline contains many suggestions that may seem obvious, but you could easily forget to mention them. Again, this outline should be used as a preliminary planning guide. For an in-depth guide to writing a comprehensive business plan, see my book *The McGraw-Hill Guide to Writing a High-Impact Business Plan* (McGraw-Hill, 1994).

Business Plan Structure

1. *Cover sheet.* Include on the cover sheet the name, address, principal contact, and phone number of the business and the date the plan was written.
2. *Table of contents.* Categorize the contents.
3. *Executive summary.* This very important summary briefly sets forth the contents, taking key sentences from each section of the plan to prepare the reader. Devote two or three pages to it.
4. *History.* Include a brief description of how, when, and by whom the company was started and its achievements, acceptance, setbacks, and current status.
5. *Product or service.* Describe the need for the product or service in today's marketplace, how it will make a difference, the benefits derived from using it, what will make the customer buy it, and any other advantages or disadvantages. Explain any special training needed to sell or use it. Include all relevant regulation. Expound on any exclusivity or uniqueness.

6. *Market description and analysis.* Prepare a customer profile. Describe what persons form your market, where they can be found, why they would purchase this product or service rather than another, and whether it would appeal to single individuals or to groups. Document quality, warranty, service, and price significance. Pinpoint the buyer and user. Point out political influences, if any. Describe market coverage, whether local, regional, national, or international.

   Prepare an industry profile. Discuss pertinent trends: past, present, and future. Offer available statistical data on sales and units. Use charts, graphs, and tables if they seem impressive. Refer to trade associations if helpful.

   Prepare a competitive profile. Stress advantages of price, quality, warranties, service, and distribution. Include operational strengths and weaknesses. Project potential market share, trends in sales, and profitability.

   Don't guess. Check your facts and note sources wherever possible.

7. *Marketing strategy.* Specify the company's goals, how they are to be achieved, and who will have the responsibility. Qualify all distribution methods (representatives, dealers, etc.) and describe any planned advertising. Include sales aids, foreign licensing, and training.

8. *Operations plan.* Disclose all present capabilities of equipment and facilities as well as future projections for offices, branches, manufacturing, and distribution.

9. *Research and development.* Explain all past efforts and accomplishments as well as future expectations. Substantiate the patentability of inventions or other advantage the company will have over the competition and the anticipated market impact.

10. *Schedule.* Describe the timing and sequential steps that will be taken to bring the company up to full speed. Take it month by month for the first year; thereafter, indicate the progress expected quarterly.

11. *Management.* In the eyes of investors, the quality of the management team often determines the success of the company, so include detailed résumés. These should cover career highlights, accomplishments, positions held, good performance records. Describe how the team has worked together in the past. List directors, consultants, advisers, and other key professionals who will be involved in company operations. Detailed resumes should be appended.

12. *Risks and problems.* These could be a red flag. Indicate them only if the potential investor wants them identified.

13. *Use of proceeds.* Judiciously present a timetable indicating how much money will be needed, when it will be needed, and how it will be used.
14. *Finances.* Present the company's current equity capital structure as well as future plans. Itemize payments made with dates paid. List all outstanding stock options. Include profit and loss statements and balance sheets. Present the current and proposed salary structure for those already on board and those who will come on board at a later date. Show projections month by month for the first year, quarterly for the second and third years, and yearly thereafter.
15. *Appendix.* Include a glossary (if pertinent) and all essential pieces of evidence, such as résumés, product brochures, customer listings, testimonials, and news articles.

Preprivate Financing

Information regarding preprivate and private financing prior to a public offering should also be included in the business plan. To explain these terms: If two entrepreneurs each put up a certain amount of money to get a company started, that's preprivate financing; they then go out and seek more money from others—that's private financing. (See Chapter 19.) It's common practice and will not raise any eyebrows when presented in a good business plan.

Special Executive Summary

The special executive summary is not a part of the business plan, but it takes advantage of the high points in the business plan. It serves as an entering wedge by the entrepreneur anticipating a public offering. It's called "special" because it stands alone.

The executive summary discussed earlier in the business plan outline usually summarizes the plan in two to three pages. The special executive summary expounds on the most enticing parts of the business plan for six to eight pages. In essence, it's a condensed business plan that shows a company to its best advantage. It's an entrée when seeking help to locate and identify potential financial sources. It can also be used as an overview for persons who don't need to know all that much about the company or for those from whom management wants to keep proprietary information. It can be changed and adapted to any particular audience. The special executive summary also serves as an informational document to create enthusiasm among brokers involved in selling the stock at the time of public offering. It certainly will make more interesting reading than a formal SEC document. A company should not go into an offering without it. Above all, a special executive summary should not be taken lightly. It is indispensable and should be kept updated. It could very well be a key to reaching the right money source.

Follow-Up

A business plan requires regular updating. This should be given top priority. After a company has gone public and has raised the needed capital, the business plan should not be cast aside but rather should be converted into an operating plan. It should also be used to reflect on and to assist the management group in keeping the company focused on its goals. Refine it; adjust it; refer to it. Use it! Use it! Use it!

FREQUENTLY ASKED QUESTIONS

Our company is ten years old. Do we still need a business plan?

More than ever. The process of writing a good plan will cause you to rethink many of the ways you do business. It is also a necessity for the underwriters.

Can I use the same plan I use for private investors?

To some extent and for the basics, yes. However, many parts of a plan for a public offering are different from a private financing. Solid projections, with substantial assumptions that take in consideration the ongoing public company operating cost, are one of the major items unique to IPO business plans.

What about financial projections?

They are needed for the underwriter to analyze the potential but are seldom used in the actual offering memorandum.

A final note for anyone planning to go public: *Failing to plan is planning to fail.*

TWO

Assembling the IPO Team

6

The Management Team

In baseball it takes a team effort to get a player out. In football a tail-back would be hard pressed to cross the line of scrimmage without having the way paved by teammates. In hockey the puck is passed from player to player until it is finally slammed towards the goal. In business it takes the same kind of teamwork to make a public company operate successfully. But as with any game, it takes leadership to make the team work as a unit. This is management's role—to provide the vision, the direction, and the motivation to make the team a winner.

Let's take a look into the relationships, responsibilities, and qualities that can be expected from those members of the team in key management positions in a public company—the people responsible for carrying out the policies established by the board of directors and the directions of the CEO for the operation of the company. The CEO is the information and communications architect of the company, informing the team what must be done, while, by working together, they make it happen. Another responsibility of a public company's management team is to make certain that the company operates within the rules of the SEC. We all know that teams perform better when they're well motivated. In a public company the motivation for management is usually the reward of salary, stock options, and bonuses, which motivate individual players to play well and ultimately makes the team perform well.

When reviewing a prospective offering, underwriters view the quality of the management team as one of the most important factors. They expect management under the direction of the CEO to foster growth and establish a leadership position in the market. The reason is obvious—a good market position results in the public's purchasing more of the company's stock, which increases the stock's value and in turn increases the value of the management team's stock holdings. Underwriters are especially pleased if one or more persons on the management team has already gone through an IPO. It adds credibility to management's role—a good rationalization for the entrepreneur to be selective in the choice of management people. But then, of course, most entrepreneurs will do whatever is necessary to make their business a success.

In today's business world, entrepreneurial CEOs are the primary creators of all new businesses. The influence of the entrepreneur of the 1980s is without parallel in our history. At the turn of this century, 80 percent of all Americans were self-employed. By 1950, this figure dropped to 18 percent. By 1970, just 20 years later, it dropped to 9 percent. The 1980s saw a reversal in that trend as entrepreneurs moved to the forefront of a free-enterprise-driven society. The results of their entrepreneurship and creativity have not only increased our quality of life but caused revolutionary changes in our daily living.

Here are just a few examples of the impact made by entrepreneurs: Ray Kroc, the founder of McDonald's Corporation, was one of the prime contributors to the concept of fast food in this country. His franchise operations opened the door to thousands of entrepreneurs who dreamed of self-employment and in the process expanded the job market. Mary Kay Ash, of Mary Kay Cosmetics, was responsible for millions of dollars being earned by second-income families, but, more important, she helped thousands of women launch entrepreneurial lifestyles. The Block brothers, Henry and Richard, not only changed the practice of income tax preparation but in the process built a $500 million company and opened the door to thousands of new jobs. David Packard and William Hewlett created Hewlett-Packard. Today it's the largest manufacturer of electronic test and measurement equipment in the world. Packard and Hewlett trained and encouraged many people who now are among our most outstanding electronic entrepreneurs. And no list of current entrepreneur success stories is complete without mention of Bill Gates and Microsoft. Today his legend is being further enhanced by all the Microsoft employees that are spinning out new companies of their own.

In the past several decades, thousands of entrepreneurs have created millions of jobs all over the world. Many thousands of new products and service ideas have been spawned in hundreds of industrial classifications. Few of these entrepreneurs could have accomplished their goals without the expertise of their management team.

The value of a good management team is undeniable, but deciding on the right people to constitute a particular team can be a genuine challenge for CEOs. It requires careful evaluation of their own skills to determine the supplementary skills that will need to be provided by others on the management team.

The CEO's decision should be based on a thorough understanding of the business and what the members of the management team can bring with them to further that business. Their education and experience in business is essential to the company. It is also crucial for the entrepreneur-CEO to consider the personality of each team member and his or her ability to deal with management problems that will be aired in public, to adapt to the frustrations and compromises involved in accomplishing short-range or long-range goals, and to handle the continuing time diversions to accommodate public investors—let alone the burdensome reports constantly required by government agencies such as the SEC. In other words, besides having special abilities, the team members must be prepared to live in a goldfish bowl, even to the point of having their salary made public. These are only some of the factors that affect the important decisions an effective entrepreneur-CEO must make regarding the management team, but they are particularly important for building a strong team to run a public company.

The entrepreneur-CEO must understand, too, that the credentials and experience of the management team will be closely scrutinized by those involved in the investment process, including regulatory bodies, public investors, private investors, underwriters, consultants, attorneys, and accountants. The management team must be able to enhance the company's ability to raise needed money. Because, simply, that's what the game is all about!

Of course, the functions of the management team differ for different companies depending on the nature of the company. For instance, some companies may require a research and development department, whereas a service company may not. An engineer-to-order manufacturing company and a fast-food company require different kinds of management. Specific management abilities function in specific areas. Here I have prepared a general list of guidelines, qualifications, and fundamentals outlining abilities needed by members of the management team for a variety of public company environments:

Administration and General Management

Planning: ability to identify obstacles, establish attainable goals, develop and implement action plans

Problem solving: ability to gather and analyze facts, anticipate trouble and know what to avoid, implement solutions effectively, and follow up thoroughly

Making decisions: ability to take input from the team and implement changes

Project and task management: ability to properly define and set goals, organize participants, and monitor a project to completion

Negotiating: ability to solicit differences from all sides, balance opinions, and fairly arbitrate for mutual benefit

Communication: ability to communicate clearly and effectively to all parties and the public in both written and oral form

Operations Management

Purchasing: ability to seek out the most appropriate sources and suppliers, considering cost, delivery time, and quality; and ability to effectively negotiate contracts and manage flow, balancing current need and dollar resources

Manufacturing: demonstrated experience in the process; open to continuous improvement techniques, people power, machinery, time, costs, and quality needs of the customer

Inventory and quality control: ability to establish suitable inspection standards, maintain accuracy, and set realistic dollar benchmarks for raw, in-process, and finished goods

Financial Management

Ratio applications: ability to produce detailed pro formas for profit and loss (P&L), cash flow, and balance sheets; and analyze and monitor all financial areas

Money controls: ability to design, implement, and monitor all money management and to set up systems for overall and individual projects

Raising capital: ability to determine the best approach, form, structure of debt/equity, short-term versus long-term, and familiarity with sources

Marketing Management

Evaluation and research: ability to conduct thorough studies using proper demographics and interpret and analyze the results in structuring viable territories and sales potential

Support: ability to obtain market share by organizing, supervising, and, most important, motivating a sales force

Planning: ability to provide promotion, advertising, and sales programs that are effective with and for sales representatives and distributors

Selling: ability to effectively demonstrate a capacity to identify, open the door to, and develop new customers by closing the sale

Product distribution: ability to manage and supervise product flow from manufacturing through the channels of distribution to the end user, with attention to costs, scheduling, and planning techniques

Product continuation: ability to determine service and spare parts requirements, track customer complaints, supervise the setup and management of the service organization

Engineering and R&D

Research: ability to distinguish between basic and applied research, keeping a bottom-line balance

Development: ability to guide product development so that a product is introduced on time within budget and meets customers' basic needs

Engineering: ability to supervise the final design through engineering, testing, and manufacturing

Personnel

Listening: ability to listen without prejudging, really hear the message, and make effective decisions

Help: ability to determine situations where help is needed

Criticism: ability to receive feedback without becoming defensive and provide constructive criticism

Conflict: ability to confront differences openly and determine resolution with teamwork

Development: ability to select and coach subordinates and pass this ability on to peers

Culture: ability to create an atmosphere and attitude conducive to high performance, rewarding work done well either verbally or monetarily

Legal

Contracts: experienced in and knowledgeable about the broad procedures and structure for government regulation and commercial law, including warranty, default, and incentives

Corporate: experienced in and knowledgeable about the intricacies of incorporation, leases, distribution, stock issues, and patents

This list covers the qualifications, abilities, and characteristics the entrepreneur should take into account when assembling a management team for a public company.

It's not necessary to have the full team assembled and in place at the time of submitting the IPO registration statement. It is perfectly acceptable to simply list the titles of positions not yet filled, followed by a statement that team members will soon come on board or the company is still searching for qualified candidates. List the qualities and qualifications desired and include the positions in the officers' compensation table. Thus, you'll show that management is aware of a personnel deficiency and intends to fill the vacancies with highly qualified candidates.

FREQUENTLY ASKED QUESTIONS

After the CEO, what management position is the most important to an underwriter?

Usually, the CFO (chief financial officer), who has the primary responsibility to understand, furnish, and interpret the past, current, and financial future of the company.

Is it okay to have family members on our management team?

Sure, but they'd better be qualified. A company with multiple family members always leads to close scrutiny. However, no one will object if they have proven to be valuable performers.

We have fashioned our firm as a virtual corporation with a lot of valuable outsource suppliers. Do we need to hire them instead?

Absolutely not. But this fact needs to be carefully documented in your business plan and you may have to put them under long-term contract.

7

The Board of Directors

There's an old story about a "smart" entrepreneur, the chief executive officer (CEO) of a company, who was advised by underwriters to be sure to get a highly qualified board of directors to help make important company decisions—people of integrity who could be objective and had good judgment.

The CEO told the underwriters there was no need for outsiders to tell him how to run his business—he'd make a killing with his company on his own. Well, he made a killing all right. He killed the company.

The point here is that IPO CEOs need and should seek the best help they can get in making important company decisions. They should begin by assembling a strong board of directors.

Good and Bad Boards

A good board of directors is composed mainly of outsiders, even though selecting outsiders often goes against the grain of the CEO. It's true that no one has the CEO's stake in the company. It's understandable if one dislikes involving outsiders in important decisions. Thus, CEOs tend to enlist people who are involved in the day-to-day operations of the company, such as the management team. *That* is a bad board of directors.

They'll deny it till hell freezes over, but employees and managers tend to rubber-stamp the CEO's decisions and to inhibit rather than encourage frank comments by outsiders. It's called self-preservation. It's hard to be objective when one's job could be in jeopardy. Therefore, it's in the CEO's own interest to choose board members who will give independent, unbiased feedback and won't be afraid to disagree or say no.

Another good reason to limit the number of insiders on the board is to preserve the CEO's own fallibility. No one has all the answers, but when CEOs can't come up with answers, their leadership position is weakened in the eyes of management. It's just not a good idea for subordinates to know when CEOs are frustrated and unable to come up with the solution to a problem, or to discover the CEOs are not the great leaders they seemed. All of us are, at one time or another, faced with decisions we just don't know how to make. Strong boards of directors can serve as psychological support teams to help CEOs make the important decisions only they can make.

Outside board members serve a very important function in a company. They are outsiders only in that they do not actively work in the company as an employee or in management. A board member could be a major shareholder (most valuable), a business associate (valuable), a retired chief executive (valuable), or an investment banker (good). Also acceptable, but ranked lower on the ladder, are lawyers, accountants, and suppliers with a financial stake in the company. The common feeling is that they should be reviewed very carefully because they may have personal interests at odds with the company's best interests. Other excellent candidates for the board are persons engaged in businesses different from the company's who can appreciate and understand the risk of running a company or who manage, or have managed, a public company.

A good board member plays many roles—from assisting in formulating long-term policies and plans to critiquing existing financial, production, or marketing practices. But the board's most powerful role is that of confidant, mentor, and peer to the CEO. With a good board, rather than the president's making decisions alone, the directors become involved in setting company policies and strategies and reviewing operating results.

Overall, the board of directors should demonstrate respect for the CEO. The directors should like the CEO and want him or her to succeed. They should have unquestionable integrity, good judgment, relevant experience, problem-solving skills, and a capability for action and risk taking. That's why a good board is hard to find.

Changing the composition of the board of directors may prove embarrassing to the CEO, especially if the board existed before the company went public, and it can be even more embarrassing if the board consisted of friends and relatives lacking real credentials. But the CEO must understand that in going public the board will assume greater responsibilities. Their credentials must be acceptable to the public, and the public must have confidence in them. To paraphrase a well-known statement, CEOs must do not what is best for them, but what is best for the company.

An Informed Board Is a Helpful Board

One of the prime responsibilities the CEO has to the board of directors is to keep it informed. Directors must be given information on a timely and continuing basis. They must have meeting agendas and pertinent background information sufficiently in advance of a board meeting to allow them time to prepare for the meeting. They must be furnished with monthly financial statements, including comparisons to budgets. At all board meetings, they must be given detailed reports on the company's progress.

Although most directors know what is expected of them, it would be a good idea for the company's legal counsel to furnish each board member with a copy of the *Corporate Directors Guidebook,* published by the American Bar Association. This book provides a general overview of the functions and responsibilities of the corporate director and will help the directors to perform their directorial functions responsibly as well as to adhere to the board's bylaws and the regulations of the SEC and other governmental agencies. Consider it must reading.

What to Expect from a Board of Directors and What Not

The board of directors does not run the company. The board of directors does not run the company; management runs the company. The board sees to it that the company is well managed.

The board of directors does not develop company strategy. The CEO and management develop company strategy. Board input can be indispensable, however, in coming up with ways to test and evaluate management strategy.

The board of directors enhances company performance. The attention of the board of directors can be turned to immediate needs, such as controlling costs, or it can apply its expertise to plan ahead for future needs, such as defining and penetrating a new market. The board must be flexible enough to deal with all matters in the best interests of the company.

Directors should be experts in their fields. It's up to the CEO to assess the management team's strengths and weaknesses and the company's direction, and then select the best candidates for board positions to fill the voids in the management plan and thereby help improve the company's performance. The entrepreneur-CEO will probably be pleasantly surprised to find the high caliber of outside people who not only are flattered but would give their eyeteeth to be asked to serve on a board of directors. The ideal board is composed of top-notch people who are experts in the industry, such as a scientist with an interest in business dealings who would benefit from the experience, a former CEO of a public company, or a former politician with a business background.

Directors must attend meetings. At the very minimum, meetings of the board of directors should be held quarterly. The frequency of meetings depends on the needs of the company. According to surveys conducted annually since 1971 by Korn/Ferry International, the world's largest executive search firm, the national board meeting average is 8 times a year. Small public companies, start-up companies, or those in the early stages of going public may find it necessary to schedule meetings 10 to 12 times a year. The Korn/Ferry survey also determined that the average outside director devotes more than 150 hours annually to company business.

Directors get paid. As far as compensation goes for directors, no two companies do it the same. Compensation can take many forms, including annual retainer fees and hourly or per-meeting fees plus expenses. In a recent Korn/Ferry survey of 31,000 companies, meeting fees for outside directors ranged from $100 to $1,000 with an average of $534. In addition, many firms have established annual retainers of $5,000 to $10,000. Smaller companies may pay no fees at all, although $100 per meeting seems to be common practice.

Another form of compensation, especially suitable for cash-short companies, is the issuance of stock in lieu of money. This practice can prove to be a disadvantage over time as it makes outside directors insiders. Let's say, for example, that a director is also a shareholder. If the board is contemplating a decision that may adversely affect the value of the shares, that board member may not come up with the desired objectivity. Also worth thinking about is that when directors become shareholders they open themselves up to directors' liability lawsuits.

Directors can get sued. In 1977 Congress passed the Foreign Corrupt Practices Act (FCPA), which stated that officers and board members should create an environment whereby middle and lower levels of managers and employees would understand the nature of corporate accountability. It urged board members to be cognizant of their responsibility to monitor the totality of corporate performance. (Chapter 28 deals more fully with the FCPA.) This well-intended legislation was probably the forerunner of many current lawsuits.

Most lawsuits filed are nuisance suits, but they are very expensive to fight. There were hundreds of such lawsuits filed in the mid-1980s against public companies, and liability insurance premiums skyrocketed. Many insurance companies stopped writing policies, and many fine prospects turned down offers to serve on boards of directors.

In response, as many states passed legislation that limited liability, SEC compliance became stricter, tighter financial accounting rules were instituted, companies policed themselves more carefully, and court awards were reduced. These cases were no longer plums for lawyers seeking to make quick bucks; plaintiffs had to prove that the company, its management, and, more particularly, individual directors were purposely negligent in performing their duties, were party to insider-trading abuses, or had committed willful acts of omissions, especially fraud. By the late 1980s, the volume of suits subsided, but much damage had already been done.

Makeup of the Board

There is no standard operating procedure regarding the number of members that must constitute a board of directors or the mix of outside directors versus management members. It depends on the scope of the company, egos, and personal preferences of the CEO.

Five directors on the board is a good number for several reasons. It's an odd number, which avoids tie votes, the taking of sides, and bitter personality battles. Three members may not allow for sufficient diversity of opinion or fill weak areas in management. Two outside directors seems to satisfy the vague FCPA rules and the feeling of the courts about the need for outside objective input. And, of course, on the inside managing directors have a high stake in the success of the company. Rounding out the board could be a major shareholder. For a small IPO company five directors is ordinarily sufficient, and as the company matures it can easily be expanded to seven. Thus, a company can add expertise from either the inside or outside to fit expanding needs without the board's becoming cumbersome and overly expensive.

Committees of the Board

Because of the proliferation of liability suits against companies, management, and boards during the late 1970s and early 1980s, as mentioned earlier, companies were compelled to become more accountable. Committees were established to validate accountability. Most OTC companies today maintain committees composed of board members, management, and outside experts that include those discussed below.

Audit committee. The audit committee is found on most boards. Comprised entirely of directors who are not officers of the company, it supervises and directs investigations into matters relating to audit functions and is responsible for a general review of the annual report. The audit committee recommends to the board of directors the retention of independent auditors and approves their work. This includes the fee arrangement, the scope of services, and a confirmation of the independence of the auditors. The audit committee also reviews the company's internal accounting procedures and controls.

Nominating committee. The nominating committee reviews the performance of the directors and recommends management nominees for directorships.

Conflict of interest committee. At least two-thirds of the members of this committee should be outside directors unaffiliated with the company or its subsidiaries to avoid the potential for favoritism. The committee's function is to oversee the company's conflict of interest policy and to keep track of significant transactions between the company, its subsidiaries, and members of management.

Compensation committee. The compensation committee reviews the achievements of executives and officers of the company and makes recommendations to the board concerning their compensation, including the awarding of bonuses, perks, and stocks.

Executive committee. The executive committee is less common than the others that have been mentioned. Its primary function is to assist management in implementing corporate policy established by the board of directors. For instance, the board may decide that certain procedures could benefit or expedite the company's operations. The executive committee would have the power and authority to act on behalf of the board in working with management to see that the board's directives are carried out.

Board of Advisers (Advisory Committee)

The board of advisers is not set up as a committee of the board, although in some corporate structures it is considered to be one. One or two board members may head the advisory committee and act as a buffer between the advisers on the outside and the board itself.

As a rule, the formal setup of the board of advisers is accomplished through an amendment of the bylaws. The advisers are appointed by the board of directors, but they are distinct from the board. In most companies advisers may not be officers, directors, or employees of the company. They are experts in various fields whose function is to consult with directors and officers of the company on technical, management, and economic factors that affect the company. Well-chosen advisers add prestige and credibility to an IPO.

Members of the board of advisers serve at the pleasure of the board of directors and receive compensation as determined by the board. They are also provided with indemnification by the company.

There are no requirements for formal group meetings by the board of advisers, although in some companies they meet as a group at least twice a year. Most commonly, individual members of the board of advisers are consulted as necessary in their areas of expertise.

For Directors Only

Directors of OTC companies and entrepreneurs contemplating an IPO should consider membership in the National Association of Corporate Directors, a nonprofit organization serving the needs of corporate directors and boards. Member benefits include an informative newsletter, *Director's Monthly,* and the Directors' Register, a unique service to help companies search for appropriate candidates to fill board vacancies. The association sponsors seminars featuring timely topics for directors. It offers liability insurance and other services of interest to corporate directors. It's an organization for all companies regardless of business size, structure, or sector, and membership fees are reasonable. For information write to: Association of Corporate Directors, 450 Fifth St., NW, Suite 1140, Washington, DC 20001.

Officers' and Directors' Questionnaire

All executive officers and all directors of an IPO, including outside directors (but excluding members of the board of advisers), are required by the SEC to complete a very extensive questionnaire. It includes some of the personal information required in the registration statement and in the annual proxy statements. Many of the questions are of a technical nature and require lengthy answers.

The questions place special emphasis on relationships between the company, its suppliers, lessors, lessees, purchasers, consultants, principals, and even relatives. Other subjects deal with fraud, misrepresentation, education, employment, legal and illegal acts, past history (with specific dates), outside stock or equity ownerships (present, past, public, and private), and any dealings with the SEC or the NASD. It's not a pleasant task to fill out one of the questionnaires, but it's a necessity.

FREQUENTLY ASKED QUESTIONS

How do I find prospective board members?

Network! Ask peers; ask friendly competitors; check with your local college department heads and ask them for recommendations; read your local newspaper, and when you see someone of potential interest, contact him or her.

Aren't top-quality people reluctant to serve on small company boards?

You'll be surprised. Many successful people enjoy the opportunity to get involved with emerging growth companies. You'll never know unless you ask.

What do I do when I need money, not a fancy board?

Quality board members bring money with them. A lot of small companies attribute their funding success to their board members.

Will suppliers work?

Suppliers make great advisory board members. They usually are up to speed on the latest happenings in the industry and if they've been at it awhile, they are a good source for additional board member leads.

8

Consultants and Advisers

Too many cooks spoil the broth. That ain't necessarily so—especially when it comes to hiring consultants for small companies, or even large companies for that matter. No matter how professional a management team may be, and no matter how well staffed the company, there are usually areas of the business that can use outside expertise. That's why consultants were born.

Consultants are people with specialized expertise. They are often retained on a onetime basis for a specific problem. Advisers, also discussed in this chapter, may serve as consultants, too, but are expected to have a broader knowledge of the business. Advisers are usually retained to advise the company's management team for a longer term and can be especially useful working through the IPO process.

Consultants

Bringing in a consultant is not the same as hiring another person on the staff of the company. Consultants should be retained only for the period of time required to assist the management team in identifying, isolating, and solving problems or deficiencies. The consultant's function is to bring a particular problem into focus and zero in on the solution.

If there is a marketing problem, for example, the consultant may advise the company when to put a product on the market, whom the product should be directed to, and where the product is likely to receive a good reception. Or a consultant can provide expertise on product improvement or production techniques. There are countless situations for which management could be served by help from a professional on the outside.

A consultant or consulting firm is not someone management turns to in desperation; rather, they should be used as a source for helpful guidance. Many consultants, where an IPO is concerned, like to get involved during the conception phases of the company. If they really know their craft, they can be very helpful in starting a company off on the right foot.

Consultants Can Come from Anywhere

Anyone can call himself or herself a consultant. Some people who call themselves consultants are self-promoters. Some work at it on a temporary basis. They are often people with good management skills who are between jobs, or they can be former CEOs who offer expertise in their particular fields.

There are over 50,000 private consultants in the United States today. Most work on their own, but there are also consulting firms that employ as many as several hundred people that range from national to international in scope. Their clients are usually major companies. They prefer long-term projects and their fees are commensurately high. Many major companies operate on the premise that the higher fee, the better the consultation. The question is whether the consultant's experience fits your company's needs. Look for proven professionals in their field who have successfully helped others with similar problems to those facing your company.

Hire When Ready!

When enlisting the aid of a consultant or consulting firm, a company should first be convinced of the need. According to a recent *Harvard Business Review* article, "Management consultants are generally hired for the wrong reasons. Once hired, they are generally poorly employed and loosely supervised." It's important therefore that the company does its homework before hiring a consultant.

Most consultants have an area of specialty. Some may claim broad expertise, but their experience may actually lie in a special industry or technical area. The company should find out this information in advance. The fact that a consultant has an excellent background in one field does not make him or her an expert in another field. The company should also determine in advance the precise problem needing a solution—thus eliminating some consultants from the running.

Consultants Are Not Always Necessary

Properly utilized, a consultant can appreciably help a company's operations, but too often management may already have the answer to a problem and only need to convince key people. The consultant can serve that purpose, but at a price. Consultants are also often asked to explore areas the company has no intention of pursuing. Yet another misuse of company money is to hire consultants to research information that is readily available.

A sharp management group can solve many consulting chores without paying unnecessary consulting fees. For instance, suppliers can usually advise a company whether it is more advantageous to buy or lease certain assets or how best to go about computerizing a business with the right kind of hardware and software. Insurance company agents are trained to determine the most efficient insurance and employee benefit plans. Advertising agencies and marketing companies interested in working with the company will usually provide sound, useful information for free. All it takes is a little talking to the people a company does business with or plans to do business with. Remember, a consultant is not the only one who can supply answers.

Consultant is not a magic word. Consultants should not be left to their own devices. Management has an obligation to stay on top of consultants' activities as well as to make certain they get the necessary support from the company's staff. Consultants should be encouraged to bring in solutions within a reasonable period of time. As mentioned in an earlier chapter: time is money.

Fees

Consulting fees can take many forms. They are often open to negotiation, but some consultants are firm in their charges; much depends on the complexities involved. Fees can be based on hourly time or a weekly amount. Some consultants ask for a fixed fee or retainer. Some companies prefer to have consultants work in-house, but some consultants will work only off-site.

The ideal way for the company to approach the consultant situation would be to contact several possible consultants. Brief them on the problem. Secure proof of their expertise and get information about similar projects they have worked on. Besides asking for their credentials and résumé, request specific proposals on how the project could be handled.

Before a final decision is reached, management should feel confident about working with the consultant and satisfied about receiving

- a realistic and reasonable charge for services,
- a determined attempt to produce results,
- a cooperative attitude toward the people involved, and
- maintenance of a continuing relationship.

The effort and time involved in securing the services of the right consultant for a particular need will pay off handsomely. The chemistry must be there, for with it comes the confidence and security the job will be done right.

Many sources are available for locating consultants: the Small Business Administration, Small Business Development Centers, Service Corps of Retired Executives (SCORE), colleges and universities, and even professional placement services. Some of the best sources may be recommendations from other companies.

Advisers

Don't even think about going public without the backing of knowledgeable advisers. More obstacles will be encountered in the IPO process than in the game of Monopoly, from finding the right underwriter to submitting the proper forms to the SEC at the proper time.

The best advisers—the most dependable ones—are those individuals or consulting firms that have been through the IPO battle from beginning to end more than once. You may have to search because there aren't very many of them out there, but they are the only sure way to go. What's more, even though the advisers may have been through the process, they'll find it different every time. The rules change from day to day with never-ending changes in federal and state regulations and the fickleness of the financial community, which wants every speculative investment to be a sure thing.

Young's Study

Dr. John E. Young, while at the College of Business and Administration of the University of Colorado at Denver, questioned hundreds of CEOs who had gone through the IPO process about outside advisers. Those shown to be most important were legal counsel, CPAs, underwriters, bankers, and printers.

Other advisers not specifically covered in the study, but who should be considered as even more important, are people who have been through the IPO process and could apply their knowledge and experience for the benefit of the company—people such as a member of the board of directors, or someone in the management team who has been involved in the IPO process before, or an experienced outside investment banker with prior dealings with IPOs. What matters is having a broad perspective of the process and being objective about what the CEO must contend with in confrontations with other professionals such as attorneys and CPAs and with the SEC and other government agencies.

Young's CEOs rated legal counsel as being "very important" before, during, and after the IPO. This was not surprising as lawyers play a key role in almost every aspect of a company's going public. It's especially advantageous to have legal counsel with a strong working knowledge of the IPO process.

Young's CEOs continued to find underwriters important advisers, but underwriters have lost some of their mystique. While it's true they are a direct connection between the entrepreneur and the money to be raised, the entrepreneur is becoming more aware of the human frailties to which the underwriter is subject. It can soon become obvious that underwriters' main incentive for working on an IPO is to make commission revenues by selling the company's stock. That motivates them to keep the stock in the public eye, but they usually lack any deep or abiding interest in the operations of the company.

CPAs who have been through the process can be invaluable in showing the company to its best advantage. The end result of any business has to do with accountability—profit and loss. CPAs with a working knowledge of IPOs can evaluate how well the company's earning stream will hold up. They can put the company in touch with interested investment sources through banking and underwriter contacts. They can also act as a bridge between the CEO and the SEC's legal department and advise the entrepreneur whether the company can be competitive in the market.

Although bankers seldom play a lead role in the IPO process, they lend a note of credibility and longevity for a company involved in the IPO process. They can advise the CEO how to deal with the banking community and how and where to get the most for the company's dollar.

Printers' contributions to an IPO can be critical, for they are involved in the process from beginning to end. On their shoulders fall the supervision of the preparation and issuance of documents, including the prospectus and registration statement, which must be flawless. As an adviser, the printer can help the company obtain quality work at the best price.

Planning Ahead

The purpose of this book is to help the entrepreneur-CEO through the stages and processes involved in taking a company public. Young's study substantiated the importance of prepublic planning. He asked hundreds of CEOs, "Now that your company has gone public, to what extent do you feel that your company should have engaged in prepublic planning?" He concluded, "Most CEOs, after having gone public, believe that they should have engaged in even more planning for the IPO process." For the uninitiated it's something worth considering. It's also something the responsible adviser should suggest.

Because his study was broken down by industries, Young was able to determine that *industry dynamism* was a factor in the purchase of stocks as far as investors were concerned. Industry dynamism refers to "hot" industries—those favored by the stock-buying public. Young concluded that "industries characterized by rapidly changing market conditions and increasing competitive entry cited a greater need for prepublic planning."

Consultants and advisers who are well versed in the IPO process should have a handle on the progress being made during the prepublic planning. They should be able to temper the eagerness of the CEO and the management team, ignore minor pitfalls, and get on with the show. Problems that are not solved in advance, whatever they are, have a way of snowballing into almost insurmountable difficulties that require inordinate time and effort to correct when you're going public.

Young's study confirms the importance of consultants and advisers and of settling for nothing less than the most qualified and highly experienced advisory people available. Once these are found, the CEO should give them good incentives to maintain ongoing relationships with the company.

FREQUENTLY ASKED QUESTIONS

What's the best way to find a consultant or adviser?

The old standby of networking is best. Ask your lawyers and accountants. Talk carefully with your industry peers.

Aren't consultants expensive?

Some are very expensive but you can find many others who are highly qualified and very reasonable. The key is to be very specific in what services you desire.

Can you expand on the term qualified?

The two keys points in being qualified are war stories and time. Consultants should be willing to spend some time with you relating war stories about their past experience, which it's hoped applies to your particular need. Time refers to the length of time a consultant or adviser has been plying his or her craft: the longer the better. Hands-on experience is important.

9

Accountants

One of the key figures in a company's going public is the accountant. If the books aren't in order, if the figures don't check and balance, the company doesn't stand a chance of satisfying the SEC requirements for public companies. Therefore, the role of the accountant is most crucial to the completion of any IPO.

For an existing company the SEC rules for registration require a company to have at least one year of audited balance sheets and two years of audited income statements. Although a start-up company doesn't have to furnish such financial information, it would be ill advised to proceed past square one without the services of a highly qualified accountant, preferably one well versed in the IPO process.

A Brief History Lesson

Accountants were not always considered integral to a public company. The historical impact of the accounting profession on public accounting practices and the evolution of the rules now in effect were long in coming.

Until the 1929 stock market crash, the U. S. accounting profession did not adhere to rigid accounting-practice standards. Even though history proves it should have shared in the blame for the crash and the subsequent depression, accountants escaped any direct responsibility. Except for mild chastisement, the accounting profession was ignored in Roosevelt's New Deal Securities Act of 1933, and this "held harmless" attitude continued into the

1970s until post-Watergate political pressure called for corporate accounting reform.

In 1976 a House subcommittee reported that scandalous episodes of corporate illegality, unaccountability, and the use of questionable business practices raised questions about the effectiveness of our system of corporate accountability. The Financial Accounting Standards Board (FASB—the accounting profession's internal rule-making body) made virtually no progress toward increasing accountability in the profession for continuing abuses, especially in large corporations. (These corporations mainly used the services of the Big Eight accounting firms, at the time of this writing referred to as the Big Six as the result of mergers and acquisitions but probably soon to be the Big Four.) The House report further stated that "the SEC's continued reliance on the private accounting profession is questionable."

A Senate subcommittee agreed with the House report and advocated more federal control, which resulted in Congress's passing the Foreign Corrupt Practices Act (FCPA) in December 1977. One purpose of this act was to make a foreign bribe by a U.S. company a federal crime, but more important it strengthened section 13(b)(2) of the Securities Exchange Act of 1934, which regulates accounting controls and financial recordkeeping of U.S. companies that are registered with the SEC.

The strengthening of accounting standards affected by the FCPA created a whole new ball game. The Big Eight firms were now forced to attest to a company's inventories, purchases, and financial status. As one result, to cover their new liability exposure, they increased their fees substantially.

Companies that experienced financial difficulties or bankruptcy had caused much shareholder disenchantment, and suing the accountants who, it was felt, did not conduct proper audits became fashionable. During the late 1970s and early 1980s, juries often found accounting firms negligent in their auditing of client companies and made substantial awards against them. The verdicts might have seemed justified by the fact that the accounting firms raised their fees and therefore made more money, which allowed them to purchase high liability insurance.

The 1980s also witnessed the coming of age of the entrepreneur. With that came a strong IPO market and a steady increase of venture capitalism and investment banking. The Big Eight firms soon found that they were missing out on many new, fast-growing, potentially valuable clients. By the mid-1980s, the large and the small were in a head-to-head battle for the audit account business of IPOs. The competition not only benefited the OTC IPOs but brought the fee structure of accounting firms more in line.

Selecting Accountants

According to law, every IPO and public company must have audited financial statements. Not only that, but when going public the company must have an SEC-qualified accountant perform the audit. To be considered qualified, the accountant or accounting firm must be a member of the SEC Practice Section of the American Institute of Certified Public Accountants (AICPA).

For the small company, hiring an auditing accountant to verify the bookkeeper's figures may seem like having to pay to have the same job done twice. Generally, start-up and early stage companies don't need a detailed or complex accounting system. In all probability, a part-time bookkeeper or comptroller can easily handle the accounting. The situation is different in IPOs. They often do better with a prestigious major accounting firm because those firms usually have contacts with SEC legal counsel, underwriters, and investment banking firms. Because, by law, every business has to prepare financial statements, sophisticated entrepreneurs seek out the services of a CPA to prepare the required reports.

Compilations

A compilation is the simplest of the CPA reports, generally performed for internal company use only. The purpose is to give the accountant a general understanding of the nature of the company's business, accounting records, and company policies. The CPA reads the company's financial statements and makes sure they are in appropriate form and free from clerical errors. The figures are supplied by management, and the CPA does not express any opinion about them.

Reviews

A review is a report that goes beyond the compilation. It provides some assurance about the reliability of the financial statements. The company accountant or CPA reviews the accounting principles and practices of the company and its industry, and analyzes and compares expected trends, past results, industry data, and internal projections. The review may also contain some of the specific procedures that would ordinarily be performed in an audit.

Audits

An audit is a confirmation of the credibility and reliability of the financial statement of a company. Every IPO and public company has to have an audited financial statement performed by an outside auditor to guard against company manipulations in the report. The accountant reviews and evaluates the effectiveness of all the accounting procedures and internal controls that are necessary to meet SEC accounting standards for public companies. The accountant must also attest to the correctness of the company's financial statements and to the company's financial position for the period covered.

It is the responsibility of an existing company going public to present the auditor with as complete and correct financial records as possible to verify the income statements. If the balance sheets and inventory verification are not possible to reconstruct, a cloud on the audit could result: a "qualified" financial opinion on the part of the auditor that could delay the offering by the SEC until a full year of audited inventory has taken place.

Preparation

It bears repeating: Companies in the early stages of doing business should make preparations for the eventuality of going public. They should start by assembling an accounting team. The team should consist of inside (often called in-house) and outside (usually a CPA) accountants as well as an auditor.

An in-house accountant should have bookkeeping and accounting experience but need not be a full-fledged accountant. The position includes responsibility for day-to-day routine bookkeeping functions and coordinating with the outside accountant. As the company grows, there may be an increasing need to bring in a full-fledged accountant.

The outside accountant is independent, not personally involved with the company, and preferably a CPA. It's important that the CEO has respect and confidence in this person, who represents a link between the company and the SEC accounting world. The outside accountant usually prepares, or at least reviews, the monthly financial statements and supervises the assembly of the company's quarterly and annual reports. The position requires someone familiar with, and knowledgeable about, SEC accounting procedures as well as able to serve as liaison between the company and auditors.

Auditing

Audit accounting is a subject warranting a closer look. Auditors must be completely independent. They must not have any financial interest or ownership in the company. SEC auditors work in teams to look for trouble in the books, so they tend to be suspicious, trusting no one, especially no one in the company. They can be expected to check and cross-check every item: that's what they're paid to do.

Audit Guidelines

SEC Regulation S-X deals with the form and content of financial statements and their ultimate certification. It spells out the importance of independent auditors and details the rules and regulations these auditors must comply with to establish their independence. It further sets out qualifications to guarantee that independence, including the following ones:

- Must have independence during the full period of the audit.
- Cannot have a financial interest in the company.
- Cannot be a promoter, officer, director, or employee of the company.
- Cannot certify another auditor's work.
- Must avoid interrelations with employees or relatives of employees of the company.
- Must perform the audit personally and not subcontract it to others.
- Cannot "write up the books" (post the general ledger—a function that must be done by the in-house accountant).

SEC rules also state that the company cannot owe the independent auditor for past audit fees.

SEC Regulation S-X seems to infringe upon the auditor's basic rights by making any contact with management or employees strictly taboo. The SEC, however, looks upon these rules as a way to assure the independence of the auditor and to make certain that favoritism in any form towards the company does not take place.

Evaluating the Auditor's Qualifications

Many ways are available to evaluate an auditing firm. One is to get recommendations from a trusted person, from someone knowledgeable about the IPO process, or from the company's IPO adviser or attorney. Although a lot of experience with the SEC is not critical for the accounting firm because set guidelines are followed by all accountants, it is nonetheless essential that the auditing firm have some experience with the SEC. For an IPO you shouldn't make a move without an auditor who has been through the registration process more than once—and recently! Also important to remember is that the managing partner in the auditing firm should be the sign-off person, the one fully responsible for the detail work of subordinates.

Another good way to evaluate an auditing firm is by interviewing. Select several promising contenders and request proposals for final evaluation. Ask such questions as these:

- What are the firm's areas of expertise?
- What is its recent SEC filing experience?
- Who will work with the company day to day?
- What are the billing methods—by the hour, by the job?
- What is the billing cycle?
- When can someone begin?
- How long will it take?
- Does the firm have underwriter or investor contacts?
- Will it give an estimated total cost in a written proposal?

In August 1997 the Nasdaq announced a requirement that "independent auditors must be subject to practice monitoring under a program as the AICPA SEC Practice Section peer review program." Ask your prospective auditing firm if they participate in this program. It is one more way to evaluate them.

Familiarity Is a Must

Every effort should be made to hire auditors familiar with the company's type of business and industry. It is also beneficial if they have experience with competitors—so long as another client is not presently in direct competition with your company. Actually, auditors are bound by an ethical code to turn down companies that may represent a potential conflict of interest.

Familiarity helps because auditing requirements differ vastly from industry to industry. An oil pipe supply company's inventory, for example, occupies many acres of outdoor storage, whereas the inventory of a fast-food franchise is turned over by being eaten every day, and a manufacturer of high-tech small parts may fit three months' inventory in a few fireproof file drawers. Bookkeeping, payable, and receivable methods vary from company to company, resulting in special rules being applied to different types of companies and to their various stages of development. The auditor must have the skill and knowledge to work through these differences—why familiarity can be a plus.

GAAP Must Be Observed

GAAP is an industry term that means generally accepted accounting principles. GAAP dictates the procedures for presenting audit information. As an example, accounting methods of private companies are generally aimed at decreasing taxable income and depreciation, and inventory booking and write-downs are adjusted accordingly. Private companies frequently switch back and forth from cash to accrual accounting methods to assist in tax adjustment, but these practices are not allowed for public companies that function under GAAP. All accounting for public companies must be done on an accrual basis.

In a case of an existing company that has operating subsidiaries, the subsidiaries must also have financials audited under GAAP. This makes for auditing headaches, especially if offshore subsidiaries are involved. Separate audits must also be prepared for subsidiaries that may be sole proprietors or partnerships. Even if the company is considering an acquisition on a pro forma basis in conjunction with an IPO and the acquisition amounts to more than 10 percent of the combined total assets, it must be audited, too. The SEC considers as "material" any assets representing 10 percent or more, and they must be audited.

Although the process of auditing an existing company that has not previously been audited can be costly and time consuming, it can be done providing the company has maintained fairly complete financial records. However, getting into the area of inventory may be a different matter.

Inventory verification within GAAP can become very complicated. It must include historical (prior) audited financials, which can present a sticky problem for the auditor who was not around when the inventory items were first counted. Consequently, many companies may find themselves in the awkward position of writing off large amounts of inventory with the audit opinion evaluated regarding past inventory procedures. In essence, the auditor says, "Since I wasn't involved in taking the inventory count, I can't truly say that all the statements are absolutely correct. But I assume they are."

For inventory accounting, the auditor must know whether the inventory valuation has been applied on a consistent basis—was the method used last in, first out (LIFO) or first in, first out (FIFO)?—as there is often a price variation in the interim. What, if any, tax adjustments were made and how they have affected the tax reporting are other possible variables as is the inclusion of overhead in finished goods inventory, a requirement of the SEC. And, of course, the method used for inventory accounting must accord with GAAP.

Before the new SEC regulations, an auditor could simply state in effect, "I was not present to observe the taking of the prior year's inventory; however, I did physically monitor the most recent inventory. Consequently, it is my opinion that all past inventories were properly conducted, and I believe all accounts are reasonable." Because this type of statement occasionally proved to be incorrect, the SEC has disallowed the practice and now insists on a clean, fully satisfied "I did physically observe all inventory."

Time Costs Money

A forward-looking entrepreneur-CEO with the goal of eventually taking the company public should seriously consider enlisting the services of an accountant to monitor and audit inventory procedures from the start. The cost will be considerably less than a fully audited financial statement and so will the aggravation. It won't eliminate the necessity of an audit when going public, but it will save time and dollars even if a different accounting firm becomes involved with the IPO. What's more, even if a company's inventory has been audited regularly, prior audits must be reviewed to assure compliance with SEC regulations.

An audit for a small existing company can take from a few weeks to possibly six months. It depends on the problems the auditor may uncover. Previously unaudited companies are typically beset with such deficiencies as poor accounts payable systems, uncollectible accounts receivable that haven't been written off or down, unreconciled bank accounts, notes payable with doubled assets pledged as underlying collateral, and incorrectly recorded depreciation expenses.

Accounting ethics require strict adherence to due diligence procedures. For instance, if the company purchased a major piece of equipment, the accountants will have to see copies of purchase orders, invoices, and canceled checks. They will be expected to inquire about possible securities fraud violations and bankruptcy filings.

Areas that can present very complicated problems for previously unaudited existing companies include personal financial dealings by officers and directors that were placed through the corporation. Even advances or loans made to officers by the company, especially in recent accounting periods, require special schedules to be filled out and reported. Most likely, too, they will have to be declared in the IPO prospectus.

All of these issues take time to resolve, and the cost varies according to the time involved. It's not unusual for an auditing firm to charge as much as $25,000 for a noncomplex audit.

Auditors Are Accountable

Auditors today must take full responsibility for their work. CPAs can be held liable for misleading or false financial data in a prospectus. If they were misled by company falsification but cannot establish that they conducted their work with sufficient diligence, they are accountable under the Securities Act of 1933 through the comfort letter we spoke about in an earlier chapter, leaving them vulnerable to lawsuits by both the SEC and investors.

Experienced auditors know that the financial statements they submit will be used in the prospectus of a company going public. They know that the prospectus basically serves as a selling document. Therefore, they can be expected to make every effort to express their findings in clear, concise, and easily understood language, down to the thoroughness of the footnotes in the financials. Their reputation rides on the effectiveness of their presentation. And so does their next job.

FREQUENTLY ASKED QUESTIONS

Do I have to use a Big Six or maybe a Big Four firm?

No. We are very fortunate in that there are many smaller firms with regional practices. They frequently have very qualified departments with a lot of experience dealing with the SEC. However, some underwriters may insist the larger, internationally known firms be used.

Will the accountant work with me on a payment plan?

Maybe when you're first starting a company, but SEC compliance rules require that the company stays current in paying accountants. Auditors are used to having discussions with management about this subject, especially for IPO companies. Talk with them, whether they're large or small, for they'll be pleased to answer your questions.

Do I have to show them all my records?

Absolutely. Auditors want to see and know about all financial transactions. They are the experts and they will tell you what they don't need. But be prepared for full disclosure.

10

Attorneys

Highly specialized . . . Past and current IPO SEC experience . . . Successful record in IPO filings . . . Compatible, intelligent, knowledgeable . . . Friendly, if possible . . . Good contacts with underwriters, investors, bankers, and brokers . . . Reasonable fee.

Well, the last may be asking too much. But the kind of counsel described above makes an IPO a happy experience. The services of qualified SEC counsel in an IPO cannot be overemphasized. In fact, they are crucial. The company must depend on legal counsel to see it through compliance with a multitude of federal and state securities laws and regulations. If all is not done according to SEC rules, which require a keen legal mind to decipher, the IPO can be stopped in its tracks.

Letting Go

Unfortunately, it's not easy to let go of the friendly legal counsel who has seen a company through thick and thin. As private companies grow and contemplate going public, however, they must be prepared to make changes unless their present or regular attorney has SEC experience. Most competent attorneys will realize their limitations and even suggest bringing in a highly competent, recognized specialist in the IPO process.

Every effort should be made to select counsel with current IPO experience with the SEC in an industry similar to yours. Although many legal firms have an active SEC practice, their experience may have been in dissimilar industries, and their involvement may be limited to ongoing companies as opposed to new filings. The SEC categorizes generic filings as SB filings that apply to general types of industries. There are also filings that apply only to oil and gas and some only to precious metal mining. Some attorneys specialize in oil and gas and others in gold mining; some have expertise in high-tech filings. Large, prestigious law firms are usually geared to handle more complicated SEC filings, whereas smaller law firms may not be. The secret is to select an attorney or firm familiar with the business of a company's going public and, we emphasize, experienced in IPO filings.

The Difference between Large and Small Law Firms

Like shoes, legal firms come in different sizes and styles. Many of them specialize in various types of services. It's up to company management to choose the firm that best fits the company's requirements as to size, compatibility, competency, and contacts in the investment community.

A large legal firm is not the answer for all companies. True, a large firm may have several hundred lawyers with many areas of specialties, which on the surface may seem advantageous. Many large corporations prefer such firms, as they can call upon the services of different specialists in one office. That arrangement may serve the purpose of a diversified, multidimensional company with many different companies under one umbrella—say a manufacturing company, a mining company, a food company, and a service company—each requiring different legal input. A smaller IPO lacking that corporate makeup wouldn't need a firm with all those attorneys where it may face the possibility of getting lost in the shuffle.

Large legal firms with many partners and associates traditionally also have many young, inexperienced junior associate attorneys who are usually assigned to work with small companies on a day-to-day basis. Because the associates must often clear their advice with a managing partner, dealings can become frustrating for the company management as well as inefficient, time consuming, and costly. Those new, bright, young lawyers, although capable and intelligent, lack experience and can make a lot of mistakes. It's a learning process for them, but it's usually the client who pays for their mistakes.

Depending on the benefits and prestige derived from engaging a large law firm versus a small one, it may be preferable for an IPO to work with a small, SEC-specialized firm. For one thing, the company will get closer attention. Junior associates or paralegals become involved usually only to help out in routine matters. Small firms can be fully competent to handle all the corporate information, including all the SEC rules and regulations. Specializing in companies that are going public, they are usually more cognizant of the nuances of prospectus writing and more aware of the current SEC environment; that's their whole business.

Getting Along

Too often the attorney's image is that of a necessary evil. Attorneys have been typecast as arrogant, nonresponsive, and overpriced. In fact, some are really nice. But rarely do they come cheap. However, in the eyes of reasonable entrepreneurs, the price is right if it gets them through the IPO.

Setting Parameters

It's up to management to set the parameters when selecting counsel for an IPO. Management should be clear about what it expects—whether it's hand-holding, assurances that the company's goals to go public are attainable, or even alternatives on how the IPO can best be achieved. Management must also cooperate fully with counsel. It's the attorney's responsibility to write a full disclosure document describing the company, its markets, the competition in the market, and its product or services.

There must be no secrets kept from counsel. The more counsel understands the company's industry, its management team, and its aspirations, the more helpful he or she can be, and the less frustrated. Forthrightness will also save time, which translates directly into dollars.

Questions to Ask

When interviewing counsel for your IPO, it's advisable for management to prepare a list of questions for a potential law firm or attorney to assist the CEO in the selection process. The following questions can prove helpful in making the decision:

- What types of registration has your firm worked with in the past?
- Do you have recent filing experience?
- Do you specialize in particular areas of business, and are they compatible with our company's industry?

- Who will be our day-to-day contact?
- What is your billing procedure—hourly, monthly, or by segments?
- Can you give us your estimated total cost, including expenses and fees?
- Do you have any useful investment contacts—underwriters, brokers, investors?
- What is your projected timetable? How long do you expect the process to take?
- When will you be able to start on the project?

Billings and Fees

IPO attorneys typically bill by time and they count not just hours but minutes. Their rationalization is that they do not sell products or services; they sell knowledge and past experience, which can be invaluable to a client.

Although hourly rates can vary from less than a hundred dollars to several hundred, a good round figure for the primary senior contact member of a law firm would be about $150 an hour. Time for junior associates could be in the area of $75 an hour, and administrative functions (typing, copying) could range from $30 to $50 an hour. These are give-and-take figures.

Total fees can vary considerably. A simple start-up through the public offering could be in the range of $20,000 to $40,000. The more complex process for an existing company with a past history is usually more costly. It requires going back into the company's past and reviewing the minutes, article and bylaw changes, patents, employment, license agreements, financing, and clarification of anything that may put a cloud on the company's operations. Depending on the complications, the fees could be as much as $80,000 to $120,000. On average, in an existing company costs approximate $35,000 to $65,000.

Law firms usually provide an estimate of the total costs. It's a safe guess that the final amount will seldom be less than the estimate. Although some firms are willing to put a cap on the project, they will usually leave an out for themselves for unanticipated exigencies. These could be article or bylaw changes, unexpected litigation, state law changes, unresolved lawsuits, or new SEC requirements. The entrepreneur can make book there will be something.

It is also unrealistic to assume that legal counsel will work on the contingency that the fee will be paid after the IPO is completed, regardless of the negotiated amount. It's best to plan on a deposit or advance. A reasonable figure would be a percentage of the total estimated fee or an estimate of the first month's work or of the first stage of work. Rarely will any substantial work be performed by an IPO law firm before an initial payment, usually made at the time of signing an engagement letter.

Other Forms of Payment

Generally speaking, the legal profession is not averse to taking a flier with the company. Many attorneys like IPOs, not only because they generate handsome fees, but because they like the idea of taking a portion of their fees in stock. The structure of the legal business in itself does not generate capital appreciation or equity buildup. Consequently, accepting stock as part payment allows lawyers to become more intimately involved with the company and gives them an opportunity to invest without actually putting out any hard cash. But paying stock in lieu of money *can* create problems. For one thing, it can dilute ownership among stockholders in the company. It can cause disagreement among the partners in the law firm. Especially in larger firms, partners who are not directly involved in the project may not feel as positive about the company's potential and would prefer the cash to restricted stock that has no guarantees.

The strongest argument against stock as payment is the potential conflict of interest. Some company managers may question whether the advice they are receiving is in their interest or the adviser's interest. Attorneys in the law firm may question a conflict of interest regarding the involvement of outside parties and whether it would be condoned by the SEC. The ability to remain objective when negotiating non-arm's-length transactions may also be questioned. These may seem extreme concerns but should not be ignored in a decision whether to offer stock for the services of legal counsel.

Double-Check the Cost

The cost of doing business with an IPO-specialized law firm is high under the best of circumstances, as mentioned earlier. Therefore, it's just common sense to make a practice of regularly reviewing counsel's billings. To err is forgivable. Not to check for errors can be expensive. Time and again, good relationships between management and legal counsel have dissolved because it seemed counsel was taking advantage in its billings. This assumption, more often than not, turns out to be unfounded. But that is why professional legal counsel is always ready to discuss, substantiate, and, if necessary, adjust billings. It's up to the company to keep the lines of communication open and frank. Establishing a good working relationship is of benefit to both company and counsel.

Legal Responsibilities

The role and responsibilities of legal counsel are covered more fully in subsequent chapters involving

- prepublic planning,
- corporate records cleanup,
- review of all contracts and agreements,
- amending articles and bylaws, and
- capital structure.

Other areas that involve legal counsel are preparing information for the SEC, advising about exemptions and their impact on the company, and developing stock incentive plans that meet SEC regulations. These are all part of the process of making the company ready to go public that leads up to the actual presentation of the registration statement and the filing.

The 1933 and 1934 securities acts (discussed further in Chapter 18) established the parameters for the legal profession's role in an IPO and the company's role as a public company. These acts were conceived and written by lawyers; their interpretation, as for all U.S. laws, was left to the discretion of the courts. Judicial decisions have played havoc with the accounting profession, resulting in accounting firms being named in shareholder lawsuits. Accountants were the first to be blamed for "improper" company financial records. Judges soon discovered complicity on the part of the legal profession, which increasingly became named in these suits after companies faltered. Today, accountants and attorneys as well as management and directors are jointly sued by disgruntled shareholders. As a result, the fees of all continue to rise.

The Multiple Counsel Approach

It's common practice today for entrepreneurs going public to continue retaining lawyers they worked with in the past or are currently working with. Companies frequently remain with the corporate counsel they have felt comfortable with even if the counsel lacks SEC experience. They may also use outside counsel in areas such as patent, trademark, copyright, real estate, or other specialties. The attorney experienced in dealing with the SEC—a securities lawyer—is another specialist who will supervise the IPO undertaking. Working with the company's corporate attorney should present no problem but rather should be of help for general business issues.

Retaining the company attorney could very well save the company hefty legal fees. Instead of paying the high hourly rate of counsel experienced in SEC matters, the company can pay its regular counsel, usually at a much lower rate, for many items needed to clean up and update company records in the IPO process. The two lawyers can complement each other as well as realize a savings for the company. In the final analysis, it's a "save and sound" idea.

FREQUENTLY ASKED QUESTIONS

So what's best, large or small legal firms?

Neither necessarily. Retain the one you're most comfortable with. Personal compatibility is a paramount consideration. The relationship of management and counsel is often likened to a marriage as you'll be practically living together during the IPO.

Do I really have to have an IPO specialist?

Not retaining counsel with IPO experience could prove deadly to your company. Going public is an extremely complicated legal specialty.

How do I qualify a lawyer?

Sounds like an intimidating process, huh? You'll find that top IPO attorneys are knowledgeable and willing to help you understand the process. They will take the time (you're paying for it) to be sure you are comfortable with the decisions you have to make. I've also found that the good ones have (by necessity) a great sense of humor.

Financial Printers

Financial printers are a breed unto themselves. They are specialists in the printing of financial documents, including registration statements, prospectuses, even stock certificates. On the surface this may sound like nothing out of the ordinary. Not so. It calls for complete involvement with the client.

As mentioned in Chapter 3, the initial registration statement and prospectus must be submitted to the SEC, the NASD, and the state securities commissions. The preliminary prospectus, called a red herring because it's cover is printed with a lot of red ink, accompanies the registration statement and is distributed to the brokerage community to solicit indications of interest for the underwriting. The final, or definitive, prospectus (without red printing) is the completed approved offering document that is used to solicit prospective shareholders and interested persons in the financial community. It's a showpiece and can include photos, graphics, colored paper, and multicolored print. Each is a unique document and calls for special attention by the printer.

A prospectus cannot be distributed if it is not letter perfect—no typos or errors allowed. After proofreading by all key parties, the printer performs an additional review to make sure all necessary elements are included and correct before going to press. No one concerned considers prospectuses run-of-the-mill printing jobs. Not just any printer can do financial printing. Recognized financial printers must stay current with the strict SEC rules, regulations, and printing requirements regarding the size of type and paper, format, and other technical specifications. Nothing short of 100 percent accuracy is acceptable.

In addition to accuracy, timeliness is critical. After layout, typesetting, and submission—then come the changes. There are always changes in a prospectus determined according to responses to a letter of comment from the SEC. The changes may be typographical. They may concern a new SEC ruling or a requirement that had not been included in the prospectus. The changes must be made quickly and accurately—usually overnight or within 24 hours. Once the SEC gives its final approval, no time should be lost in getting the prospectus out and into the hands of the underwriter and selling group for distribution to the public.

To expedite the printing, management (with a lot of help from its legal counsel) needs to ensure that each proof is promptly reviewed by all the key parties. It is usual for management to authorize one person to communicate and coordinate the project with the printer. Many companies simply rely on their SEC-specialized counsel to handle that chore. Another time-saver is to assign one person, a secretary or the central editor, to submit corrected copy to the printer with all the correct spelling, punctuation, and content, thus avoiding a lot of confusion and allowing the printer to move fast.

You need 100 percent cooperation, dedication to the job, and know-how from the printer, which probably explains why there are only about 20 qualified financial printers in the United States today. (Lists are available through legal counsel and most brokerage houses and underwriters.)

Confidentiality is another reason for using experienced, qualified financial printers, who are well aware of the importance of keeping inside information from leaking. They are accustomed to working behind a veil of secrecy and know the implications. They know that companies they work for must be able to trust them and feel comfortable with their security precautions.

Costs

Financial printing is not cheap. As of this writing, a one-color run of 30,000 to 40,000 copies could cost approximately $20,000. Four-color runs can easily amount to $60,000. It takes a lot of paper to cover the territory: copies of the prospectus must be furnished to all prospective purchasers of stock, whether they buy or not.

It's also customary to keep a supply on hand for at least a year after public trading starts. The prospectus can be used as a public relations tool also. Copies are sent to brokers, financial publications, and magazine publishers, and they are used in media kits. The quantity required is usually determined by the company's attorney, the underwriter, the printer, and the public relations (PR) firm hired to promote the company.

Qualifying the Financial Printer

The company's attorney usually has the best access to qualified financial printers. Recommendations can also come from the IPO adviser, the underwriter, and the financial PR firm. Because the outlay for financial printing is substantial, a wise management team will ask for several recommendations. There aren't that many printers to choose from, but it's important to find the one that can offer the best deal for price and performance. Printers with computerized equipment are capable of accepting floppy disks and other electronic word-processing input directly from the attorney's office and thus saving time and money.

Following are some pertinent questions a company should ask a potential financial printer:

- Could we have a list of your recent clients?
- What type of facility do you operate?
- May we have samples of recent similar jobs?
- How long have you done financial printing?
- Do you expect computer disks, hard copy, or both from us?
- Can you give us an estimate of the cost of the complete job, breaking out any extras?
- Who will be your contact person?

Management should carefully evaluate the responses to select a printer that will fulfill the company's requirements and with whom company personnel can work comfortably.

Ancillary Services

Stock certificates are also printed by financial printers, although no longer exclusively. Few public companies any longer use the elaborately engraved certificates of earlier days but now choose preprinted certificates, simply inserting the company name and logo for a customized look.

Most financial printers also provide full conference room facilities complete with bar and kitchen to offer clients comfortable surroundings where they can proof their documents and make last-minute changes before the documents go to press.

Financial printers are also geared to handle the distribution of both the preliminary and final prospectus to broker-dealers and other members of the financial community. The printer will sort and deliver copies to the various places and people specified by the lead underwriter—the service isn't free but it relieves the company of a burdensome task.

FREQUENTLY ASKED QUESTIONS

Why can't I just use my local copy shop?

The process is very complicated and takes a through understanding of SEC guidelines for these types of documents.

Is it true that some financial printers have beds adjoining their conference rooms?

Not many, but some do. All-night and 24-hour-plus sessions are not unusual at the last minute before an offering is released.

Who attends these sessions?

The whole IPO team. Company management, accountants, legal counsel from the company and the underwriter, possibly PR representatives, and the underwriter's key people.

Financial Public Relations

Financial public relations (financial PR) as it pertains to public companies traded over-the-counter—especially small ones—is usually sadly lacking. The reason is that, unfortunately, management people in too many small companies just don't comprehend the value of financial PR. In fact, it's often a totally foreign subject to management, which doesn't understand how important it is to get out information about the company to brokers to keep them hyped up, to members of the public so they'll buy the stock, to shareholders to keep them from selling their stock, and to the media in general. Too few people in management think "out of sight, out of mind" could possibly pertain to their company.

A wise entrepreneur knows, "You gotta sell the company to sell the company." Entrepreneurs astute enough to include financial public relations in their business program, even on a limited basis, stand a greater chance of success than those who neglect it.

The Public Relations Mystique

There's really no mystery about public relations except perhaps in the minds of some members of management teams. Financial PR is simply a means of informing the public what a company is doing in such a way as to make the public take notice and take the kind of action that enables the company's goals to be reached—that is, buy the company's stock.

Public relations begins within the company in the day-to-day conduct of business. It's the shine on a salesperson's shoes, the smile on a face, a friendly greeting, a welcome attitude by a receptionist, a call put through promptly by a telephone operator. It's a cordial letter by the company president. It's employees who think and speak well of the company. Public relations is, in essence, a state of mind with a positive attitude toward anyone who hears about, reads about, or comes in contact with the company.

Four Steps to Effective Corporate Financial PR

Embarking on a financial public relations program can be divided into four basic steps.

1. Analysis. PR people will first analyze the public's attitude toward the company: Is it positive? Negative? Indifferent? They may resort to a public opinion poll or an attitude survey. They may randomly ask people what kind of feelings they have toward the company or industry. Or the PR people may have enough research on hand to proceed with the next step.

2. Interpretation and policymaking. After an understanding of public opinion about the company has been gained through formal or informal means, the next step is evaluating these opinions in order to formulate policies and objectives. Then the PR people must prepare plans to achieve these objectives. Effective corporate financial public relations revolves around the interpretation of public opinion, planning, and decision making. Plans should cover existing factors and conditions—products, markets, sales performance (if significant), competition, policies, dealers and distributors, and the various people the company wishes to reach. The objective is always to create an interest in the company as one that should be invested in. Specific needs and goals must be set forth to reach this objective. Methods include human interest stories, news releases, or other forms of communication such as broadcasting, TV, or printed material. The methods should take into consideration the results of research, including attitudes and public opinion. The goal is to reach all interested parties—shareholders, investors, underwriters, and the financial press.

3. Communication. The basic message to be communicated should be established and agreed upon. The target audience should be clearly defined in order to reach the greatest possible number of those at whom the message is aimed. Appropriate media should be used, whether brochures, newsletters, newspapers, the Internet, and even broadcasting. The more people who become interested in the company, the greater potential for the stock's rising in value.

4. Continuing evaluation. PR should not be considered a one-time effort. The results of programs and the effectiveness of techniques should be constantly evaluated. Although the corporation may have gained approval today, there is no assurance it will continue through tomorrow. Attitudes and opinions of individuals change with time, with new points of view, and with information from competing sources.

Markets also change. New markets develop. Income levels and populations shift, changes that may necessitate company diversification. Technology may change. The need for venture capital may arise. All of these factors require a company to be prepared to alter its strategy. It will pay off in increased profits and future growth for a company to constantly reevaluate its public relations program.

To reiterate: A financial public relations program begins with building a favorable image and a friendly climate of opinion in which to operate. Maintaining them is critical to a company's success. It stands to reason that if a company is perceived to have growth potential, chances are it will have more buyers of its stock.

The Public Relations Difference

There is a difference between financial and other public relations. In nonfinancial PR, the company is mainly concerned with its community image, its customers, its suppliers, its employees, and its standing in the industry. In financial public relations, the focus is on those areas that affect the public's impression of the company financially. Of key concern are existing and prospective shareholders. The goal is to attract new shareholders while retaining the old ones, because the more a company has of both, the greater chance its stock has of going up in value.

The CEO of a company is rarely involved in the sale of its stock. Sales are usually handled by brokers, market-maker contacts, printed material, news releases, and the efforts of financial public relations.

The Rewards of Financial PR

In most companies, the CEO or a key member of the management team will have the responsibility for implementing and overseeing the financial PR program, thus making it even more important that they have an awareness of all the areas financial PR encompasses. It's through financial PR that management is able to maximize the company's progress and development, not only for itself, but for all shareholders.

Take the price the company's stock sells for. The higher the current price, the fewer additional shares must be issued for company transactions, such as expansion or acquisition, which translates to less stock dilution. It's simple arithmetic. Instead of selling 20 percent of the company for $20 million to consummate a deal, you may have to sell only 10 percent for the same $20 million if the stock appreciates in value. That means more shares remaining for the company less dilution) and higher value per share for the shareholders. Also to be considered is that with the increase of the trading price of the company's stock, management's personal net worth increases, which naturally makes for a more contented management.

Any stock on any exchange or market faces a potential demand every day it's traded—and that demand usually originates in the concerted efforts of public relations. Stocks go up when there are more buyers than sellers. Stocks go down when there are more sellers than buyers. If a company is perceived to have growth potential, chances are that it will have more buyers. It's the job of the financial PR firm to let the public know that the company is there and that good things are happening to it.

Unfortunately, a common cry among financial PR people is that many corporations think of them only as a means to put out fires, and too often the PR people have good reason for complaint. But hiring a qualified financial public relations firm is one of the best investments an IPO can make. Public relations can set the fires that an IPO needs to gain the recognition and acceptance that it seeks.

Today's investors are more sophisticated. With new stock disclosure laws, there is less manipulation of stocks, and many other choices are available to investors, such as bonds, money market funds, and real estate. For a public company, especially an IPO, to get the investor's attention requires a serious attempt to reach the target audience. You can't just sit back and wait for market analysts to find buyers and hope to make an impact on the market. Financial public relations can help make your day.

What to Expect from Financial PR

- Financial public relations can develop exposure for a company's business. It can make the potential investor aware of the company's product, marketing approach, personnel, philosophy, and benefit to the industry. This is not to negate the advantages of advertising, but the costs could be considerably less than the cost of a full-page advertisement in a newspaper or magazine.
- Financial public relations can provide information to clients, investors, brokers, and analysts, influencing their decisions to purchase or retain a stock.
- Financial public relations can, over a period of time, develop a favorable reputation for a company, especially if it accurately reflects what the company is doing.

What Not to Expect from Financial PR

- Don't expect financial public relations to communicate ideas or information about a company's performance, plans, attitude, or potential that don't exist.
- Financial public relations cannot guarantee that a company's publicity message will appear in a specific media at a specific time.
- Financial public relations cannot persuade media to run anything but accurate, newsworthy information.

Making a Commitment

Financial PR requires the same kind of commitment on the part of the president and management of an IPO that they give to manufacturing, distributing, and selling the best quality product possible. PR can't be treated as a stepchild. What's more, company management must get involved in the decision-making process of financial public relations if they want it to work. And they must regard the cost, which won't be cheap, as an integral expense of doing business. They must also be able to communicate that positive attitude to the entire company staff.

Let's look at how a few of the major companies regard financial PR. At Reynolds, the public relations staff is designated as an arm of the president's office. At AT&T, the public relations director reports directly to the president. At Standard Oil, the public relations manager reports to the executive vice president. If those successful companies that some people may feel don't need financial PR wouldn't make a move without it, shouldn't that serve to convince IPOs and smaller public companies of the value of financial public relations?

Choose a Professional

A professional financial public relations firm is the only way to go. You will get experts at getting the attention of the right people—the brokers, underwriters, and investors—who can make a difference. Even if a company is large enough to have a full-time person assigned to "investor relations," it's not enough. There aren't enough hours in the day, what with other obligations full-time people get involved in, to implement a comprehensive financial public relations program without outside professional help.

Why short-change the program? Management wouldn't think of doing legal work without engaging professional counsel. It would not, and could not, audit its own certified accounting. By the same token, it's much more cost effective and time effective to engage professionals in financial PR. They have established contacts with the media and investors; they know how to set up a continuing, consistent, and reliable program.

To make the program work, there must be a commitment between the financial public relations firm and the company because the result reflects corporate policy, insight, and planning.

Start Early, Stay Late

The importance of establishing an early relationship with a financial PR firm can't be overemphasized. In fact, if at all possible it should be done before going public. There's too much at stake for management to put the matter off until later. Hiring professional PR people can be expensive but worth every penny in selling out the initial public offering.

Continuing the services of the financial PR firm after the company has gone public is a natural next step, especially through the first year, with a focus on holding and gathering further support for company stock among shareholders.

Of course, an effective financial public relations program extends beyond simply maintaining positive relations with shareholders. Although an outside entity, the PR people will be working as part of the company's management team. Activities should be directed to include employees, potential shareholders, the financial press, analysts, and concerned members of the community, all with an eye on the goal of earning the company the favorable recognition it seeks.

Where Do You Find Them?

Identifying financial public relations firms is a fairly simple task; finding a good one is another matter and the subject of the following section.

Firms that specialize in financial public relations, sometimes referred to as "investor relations," spend a lot of their time with the analysts (see Chapter 30) on brokerage firms. They wine and dine them, all in the supposed interest of their public company clients. You should inquire of your underwriter—better yet of several—which PR firms they would recommend.

Another professional to ask to recommend public relation specialists is your attorney. But be cautioned, attorneys often cringe when you start talking about "hyping" your stock. On the other hand, if your securities attorney recommends a PR firm, it gives the firm a lot of creditability as well as reinforcing your belief that you have an attorney who understands what public company financial marketing is all about.

Evaluating the Financial PR Firm

Three basic areas should be evaluated before making a final selection of a financial PR firm.

Standard Public Relations Functions

Management should ask the financial PR firm to submit samples of its work as well as recommendations to show that it can perform the job required by management, including assisting and guiding the company in putting together and properly disseminating shareholder letters, press releases, quarterly and annual reports—all with professionalism. It should go without saying that management would expect the firm to familiarize itself with the company's philosophy, people, business, and industry. The public relations people should be expected to prepare an analysis of the market for the product or service. They should also have a keen understanding of the company's position and potential in its industry and know all about the competition and what it is doing.

It is also the responsibility of the financial PR firm to make certain that all written material submitted to management is free of errors in spelling, sentence structure, and punctuation. Management should expect the financial PR firm to be accomplished in writing articles, company brochures, employee newsletters, financial news releases, annual and quarterly reports, employee manuals, external publications, general publicity, press information kits, speeches, and promotional literature, and in engaging in investor relations, press relations, and PR counseling. Management may decide that some of these areas could be better accomplished in-house or by a regular PR firm. Even so, these are areas about which a financial public relations firm should have a working knowledge.

Management should also be able to call upon its financial PR firm for recommendations about ancillary services, such as market planning, special events, marketing research, finished art, media analysis, photography, catalogs, sales contests, dealer sales ads, industrial exhibits, press tours, marketing counseling, broadcast production, illustrations, media buying, print production, incentive programs, convention planning, direct mailings, video presentations, logos and trademarks, packaging, sales meetings, technical literature, letterhead and sign graphics, premiums, slide presentations, originating and maintaining Internet sites, and price and parts lists to name a few. These are services usually handled in-house or by advertising agencies, art services, media companies, broadcast companies, and PR firms. However, a financial PR firm should be aware of the need for these services when they arise and should be able to counsel management and make suggestions.

Broker Contacts

The Street contacts of a financial public relations firm can be of immeasurable benefit to an IPO. These could include personal introductions to individual brokers, broker-dealers, financial analysts, and market makers as well as individual investors. If the choice between one financial PR firm versus another comes down to a toss of the coin, common sense says to choose the one that has the best contacts in the financial community.

It also pays to take the time to personally make contact with some of the clients of the financial PR firm to find out if the CEOs of these companies were satisfied with their broker contacts.

Other steps to take in gathering information about a financial PR firm include the following:

- Verify the experience the financial PR firm professes to have in the industry.
- Determine if any of its clients might present a conflict with your company. If your company is in the computer business, for example, and the financial PR firm represents other companies in the computer business, the PR firm may have difficulty finding your IPO unique.
- Make sure the firm doesn't have more accounts than it can handle, leaving it without enough time to give your company the kind of service you expect to receive.
- Make certain that the broker contacts are right for your company.
- Look for assurances that the firm is capable of providing on-time service and meeting important deadlines.

Compatibility

It's extremely important that the financial public relations firm and management are philosophically compatible. Several meetings should give managers an indication whether there is mutual respect and they would enjoy having the firm on their team.

FREQUENTLY ASKED QUESTIONS

Why can't I use my advertising firm for investor relations?

You can if you're sure that your advertising firm is well qualified and active in the area of financial PR. Even if most financial investor relations companies are used to working with advertising firms, they inhabit two different worlds.

Why are broker contacts so important?

Stock brokers are on the front line. They have daily contact with investors. A good financial PR firm knows a lot of brokers personally and have developed a personal rapport built on brokers' trust that the PR firm represents good stocks.

How else do financial PR firms differ from advertising firms?

The media used are different. Advertising firms know newspaper, magazine, radio, and TV advertising rates. Financial PR firms know the business editors in the media. They know how to get your story out in the form of press releases and company interest stories.

13

Transfer Agents

Transfer agents are the recordkeepers of all stock transactions and shareholder information for a public company. Shareholder information includes all the pertinent data about a particular stock and its purchaser: the shareholder's name, address, Social Security number, and the number of shares and the date purchased.

A registrar serves as a cross-check on the transfer agent and has the responsibility of making sure that the company's stock is not overissued. Registrars keep track of all the certificates that have been lost, destroyed, or canceled along with an accurate accounting of the exact number of shares and certificates outstanding at any given time. The functions of the registrar and transfer agent are normally held by the same firm and referred to collectively as the transfer agent.

An over-the-counter company may, if it chooses, keep records internally with a day-by-day transfer journal and shareholder's certificate ledger. However, the NYSE and the AMEX require that the jobs of the transfer agent and registrar be handled by outside independent services, which is really the best way to go. No matter how small the IPO, the company is ill advised to do the job itself because it can become an administrative nightmare as well as a financial liability. Any inaccuracies can subject the company to claims for mishandling its stock. Most underwriters make it mandatory that all companies doing business with them retain independent registrars and transfer agents.

The services that transfer agents provide extend beyond simply transferring stock and recording the transaction. A client instructs his or her broker, Paine Webber for example, to buy 100 shares of General Motors. The broker may have to buy them from another broker, Merrill Lynch for example, on the client's behalf. The shares are delivered to Paine Webber, which in turn delivers the certificates to the transfer agent with instructions to cancel the Merrill Lynch certificates and issue a like amount in the client's name. The transfer agent also becomes involved in the issuance of new shares. Let us say that a company works with an underwriter to raise capital by selling an additional 5 million shares. The transfer agent issues the shares to the buyers and makes sure the certificates issued are valid, fully paid for, and nonassessable.

The transfer agent must also report to the IRS when cash dividends are paid (a 1099 form for U.S. citizens or a 1042 form for foreigners). It's the transfer agent's responsibility to comply with relevant SEC regulations.

Other essential services provided by the transfer agent are

- preparing and mailing proxy cards and proxy material to shareholders of record and notifying shareholders of the annual shareholder meetings;
- tabulating and certifying proxies;
- providing mailing lists of shareholders for quarterly, annual, and special reports as well as for newsletters and required SEC reports;
- determining and preparing stock dividends and issuing stock dividends, cash dividends, and stock splits;
- providing a complete mailing service that includes stuffing, sorting, and postage application;
- corresponding with shareholders concerning lost or undelivered dividend checks and verifying their payment;
- handling correspondence with shareholders, brokers, banks, and underwriters concerning shareholders' accounts and address changes; and
- verifying signatures of assignors and guarantors.

The position of a transfer agent is highly specialized. Independent transfer agents are regulated by the SEC and are subject to outside audits. As a further safeguard, the SEC reviews recordkeeping procedures through occasional unannounced visits.

Transfer agents are hired by the public company. They can be found through word of mouth, through attorneys, underwriters, and brokers; and they include many banks. Transfer agents play a key support role for public companies. Therefore, the CEO of an IPO should take the necessary time to search for a qualified, independent firm that can handle the job rather than try to do it internally. A reputable transfer agent will encourage investigation. It's worth looking for one that instills trust, confidence, and offers service at a competitive price. And it is always worthwhile to cross-check the performance of applicants with other publicly held companies.

FREQUENTLY ASKED QUESTIONS

Can I use my current bank as transfer agent?

Sure can if it furnishes this type of service. Most large banks have a transfer agent department and would be pleased to add this to the list of services they furnish your company.

Does the transfer agent have to be physically located in my town?

No. In fact, many companies located in smaller towns use transfer agents in other parts of the country. Top transfer agents are well computerized in their operations and need a large number of accounts to operate efficiently. Consequently, transfer agents seldom locate in smaller towns.

How about the expense?

Transfer agents work on a "piece" basis—they get paid for individual tasks. Each time a stock transaction takes place, the transfer agent gets a set fee usually paid by the buyer or seller of the stock. In addition, if the company requests a copy of its current shareholder list or asks to have a mailing sent out (the annual report or a shareholder letter), the transfer agent bills these costs to the company. Obviously, the expense varies considerably depending on use.

Before the Offering

Incorporating the Public Company

From a legal standpoint, a public corporation is different from a privately held corporation. Much of the difference arises in the wording of the charter, or articles of incorporation, and the corporation's bylaws. It is therefore imperative that legal counsel retained by the company be completely familiar with the specific terminology used to set up public corporations. The following explanation should help the entrepreneur to better understand the differences.

State Laws

Incorporation laws vary from state to state, and they vary in complexity. Some state laws are more liberal and flexible than others. One of the most conducive to incorporating public companies is the state of Delaware; and as a result it has more incorporations by public companies than any other state. There are many subtleties to Delaware's incorporation laws. They are among the least strict and least confining, allowing a liberal interpretation by the Delaware courts, which is why public companies throughout the nation consider Delaware the most attractive location for incorporation. Many states are now changing their laws to be as inviting for incorporation as Delaware in an effort to discourage companies from switching to Delaware when they grow larger.

Actually, it makes sense for a company to incorporate in the state where its primary business is located because it must conform with other laws of that state regardless of where it is incorporated. So it's worth having legal counsel investigate the advantages and disadvantages of the resident state's incorporation laws. But management must also consider whether its lawyer's recommendation for the home state is based on the lawyer's familiarity with that state's laws and filing procedures, and must then weigh the benefits of filing in another state.

The following are some specific points to consider in deciding about incorporation:

- Fees: Public companies require larger numbers of authorized and outstanding shares than do private companies. Many states, in fact, set their fees according to the number of shares declared.
- Directors: Some states have laws governing the ratio of directors to shareholders. The more flexible the law, the more latitude for the company.
- Indemnification: The 1980s saw an increasing number of shareholder lawsuits against principals of public companies, making the state's officer and director indemnification laws a very important consideration in deciding where to incorporate.
- Doing Business: The Model Corporation Act lists activities that do not constitute doing business in a state. If the company's primary offices or facilities are located in a state other than the state of incorporation, it may not be considered to be doing business in that state. The company may be required to file as a foreign (out-of-state) company. Check this list carefully.

Articles of Incorporation

It is important to note that some portions of the articles of incorporation differ between public and private corporations. The numbering of articles can also vary, as not all articles apply to all corporations. The following paragraphs summarize the primary areas of a set of articles of incorporation and are provided to give the lay reader some grasp of this area. The articles for your company could vary considerably, but you should not be bashful in asking questions of your legal counsel. It's important that you understand the nuances.

Article I: Corporate Name

Before finally deciding on a name, a search must be conducted through the state secretary of state's office to determine if the proposed company name is available. It is common practice to reserve specifying the corporate name until the actual incorporation filing.

Article II: Purpose

It's best to state the corporate purpose in broad, general terms to allow for changes in direction or for expansion. The more liberal states allow such statements as "to engage in any lawful business," or "to establish a retail shoe outlet and any lawful business." Some states require the purpose to be defined more specifically, such as "to operate a single location, retail only, children's shoe sales outlet." The broader the better; otherwise, an amendment to the articles of incorporation may be required.

Article III: Duration

This article sets forth the length of time the corporation will exist. Generally, "perpetual existence" is the best way to handle it.

Article IV: Capital Stock

This article designates the classifications of stock to be issued (common, preferred) and par (face) value and the number of each type of share authorized. For later flexibility, these items should also be stated as broadly as possible. At a minimum, both preferred and common should be designated. Because of the complexities, this article is generally subdivided into the following four sections.

Section I: Classes and shares. This section simply states, "The authorized capital stock of the corporation shall be [number] shares of Common stock, ___ Par Value, and [number] shares of Preferred stock, ___ Par Value."

Many states charge incorporation filing fees according to the number of shares authorized. Consequently, some companies purposely keep the number low—1,000 or less—but that policy won't work with a public company. For example, if a company expects to raise $8 million at $5 per share, 1.6

million shares are required. Further, if the 1.6 million shares offered to the public represent only 20 percent of the company, there will be 8 million shares outstanding. If the public company plans to do additional financings or make acquisitions for stock, it will initially need to authorize, at a minimum, four times the expected number of shares to be outstanding at the initial public offering, which could bring the total number of the company's authorized shares to 32 million.

These decisions must be made before incorporation because increasing the number of authorized shares after incorporation requires changing the articles, for which shareholder approval must be obtained. The process can be very costly to a public company with hundreds or thousands of shareholders. For example, suppose the company wants to make an acquisition. Without those authorized shares, the company must first call a shareholders meeting, then distribute proxies, then hold the meeting to obtain authority to increase the number of shares, and then make the acquisition. The process could well take several months. Therefore, an adequate number of shares should be authorized initially to cover any contingency.

Section 2: Preferred stock. Public companies may issue preferred stock. Private companies rarely do because preferred stock is similar to a debt in that it requires the paying of dividends (like interest), which are taxable to the company.

It's up to the board of directors to determine dividend amounts, accumulation time, and voting and convertibility of preferred shares. (Convertibility, depending on the specific incorporation laws of the state, means the company may be allowed to issue preferred stock as a debt instrument that contains a voluntary or involuntary conversion to common stock at a predetermined time in the future.)

Section 3: Common stock. The broad rights pertaining to common stock are at the discretion of the board of directors. Basically there are four designations of common stock:

1. *Authorized.* These are the total number of shares of stock the company is authorized to issue according to the laws of the state where the company is incorporated.
2. *Issued.* These are shares of authorized stock that are issued to stockholders for some consideration.

3. *Outstanding.* These are the issued shares that are actually held by stockholders.

4. *Treasury.* These are issued shares that the company has repurchased and replaced in the corporation's treasury to be resold, redistributed, or canceled.

Usually, an opening phrase on certificates of common stock state that it is second in line to preferred stock in case of liquidation and for dividends. There may also be a statement about voting rights, usually one vote per share (preferred stock is generally nonvoting). Particular classes of common stock, however, may carry multiple votes. These are all decisions made by the board of directors with advice from legal counsel.

Section 4: Proxy rules. This section simply authorizes the board of directors to adopt a resolution whereby shareholders may certify in writing to the corporation that their shares are held (controlled or voted) by one or more persons.

Article V: Voting

This article declares that "cumulative voting in the election for directors is not authorized." In essence, it bans an old practice whereby a few persons holding a distinctive class of common stock could rubber-stamp the decisions of the directors of the corporation. Cumulative voting is now prohibited by the SEC and the stock exchanges.

Article VI: Preemptive Right

This article states that shareholders do *not* have the right to acquire, before others, unissued or treasury shares of stock or warrants.

Article VII: Registered Office and Agent

Article VII gives the address of the registrar of stock for the company and names the specific person acting as registrar. This is primarily for the public's protection so that anyone wishing to contact the secretary of state regarding the company will have a specific person to refer to; as a rule, it's usually the company attorney.

Article VIII: Board of Directors

This article discloses how the directors are compensated, the length of time for which they are elected to serve, and procedures for elections and filling vacancies. The article is often divided into the following five sections:

Section 1: Number. This section establishes the number of initial directors.

Section 2: Classification. This section divides the directors into three classes as equal in number as possible. Generally, the term of office of Class 1 directors expires at the first annual shareholders meeting; Class 2 directors are elected for two years; Class 3 directors are elected for three years. At each annual meeting it is common procedure for all directors to be reelected. The chairperson and the president are almost always Class 3 directors, assuring them of a three-year tenure as board members. Classification of directors is one form of a hostile takeover defense for public companies.

Section 3: Initial directors. This section notes the names and addresses of the initial directors.

Section 4: Nominations. This section establishes the procedure for nominating and electing directors. It specifies shareholder nominations and time restrictions.

Section 5: Powers of the board. This section sets forth the powers of the board within the confines of state statutes, including the power to manage and govern; to make, alter, or amend the bylaws; to fix the amount to be reserved as working capital; to authorize and cause to be executed mortgages and liens; to designate one or more committees; to sell, lease, exchange, or otherwise dispose of assets of the corporation; to merge, consolidate, or exchange all the issued shares of the corporation; to distribute to the shareholders, in partial liquidation, portions of the corporation's assets in cash or in property.

Article IX: Conflicts of Interest

This article is usually comprised of two sections.

Section 1: Related party transactions. This section states that contracts between the corporation and companies that the corporation has an interest in are not affected or invalid because of those relationships. However, the SEC requires that directors with joint interests must disclose those facts and also must abstain from voting on issues that affect those companies.

Section 2: Corporate opportunities. Section 2 says, in effect, that if the board has rejected taking specific action on a corporate opportunity, such as an acquisition, merger, new product, or employee, members of the board are free to pursue the opportunity personally.

Article X: Indemnification

Article X deals with the process of protecting or providing security against damages or loss as a result of actions taken by the company. This article has become one of great concern but the subject is too complex to fully cover in this book. There are many areas of concern for directors, officers, employees, and agents of a company regarding what may be considered their personal responsibility. Improperly written indemnification clauses can result in devastating financial losses to the company and those involved with the company.

The extent of "allowability" in indemnification allowability clauses depends on the law of the state of incorporation. Delaware offers the best protection, but, unfortunately, few other states have followed suit. Many states' indemnification laws are simply not conducive to incorporating public companies, which is why it's so important to have a good lawyer who can make the proper determinations in this very significant area.

Article XI: Shareholder Meetings and Votes

This article determines the time and place for shareholders meetings according to the corporation's bylaws. State laws set a specific minimum for a meeting quorum, but generally one-third of the shares entitled to vote will constitute a quorum. The affirmative vote of a majority of shares represented at a shareholders meeting is usually sufficient to pass a measure. Thus, in actuality it takes only one vote of more than one-sixth of the total shares (quorum = ⅓ plus 1 vote over a majority present = 16.6 percent).

Some state statutes establish different quorum and voting standards, and some require higher numbers than a majority quorum for dissolving a company, selling off assets, or approving acquisitions or mergers. Legal counsel should be cognizant of the specifics of these laws.

Article XII: Amendments

This final article addresses the amendment of articles of incorporation, usually requiring, at a minimum, the affirmative vote of a majority of the shares.

Bylaws

Bylaws are the rules governing a corporation. They are voted on at the organizational meeting of the board of directors. They amplify the articles to cover in detail all areas of corporate responsibility, as outlined here:

1. Offices: location of the principal offices and any additional offices including those of subsidiaries
2. Meetings of shareholders: time and place for annual and special meetings; notices of meetings; fixing of record date; proxies; how formal and informal meetings must be conducted; voting privileges; required quorum
3. Board of directors: general powers; number of directors; terms of office; qualifications; notice of meetings; regular and special meetings; quorum; action by consent; conducting of meetings; compensation; filling of vacancies; resignation; removal
4. Officers: number; elections; terms; removal; vacancies; president; chairperson; vice presidents; secretary; treasurer; assistant secretaries and treasurers; salaries; method of selecting officers
5. Contracts, loans, checks, and deposits: contracts; loans; checks; drafts; deposits; authority to sign checks
6. Certificates for shares and their transfer: what certificates to look like; who can sign them; transfer of shares; limits on transfer; cancellation; lost, stolen, or destroyed certificates
7. Seal: form of corporate seal
8. Waiver of notice: who has the authority
9. Amendments: who can make them

FREQUENTLY ASKED QUESTIONS

Why can't I just use my existing corporation?

You can and usually should. However, you most likely will need to "amend" your current articles and bylaws to conform with what is needed in a publicly owned company.

Can I save some money by doing the amendments after we have signed an underwriter?

Not advised. In almost all states, amendments of articles require a full shareholder vote. This takes valuable time away from the task at hand, which is to get your registration documents filed with the SEC. Also, it's not unusual for a company to issue more stock before an underwriting, often to offset the cost of an IPO. It's a lot easier to get shareholder approval when there are fewer shareholders of record: it takes a lot less management time to explain the changes and the reasons for them when you're working with a small group of insiders.

My company has been around for a long time; does that make a difference?

Sometimes yes. If you have a lot of company history and some of it's negative, your legal counsel may advise you to start a new corporate entity. Frequently, this makes the due diligence tasks easier and saves having to hang a lot of "dirty wash" on the line.

15

Stock Control

When entrepreneurs anticipate going public, their fantasy is usually to own the lion's share of the company stock. As reality sets in, they grudgingly accept that 100 percent ownership of a public company is not only unrealistic, it's impossible. Nevertheless, they determine not to give up more than 49 percent stock ownership of the "baby." It is highly unlikely that they will retain even a majority ownership in the stock itself, but all is not lost. The founders of a company that goes public will almost always retain control of the company through voting stock, which for all practical purposes amounts to control of the company.

A five-year study by Venture Associates Ltd. revealed that the founding members of companies that received public financing in the $4 million to $10 million range retained, on average, from 20 to 40 percent voting-stock control. The study also revealed that in many cases, according to various IPO advisers, founders of potentially viable public offerings that insisted upon retaining at least 51 percent voting-stock control never realized their dreams of a successful public offering. Of course, many public companies have been successful in their entrepreneurial pursuits without giving away very much of the store. Quantum and Apple are two such companies; they raised the capital they needed but gave away only 15 to 20 percent to the public.

Quantum Computer, for example, raised $32 million in its public offering of only 15 percent of the company. At the time, the company's five top officers and founders owned only 10 percent of Quantum, but it had an IPO valuation of $21 million! It bears mentioning, however, that before the public offering, private financing from individuals and outside investors gave the company crucial millions it needed for research and development. Quantum also had money for building and testing prototypes, for establishing marketing and sales organizations, and for a vast distribution network. For that financing, the investors received a considerable piece of the action. But then the Quantums and Apples are exceptions to the rule.

Percentages Do Not Necessarily Mean Control

It is important to keep in mind that shrunken stock percentages don't necessarily mean loss of control. Management of a number of large, successful, old-line companies today hold as little as 2 to 8 percent of the voting stock but still retain firm control of their company. An example is the Ford Motor Company with annual sales exceeding $40 billion. It is unequivocally controlled by the Ford family, including various Ford foundations. Between them they vote less than 6.5 percent of the total stock outstanding, but they hold the top management positions and name the directors—evidence that it's not so much the actual physical ownership that's important but the control of voting stock that influences the direction of a public company.

To further clarify the question of percentages and their effect on voting stock, let's look at a hypothetical case of a typical low-priced OTC stock offering. The Horatio Alger Company is composed of four founding principals; each has contributed several years of concentrated effort and labor plus $100,000 of family and friends' money. Each owns or controls 25 percent of the company stock.

Now the company's sales are starting to really take off and the founders need additional capital to support the effort. They decide to go public. An offering is structured whereby 40 percent of the company will be offered to the public for $10 million. An additional 15 percent is offered and subscribed to by private placement investors for $900,000, a sum used to underwrite the cost of going public and for essential operational capital for the interim. At the time of public issue, the founders, including the board of directors and corporate management, directly control 45 percent of the outstanding stock.

The private investors became involved with the company because they liked its potential, so they will put their voting power behind management all the way. They know their best interests will be served by going along with management's recommendations. Consequently, management, including the board of directors, effectively controls not 45 percent, but 60 percent, of the outstanding stock.

As far as the 40 percent purchased by the public is concerned, investigation has shown that public shareholders normally vote, at minimum, 50 percent in favor of management's recommendations even when management is doing an extremely ineffective job in running the company. Such voter apathy gives management an additional 20 percent vote control, which, added to the above 60 percent, gives it total control of 80 percent of the company's stock along with the votes of the board of directors and corporate management.

FREQUENTLY ASKED QUESTIONS

Dilution puzzles me; can you help?

The word *dilution* when used in stock transactions puzzles a lot of people. It means simply that with each round of financing, the old shareholders own a smaller percentage of stock, although most times the stock is worth more. Let's see how control might work.

Right now, Danielle owns all the stock of her company, E-M, Inc. To keep it simple, let's say she was issued 100 shares. She wants to take her company public and to do so she is going to sell 20 percent of her shares to raise the money to offset the cost of going public and then sell another 40 percent to the public. Does that mean she will end up selling 60 percent and owning 40 percent of the public company (20 percent private + 40 percent public). NO!

	Shares Outstanding	Percent
Original		
Danielle owns 100 shares	100	100%
First Round		
Danielle owns 100 shares	100	80%
She sells 20 shares to private investors	+20	20
Total Outstanding	120	100%
(40% of 120 shares outstanding = 48 shares)		
Second Round		
Danielle owns 100 shares	100	59.5%
Private Investors	20	11.9
Public Investors	48	28.6
	168	100.0%

So does this mean that Danielle owns 59.5 percent after she sold off 20 percent and 40 percent?

Well, yes and no. Can you figure it out? (Clue: prevaluation and post-valuation)

16

Valuation and Pricing

A major bone of contention between the underwriter and the entrepreneur of an IPO is the issue price of the company stock. The entrepreneur just knows that the stock is worth much more than the offering price of the new issue. But the underwriter wants to create a demand for the new issue—and do it quickly. And the best way to do that is to offer the stock at a price low enough to encourage potential investors to flock to their brokers and buy it before the price begins to rise.

Eventually, of course, the entrepreneur grasps the gist of the psychological game and grudgingly accepts the expert advice of the underwriter. The two finally reach an agreement that neither is really quite happy with. On larger offerings, this process usually goes on until the day the issue is cleared for selling. For smaller offerings where less money is at stake, both company and underwriter seem to agree on the stock price much sooner.

Preliminary Considerations

Before the wrangling about value and pricing occurs, the type of security to be offered must be determined. The first one usually discussed is straight common stock, which typically grants the holder voting rights of one vote per share. Dividends, if any, are paid after those on preferred stock are paid. There are alternatives that management may want to consider as common stock can take many forms.

If the company has a very strong balance sheet and a long-standing management team with a successful record, the company may want to consider offering a nonvoting common stock that is first in line for dividends or a class of common stock that has less voting power, perhaps one vote for every two shares held by nonmanagement. An example of nonvoting stock is that of Coors Brewery, a publicly held company in which the public has no votes: all of the voting stock is controlled by the Coors family.

Warrants are another form of security. They offer the investor a right to buy a specified number of shares of common stock at a predetermined price and time. By way of example, an "A" warrant could be exercisable 12 months from the initial effective date of the registration statement for a 3-month period at a 50 percent premium over the initial offering price of the common stock. Thus, if the IPO price was $6.00 per share, the warrant would be priced at $7.50 per share when it was eventually purchased. The owner of the warrant would be able to exchange the warrant at whatever price the common stock was selling for at the time of the exchange. The stock could be trading at $8.50 a share at that time. Or put another way, let's say the investor has the right to buy the warrant for $2.50 and the stock goes up to $8.50 per share. The owner of the warrant simply buys the warrant for $2.50 and exchanges it for a share of stock, making a $1.00 profit. A "B" warrant might be available for two years' redemption at a 100 percent premium, or $12.00 per share. The owner would not want to exercise it until the stock reached at least $13.00 (an 8.3 percent gain).

The general attitude about warrants and their attraction is that offering warrants is the company's way of saying it is confident the company will succeed. That's why warrants are occasionally attached to a common stock offering as a unit, which means that with each purchase of a share of stock the company *gives* the buyer a warrant that can be exchanged for a share of stock at a specified time for a specified price—regardless of the stock's price at the time. Some companies use the unit plan as a merchandising device to entice potential investors to buy the stock.

Management should be aware that, when exercised, warrants dilute all the shareholders' positions. If a completed IPO has 3 million shares outstanding, for example, of which 1 million are held by the public (33 percent of the company), and if the shares are sold as a unit—one warrant for each share and each warrant entitling the purchase of one additional share—the company will be 50 percent publicly held after all the warrants are exercised.

Another question is whether warrants should be commissionable to the brokers; they often are. Warrants can be attached (not tradable on their own) or detached (separately tradable). If the warrant is separately tradable, it has a market value of its own and it trades in the market.

Warrants can provide benefits to companies and attractive commissions for brokers. But before going into warrants, a matter that can be very complex, the company should look into every aspect carefully and discuss the possibilities in detail with legal counsel, the accountant, and the underwriter.

To repeat: A warrant is a right to buy. If the warrant is to be exercised, money must be put up.

Alternatives

Instead of common stock, the company can offer preferred stock with a dividend provision. Or the company can offer a convertible debenture, which converts preferred stocks or bonds into specified shares of common stock at a specified time with an advantageous ratio. Normally, this type of offering is not feasible for start-up or early stage public offerings. Convertible debentures or preferred stock offerings require a consistent positive cash flow to meet regular interest payments or to retire bonds. Furthermore, if there is no established market for the common stocks, convertible securities are unlikely to attract investors.

All types of unit offerings should be carefully scrutinized for investor market reception and current market trends. Even more important, they should be examined for their long-range implications, which could prove that the company gave away more of the store than it should have, and the entrepreneur may end up owning too little of the company.

Selling Shareholders

Selling shareholders are usually principals of the company who sell some of their personally held company stock at the IPO with the proceeds for their personal benefit. Or assuming the stock has increased substantially in value, the venture capital firm that provided initial equity financing may sell some of its stock to regain its original investment. This means of "turning" its investment, which can represent a sizable sum, is seen mainly with large, mature, and successful companies.

Existing shareholders of companies with small, low-priced offerings and shareholders of most newer companies seldom relinquish their stock positions as it could result in a loss of some control of the company. In the case of more mature companies that are profit producers, stock sales permit original insiders to take out a percentage of their initial investment.

Where the total proceeds needed by the company are too small to justify an IPO, existing shareholders can sell some of their holdings to increase the total offering size and make the offering meaningful. This usually happens with more mature companies with a proven track record for profits.

Valuation versus Pricing

Value and price are two important factors in an IPO. *Value* refers to the estimated valuation of the company and the total dollar amount expected to be raised based on the capitalization of the company. The underwriter will generally conduct a survey of competitive or comparable public companies, which will help provide a preliminary valuation. Other points that enter into a valuation include the following:

- Efficiency ratios (sales per employee)
- Leverage ratios (debt to equity)
- Interest coverage
- Profit margins, gross and net
- Use of proceeds
- Earnings ratios (net as a percent of sales to net worth of assets)
- Operating history
- Operating base (regional, national, or international)
- Quantity and experience of management
- Product differentiation and innovation
- Single or multiple product company
- Patent/proprietary product position

Price refers to the price per share to be asked and is primarily based on what the market will bear. Aiding in the decision-making process is information furnished in the company's business plan, which details existing operations and projected future operations.

On offerings for large companies, underwriters prefer to come out with at least 500,000 shares. Sometimes they may go along with a minimum of 300,000 to 350,000 shares of public float—the stock owned by public stockholders. They want to obtain a broad distribution of the stock and provide for liquidity in the aftermarket. Another reason for the minimum is that institutional investors usually purchase blocks of 10,000 to 50,000 shares. Because

SEC rules require owners of 5 percent or more of the outstanding shares of a company to disclose what they do with the stock, many major buyers of large blocks of stocks of a company will buy only up to just under 5 percent of the outstanding stock to avoid the reporting requirements. They may also be concerned that substantial buy or sell orders create large fluctuations in the market.

The average national offering falls between $20 million and $30 million. Underwriters prefer offerings in the $10 million to $50 million range, involving 10 to 40 percent of the company. Some offerings start at the $5 million figure, but most offerings in the $5 million to $10 million range are underwritten by regional rather than national firms.

Price-Earnings Ratio

IPO entrepreneurs should be familiar with the PE (price-earnings) ratio of companies in their industry. This standard measurement of the price of the stock versus the earnings of the company is figured by dividing the stock price by the earnings per share. For example, if a stock is selling for $15 per share and the earnings per share are $1, the stock is selling at a ratio of 15 to 1.

The PE ratio is the prime standard for performance comparison. It is used both for current/historical and future/projection analysis. After the market crash of 1929 and throughout the depression years of the 1930s, the United States had a major concern about debt. Consequently, the debt-to-equity ratio, which compares the liabilities of the company with shareholder equity, was considered an important analytical tool when valuing a prospective IPO. Today, while the debt-to-equity ratio is still considered, the most popular ratio is price-earnings, sometimes referred to as the PE multiple.

PEs that are based on the last 12 months of earnings are referred to as "trailing earnings." Earnings that are shown "as reported" are based on the total number of shares outstanding as of the date of issue of the financial statement. PE ratios are also often shown as projected, reflecting the company's projections for the amount of earnings per share at some point in the future, usually the next quarter or year.

All popular stock guides, and many daily stock quotation services, publish current PE ratios. They are also published daily in *The Wall Street Journal;* and there are also category and industry listings, such as for electronics or autos.

It's not unusual for companies in the same industry to show large discrepancies in their PE ratios. A particular company may be the subject of a takeover attempt or may just have received a large long-term contract or announced a significant new product. On the downside, a company may have experienced negative earnings for several quarters or may be a defendant in a major lawsuit—it doesn't take much to affect the PE ratio of a company.

Pricing

The pricing of an issue is as difficult as the valuation of a company. The financial industry itself has some psychological quirks that affect pricing. Most underwriters are conditioned to follow historical traditions in pricing a stock. The price shouldn't be too high nor too low to appeal to their targets. Stocks under $5 a share, for example, might be considered too risky, and stocks over $20 may carry too much prestige for the issue. Whereas some brokerage houses feel that stocks under $10 a share appear too speculative, stocks above $20 a share keep too many investors away because they can't make a large enough purchase. The purchase price of a round lot of 100 shares at $30 a share would be $3000, which may be just high enough for an individual investor to say no. There are fixed psychological points that influence the underwriter's pricing positioning.

One formula for pricing that underwriters like to use is "discounting." Underwriters often attempt to price a new stock issue at 15 to 30 percent below what they consider its true market value. This creates an incentive for investors to put their money into a new issue and offers the prospect of showing an immediate return, at least on paper.

Timing is also critical in price setting. Late-breaking bad news about the IPO's industry could prove disastrous. Underwriters will keep a close watch on the industry and on competitive companies, and the final price may not be set until the day of an offering.

Valuation and pricing for larger underwritings are often based more on intuition than on facts. A general range may be agreed upon early in the IPO discussions and refined as the registration statement is prepared. When the preliminary prospectus is distributed, the managing underwriter solicits and receives indications of interest from the up to 40 brokerage firms that are involved in the selling syndicate.

The underwriter prepares an indications-of-interest book, which details the interest on the part of the selling syndicate. It shows how many shares each firm is willing to subscribe to and the price at which it believes it can sell the shares, input that is used in the final price determination. Syndicate interest indicates to the underwriter how many shares the market can bear and how much of the company will have to be given away for the least number of shares. All the preceding information plus any that research has turned up on valuations and PE ratios go into the underwriter's final price determination. At that point the number of shares to be offered and the price at which they will be sold is printed in the final prospectus.

Low-Priced Issues

Valuation and pricing for smaller IPOs with low-priced issues and total offerings of $6 million or less are much simpler. On smaller deals, the company basically informs the underwriter that it has put together a business plan and tells the underwriter how much money it will need. For example, a company may tell the underwriter it will need $4 million to implement the business plan and explains how it intends to use the money. If the company's presentation is based on a solid business plan that the underwriter can feel comfortable with, the underwriter proceeds to determine a price for the stock.

Repositioning

At some point in time a company may exhaust its trading capability in low-priced stocks and may decide to reverse-split them. A reverse split of 10 to 1, for example, would leave holders with 1 share in place of the 10 they had owned before the split; 10,000 shares would become 1,000 shares. If 1 share was worth 40¢ before the reverse split, the holder of 10 shares would now own 1 share worth $4. From the company's perspective, a public share float (number of shares held by the public) of 100 million would drop to 10 million and show a PE ratio more acceptable to investors.

The reverse stock split can be attractive to regional brokerage firms whose house rules prevent dealing in low-priced stocks. Now, with a higher price per share, they can become involved in selling the stock.

Successful small underwritings are often compelled to perform reverse splits, not only to reduce the number of shares outstanding, but to post attractive earnings per share and PE ratios. Shares must show some value before they can pay off in dividends.

FREQUENTLY ASKED QUESTIONS

My company is three years old and profitable; can I just sell a debt issue like a convertible debenture?

Probably not. Investors in new issues like the risk of unlimited reward in common stock that goes along with emerging growth companies. Convertible debentures are reserved for mature companies with time-proven solid earnings.

Isn't the pricing of a company's stock pretty scientific?

In theory yes, in actual practice no. PE ratios and industry comparisons are used but the final pricing, just like the stock market itself, has a lot of emotion attached.

Is it the company or the underwriter who determines the offering price?

Both. Although the company has the final say, it's the underwriter who tells the company at what price it feels it can sell the issue. Because the price is usually determined right before the actual offering takes place (sometimes just hours), the company most often is the one to concede. It's pretty hard to turn down an offering after your management has spent months and almost countless dollars preparing for the deal.

17

The SEC

Every aspect of going public is regulated by the Securities and Exchange Commission (SEC), a quasi-judicial administrative agency of the U.S. government that is responsible for the administration and enforcement of the securities laws. It was created by the Securities Exchange Act of 1934, which was passed to regulate the securities exchanges and the over-the-counter market. Under the Securities Act of 1933, the SEC supervises the registration of securities issues and guards against fraudulent sales practices; the 1933 act provides that all pertinent information about securities must be available to buyers.

The commission is composed of five members who are appointed by the president. Only three may belong to the same political party, and each is appointed for a five-year term; the president designates the chairperson. The commission's staff includes lawyers, accountants, engineers, securities analysts, examiners, and administrative personnel. The SEC has nine regional offices located in Boston; Washington, D.C.; Atlanta; Chicago; Fort Worth; Denver; Seattle; San Francisco; and New York plus additional branches throughout the country. Its operations are organized into several divisions discussed below.

Division of Corporate Finance. This division reviews registration statements filed by companies under the 1933 act. It furnishes interpretations and advisory services for issuers, underwriters, and their lawyers as to statutes, rules, and regulations. The initial reviewing of registration statements, the major task of this division, is the responsibility of regional branches.

Each regional branch is staffed by attorneys, accountants, analysts, and examiners.

Office of the Chief Accountant. This office has final authority over accounting matters. It makes policy determinations regarding the form and content of financial statements and decides complicated accounting disputes, from consolidated financial statements to fair practice procedures.

Division of Trading and Markets. This division assists the commission and the National Association of Securities Dealers (NASD) in the regulation of brokers, dealers, and investment advisers, and in securing the cooperation of management of the securities exchanges.

Division of Corporate Regulation. This division assists the commission in the administration of the Public Utility Holding Company Act of 1935, the Investment Company Act of 1940, and the Bankruptcy Act, and in making sure that the parties involved comply with the regulations.

Office of the General Counsel. This office handles litigation for the commission. It prepares legal opinions and dispenses legal advice on behalf of the commission and its various divisions; and it resolves differences of interpretation. It has broad powers and can, for instance, offer immunity on insider trading charges. It serves as a watchdog over international trading.

Office of Policy Research. This office, headed by the chief economist, analyzes proposals for modification of rules and regulations and prepares statistical data for internal and public publications.

Investigation and Enforcement

The SEC has the power to investigate complaints from the general public about securities violations as well as from federal and state agencies, and it has the power to enforce penalties for violations of its rules and regulations. The first step after it receives a complaint is a preliminary investigation. Most investigations are performed by regional offices with informal interrogation of witnesses. If indications are that a violation may have occurred, the matter is returned to the commission, which can order a formal investigation.

If a formal investigation upholds the charges, the commission considers further proceedings. If the charge is against broker-dealers, the commission may institute administrative proceedings under the Administrative Procedures Act that are aimed toward remedial sanctions against persons or companies involved in the securities industry. The firm may be expelled or have its license suspended or revoked. An individual may be censured and temporarily or permanently barred from employment in the industry. Alternatively, the commission can request sanctions against violators by court order from a U.S. district court. A third possibility, reserved for willful violations, is for the commission to refer the matter to the Department of Justice for criminal prosecution.

Information Availability

Because the SEC is the primary repository for all public company filings and information, it is obligated to maintain public reference facilities in its regional branches. The SEC is also obligated to provide members of the public with copies of all public company filings at a nominal cost, including opinions of the commission, statements of policy, and interpretations. By law the commission's decisions, reports, orders, rules, and regulations are always published. A summary of the releases are available by subscription to the daily *SEC News Digest* (from the Superintendent of Documents, Washington, D.C.). The commission also publishes reports on insider stock transactions.

The SEC staff provides advisory and interpretative assistance to members of the public and prospective registrants, including information forms and a list of available items. The SEC staff will also arrange for informal discussions on subjects pertaining to securities.

FREQUENTLY ASKED QUESTIONS

Is the SEC the only regulatory agency involved with IPOs?

The SEC handles IPO regulations on the federal government level, but every state also has state regulations that often supersede the SEC.

Can I contact the SEC for more detailed IPO information?

Certainly. Every SEC office supplies a large variety of information on many aspects of the regulations on going public. You will find indexes to this information on the Internet at http://www.sec.gov/ along with the addresses of SEC regional offices.

Are SEC regulations written in language understandable to the non-professional?

Hardly. Although I recommend that CEOs establish some familiarity with the SEC regulations pertaining to IPOs (overviews are contained in this book), it's best to discuss the always changing fine points with your legal counsel.

18

Federal Securities Legislation

The Securities Act of 1933 and the Securities Exchange Act of 1934 were passed in response to misuse and abuse of the system. The 1933 act brought about truth-in-securities disclosure, and the 1934 act regulates the industry through the Securities and Exchange Commission.

History

During the six years of his presidency, from 1901 through 1907, Theodore Roosevelt led the attack on business monopolies and trusts. In 1907 a financial panic erupted on Wall Street; stocks plunged and many small businesses and banks closed. The stock exchange came under fire, and in 1909 the Hughes Committee, following an investigation, recommended that the exchange regulate itself. In 1912 Congress formed the Pujo Committee, whose investigations raised suspicions about many leading trust companies and provided the foundation for the regulatory laws written in the early thirties.

The U.S. economy prospered as a result of World War I. Except for a brief recession in 1921 when the securities and commodities markets saw heavy losses, investments flourished in the U.S. business community—the stock market in particular. The unbounded investment enthusiasm was further promoted by cheap 10 percent margin credit. Euphoria continued until Black Thursday, October 24, 1929. The Great Depression followed.

Three years after the crash in November 1932, Franklin D. Roosevelt was elected president. By the following May, Congress had passed the Securities Act of 1933. The reasons for this fast action were twofold. First, Roosevelt had campaigned for financial reforms; second, the Senate Committee on Banking and Currency Reforms had completed a 17-month study that uncovered many unethical practices—including fraud perpetrated by exchange officials, bank officials, and important Wall Street figures. As a result of the study, a draft National Securities Act, modeled after the British Companies Act, was submitted to the House on April 10, 1933. With a speed unheard of today, the Securities Act of 1933 (1933 act) was signed into law on May 23, 1933—just six weeks after its introduction. Sometimes referred to as the Truth in Securities Act, it is the foundation for the many rules and regulations governing entrepreneurs today. It regulates documents with two main objectives: (1) the registration of securities before their sale to the general public and (2) civil and criminal penalties for fraud connected with the registration of securities.

A year later, Congress passed the Securities Exchange Act of 1934 (1934 act), which brought all stock exchanges under government control for the first time. The 1934 act regulates people with two main objectives: (1) the registration of security exchanges and of broker-dealers and (2) the regulation of business practices in the securities industry.

In addition, the 1934 act established the Securities and Exchange Commission (SEC) to administer both acts and to protect the interests of investors and the public.

The Securities Act of 1933

The intention of the 1933 act is to ensure disclosure of all the sources of information about a company in a carefully and uniformly prepared document called the prospectus. The disclosure philosophy was explained by President Roosevelt:

> There is, however, an obligation upon us to insist that every issue of new securities to be sold in interstate commerce shall be accompanied by full publicity and information, and that no essentially important element attending the issue shall be concealed from the buying public. This proposal adds to the ancient rule of caveat emptor, the further doctrine, "let the seller also beware." It puts the burden of telling the whole truth on the seller. It should give impetus to honest dealing in securities and thereby bring back public confidence.

The 1933 act requires disclosures by any company that intends to sell securities in interstate commerce or through the mail; these disclosures are made in a registration statement and prospectus filed with the SEC. The registration statement details business and financial information about the company as well as the securities being offered. The intent is to assure full and fair disclosure of relevant information to allow an investor to make an informed decision regarding the purchase of securities. Securities cannot be sold until the registration is approved.

Contrary to popular belief, the SEC does not review the validity of an offering but only compliance under the act. The merits of the securities themselves or of the companies offering the securities must be assessed by the investor.

The 1933 act also contains provisions about fraud that apply to officers, directors, controlling shareholders, underwriters, and all those who sign the registration statement. Also liable are the experts who assisted in the preparation of the registration statement or who are actually named in it. Civil and criminal penalties may be imposed for misrepresentations, misstatements, or omissions in the registration statement.

The actual forms and the information required in a registration statement are discussed in depth in Chapter 23.

The Securities Exchange Act of 1934

The purpose of the Securities Exchange Act of 1934 was to establish rules regarding public companies, establish the regulations governing the securities industry and its personnel, and provide enforcement guidelines to the securities laws.

For public companies, the 1934 act is notable in the areas described below.

Periodic Reporting

- *Form 10K*. This is an annual report that includes audited financial statements as well as information about the company and its management. (See Chapter 28.)
- *Form 10-Q*. This is a quarterly report with unaudited financial statements and management discussion of continuing operations (see Chapter 28).

- *Form 8-K.* This form is to be filed with the SEC whenever significant events occur within the company, its control, or management that could affect an investor's decision about the stock (see Chapter 28).

Proxy Solicitations

Regulations cover events such as elections of members of the board of directors or approval of major divestitures or acquisitions that require shareholder approval. (See Chapter 28.)

Foreign Corrupt Practices Act (FCPA)

This act contains statutory requirements covering the establishment and maintenance of proper accounting records. (See Chapter 28.)

Tender Offers

Under the 1934 act, the SEC regulates both the manner in which tender offers are made and management tactics that can be employed to resist tender offers.

Insider Trading

Insiders such as directors, officers, and shareholders are required to report to the SEC changes in their holdings in the company via Forms 3 and 4. There are stiff penalties against trading on inside information not available to the public. (See Chapter 28.)

The Industry

Other portions of the 1934 act set forth in detail rules pertaining to the securities industry itself. The act gave the SEC authority over net capital and margin requirements and restrictions on broker-dealers and members of the stock exchanges, including the OTC market.

Other Significant Legislation

Other federal legislation that regulates portions of the securities industry include the following:

- The Public Utility Holding Company Act of 1935 requires the registration of all public holding companies and utility companies.
- The Trust Indenture Act of 1939 requires relevant information on the issuance of corporate bonds and debt securities.
- The Investment Company Act of 1940 requires the registration and regulation of investment companies and mutual funds and is intended to protect investors.
- The Investment Advisors Act of 1940 provides for the registration and regulation of investment advisers.
- The Securities Acts Amendment of 1964 was the result of the SEC Special Study of Securities Markets. It broadened basic securities laws, such as disclosure requirements and the regulation of brokers and dealers.
- The Securities Investor Protection Act of 1970 established the Securities Investors Protection Corporation (SIPC), which supervises the liquidation of securities firms and the payment of claims brought by their customers.

FREQUENTLY ASKED QUESTIONS

How often do the various SEC regulations change?

Almost constantly. Although the original rules and regulations were adopted in the mid-1930s, the changes seem to come constantly—the reason that entrepreneurs need to have qualified securities counsel.

Is there a way that I can keep track of the changes?

The SEC Web site at http://www.sec.gov/ has a lot of information, including a section that lists new rules, changes in old rules, and proposed new rules and changes.

19

Regulation D and Alternative Methods of Private Financing

Simply stated, it's against the law to sell stock unless you are licensed to do so or can qualify for an exemption from the SEC rules. The very worst that can happen is that you'll have to pay penalties or you can be put in jail. For instance, section 5 of the 1933 act clearly states that "it is unlawful for any person, directly or indirectly, to sell a security unless a registration statement has been filed, or to sell a security or deliver a security after the sale unless a registration statement has been declared effective." The 1933 act does contain some exemptions, but they fall short of really helping the "little guy."

Regulation D, commonly referred to as "Reg D," which became effective April 15, 1982, is not just another exemption. It is *the* exemption for small businesses that want to raise money by selling some of their stock. It is also a form of taking a company public without the burden and expense of full registration with the SEC. Reg D may also serve as a welcome alternative for some entrepreneurs.

For decades, the principals of many small U.S. businesses have complained about the expense and trouble of complying with government regulation. It goes back 200 years to Adam Smith's push for a new era in British economic policy. Smith sought to "strip away the shackles of government regulations and constraining ideology, and replace them with the freedom of individual initiative and economic enterprise." Well, some things can't be rushed. The same kind of utterance came from Ronald Reagan when he said in 1978, "For several decades, an ever-larger role of the federal government has sapped the economic vitality of the nation." The result of this early Reaganomics movement was to remove some of the federal restraints on raising capital. In 1980 Congress enacted the Small Business Investment Incentive Act.

One of the agencies affected by this act was the Securities and Exchange Commission, which promulgated Reg D. This regulation, along with its revisions, has broadened the exemptions to the SEC's regulations, thereby easing restrictions on equity fundraising. Reg D also returned many responsibilities of government to the states. Some states took this opportunity to adopt their own version and, consequently, entrepreneurs who are contemplating using Reg D had better check their own state's securities regulations before relying completely on the federal version of Reg D.

Preprivate

Before a public offering, entrepreneurial financing of brand-new start-up companies has been known to come from any number of sources—from grandma's cookie jar to funds solicited from friends or rich relatives. Some came in for a piece of the action, some as a loan, and some as both. Start-ups are often financed in three stages: preprivate, private, and—the final stage—the initial public offering.

Preprivate financing usually takes place during a company's formation stage. First, the entrepreneur and the prospective management team formulate a business plan. They identify the key team players, design a prototype product or service, and, it is hoped, have substantial market research available. The next step would be to legally form the company and then devote the time and attention that must be given to the intended business and, more important, to the more formal fundraising process.

Preprivate financing could take the form of debt, equity, or a combination of both. The amount to ask for depends on what is necessary to get the show on the road. It could be as small as $5 (for a Kool-Aid stand) to $100,000 to as much as $1 million. The use of the proceeds should be calculated to provide bare-bones financing for the initial incorporation and legal costs, and for limited company operations. Enough should be included to offset the necessities and cost of having to raise additional capitalization the first go-around.

Typically, the providers of the founders' financing are the members of the management team and close family and friends. In order for the company to be legally prepared to receive the funds, the parties should have a legal agreement, which need be only a simple preincorporation or presubscription agreement. As a hypothetical explanation, the entrepreneur tells the money source about this great idea for a company that's going to be started but needs money to get it going. For $5,000 (or whatever amount) the potential investor will be given an agreement that gives him or her an undiluted percentage of the company. Based on the investor's reliance on the entrepreneur's intentions, the investor agrees to give $5,000 for x percent of the company—an agreement called a preincorporation or presubscription agreement. Often, the founders, if other than the management team, are offered options to further their equity positions.

The risk-reward ratio at this level of financing is obviously very high. At the time the company may not have completed its business plan or comprehensive market research; may not have completely developed, tested, or market-tested its product or service; and may not yet have a fully identified, much less working, management team. All of these uncertainties make the company a high-risk investment, and the pricing of its stock or terms of its debt should reflect this; thus, depending on the total amount invested, a 5 to 20 percent value would not be unreasonable.

For the entrepreneur, a brand-new, clean corporation makes an ideal IPO. From an accounting standpoint, there is nothing to audit, which means spending a minimum of time and expense. From a legal perspective, there is nothing to refer to as the company is structured from scratch. Its articles and bylaws will reflect that it is "to be" a public company. (Refer to Chapter 14.)

If preprivate financing is necessary for a company already in existence, it would be best handled as a debt with options attached and with provisions to convert it to equity, thus eliminating a lot of the complications involved in corporate cleanup.

Private

Private financing is the second step taken in a company's financial organization on its way to achieving an initial public offering.

The second-level private financing is undertaken after the formation (preprivate) stage is completed in both the company's operations and its overall financing scheme. By the time the preprivate financing has been accomplished, a detailed business plan should be substantially completed. The company's product, if it is new, should have gone beyond its design state and its first-generation or second-generation prototype. If the company is a service company, then a very limited beta test should have been performed (a survey that gives an indication of the viability of the service in the marketplace). In addition, key management people should be in position to come on board full-time. In all probability, the CEO is already devoting full time to the company.

At this juncture, the business will have been incorporated to fit a public company status, and a securities attorney experienced in SEC matters retained. At a minimum, identification of, if not the retention of, an accountant experienced in SEC regulations has been finalized and the firm involved in setting up the corporation's books to meet the SEC's accounting requirements.

It is also at this point that the company needs to implement the more formal vehicles or types of legally accepted paper forms used in sophisticated financings. The balance of this chapter addresses these financing vehicles.

Regulation D (Reg D)

Reg D reduces registration requirements and costs; it has opened the door to substantial exemptions to the 1933 act. The technical provisions, which were always subject to varying interpretations, have also been eased. The process now is simpler, which in turn has lessened the chance that the offerer (the company) may be subject to recision (giving back monies raised) to the offeree (investor) if a technical provision happens to be mistakenly violated.

Some risks continue under Reg D, but compliance is significantly easier than before it was introduced. It also provides the company, its officers, and its directors with an *insurance policy* against possible charges of securities fraud.

Reg D consists of six basic rules. The first three are concerned with definitions, conditions, and notification. Rule 501 covers the definitions of the various terms used in the rules. Rule 502 sets forth the conditions, limitations, and information requirements for the exemptions in Rules 504, 505, and 506. Rule 503 contains SEC notification requirements. The last three rules deal with the specifics of raising money. Rule 504 generally pertains to securities sales up to $1 million. Rule 505 applies to offerings from $1 million to $5 million. Rule 506 is for securities offerings exceeding $5 million.

Rule 501

This first rule defines key terms in the regulations that are applicable to the offering and sales under Reg D.

Accredited investors. The SEC has long had a definition for *accredited investors*—investors "sophisticated or wealthy enough" to be able to assess an offer or stand the risk of the investment without further information. Before Rule 501, it was up to an attorney, accountant, or stockbroker to decide whether a potential investor met the very vague SEC requirements. Now the rule spells it out. Accredited investors include the following:

- Banks
- Savings and loans
- Credit unions
- Corporations and partnerships with total assets in excess of $5 million
- Broker-dealers
- Insurance companies
- Registered investment companies
- Nonprofit organizations with over $5 million in assets
- Business development companies (as defined under the Investment Companies Act of 1940)
- Small Business Investment Companies (SBICs)
- Minority Enterprise Small Business Investment Companies (MESBICs)
- Employee benefit plans subject to the Employee Retirement Income Security Act (ERISA) (with some restrictions)

More applicable to the efforts of most companies to raise money privately are

- directors and officers of the company,
- individuals whose net worth exceeds $1 million,
- individuals whose income exceeds $200,000 annually (during the last two years as well as expected in the current year), and
- individuals whose joint income with a spouse exceeds $300,000 for two years.

The term *accredited investors* surfaces again in rules 504, 505, and 506. In conjunction with accredited investors, the term *reasonably believed* is often mentioned. These terms will be used extensively by a company's legal counsel or underwriter as they and the company have a legal obligation to declare (reasonably believe) if an accredited investor meets the requirements of Rule 501. If the company actually believes *and* can prove it had reason to believe an accredited investor meets Rule 501 requirements, it would have no continuing liability as far as such an accredited investor is concerned. As an extra precaution, however, the company should have the investor attest to the accredited-investor facts and qualification in writing. This accredited-investor document should be part of every offering memorandum.

Purchaser representative. A purchaser representative is a person who is not an affiliate, director, or other employee of the company, or an owner of 10 percent or more of the company, or an owner of any class of the equity securities of the company. Furthermore, such persons should possess sufficient knowledge and experience in financial and business matters to make them capable of evaluating, on their own or together with the purchaser, the merits and risks of the prospective investment. In addition, they must acknowledge in writing that they are acting as a purchaser representative, and they must make certain written disclosures as to the identification of the ultimate purchaser. This applies particularly to syndicates, multiple syndicates, and partnership holdings.

Number of purchasers. Rules 505 and 506 limit the number of purchasers, but accredited investors are not included in the total. The rules further state that the company may sell its securities to an unlimited number of accredited investors in addition to a specified number of other purchasers, such as officers and directors. This also applies to loosely related parties, who in some cases may be counted as a single purchaser.

Rule 502

This rule establishes the general conditions pertaining to the exemptions. Notable are the following areas:

- Qualifying for an exemption under Reg D is not dependent on the size of the company.
- The exemptions are applicable only to the issuer and not its affiliates, such as subsidiaries, or to others, or for resale of the issuer's securities.
- Some offerings of the "same" securities may be considered as a single offering (that is, *integrated*) if they are made within six months of the start or termination of the Reg D offering. This can save legal and registration costs, but technicalities are involved, so it's best for the entrepreneur to seek knowledgeable legal advice on how best to handle integration.
- To further clarify the somewhat confusing interpretation of Reg D: there can be no general solicitation or quasi-public advertising con-

nected with the offering. And to add to the confusion, Rule 504 explains how this type of situation can be circumvented.

- Another general condition is that certain procedures must be followed by the issuer to guarantee that the securities are not being purchased for resale. The issuer must make certain that the purchaser is not an underwriter or an agent for an underwriter. Further, the issuer must provide a written disclosure of this resale limitation, and the certificate itself must contain a legend specifying the resale restriction. This may seem like a no-win situation, but take heart; Rule 504 contains ways of avoiding this problem also.

Rule 503

Rule 503 sets forth the information that must be filed with the SEC. It also specifies the timing and the types of forms that must be used in the filing.

The company (issuer) must file five copies of the notice of sales of its securities with the SEC on the required Form D, one of which must be hand-signed. This filing must be made within 15 days after the first sale and thereafter every 6 months, with a final filing within 30 days of the last sale. Compliance in filing is extremely critical. Should the issuers not comply, they run a high risk that the SEC will rescind the entire offering and require all monies received be returned to the stock purchasers if they so desire.

The SEC also has the right to request in writing that the issuer provide the SEC with copies of all the information provided to the purchasers of the securities, thus making the information a public record. Although the SEC rarely takes this kind of action, don't bet on it.

Rule 504

This rule is considered by many as the perfect answer for the company just starting out that needs to raise less than $1 million but can't afford to go through the whole SEC registration process. Until the company grows to a point where it can afford it, Rule 504 offers it an out through the following:

- An exemption to raising up to $1 million
- No disclosure criteria
- Few general solicitation and resale restrictions
- No limit on the number of investors required
- Audited financials not required

Actually, Congress's original intent for Rule 504 was to "set aside a clear and workable exemption for small issuers to be regulated by state blue-sky requirements, but, by the same token, to be subject to federal anti-fraud provisions and civil liability provisions." A Rule 504 exemption is provided for almost any type of organization, including corporations, partnerships, trusts, or other entities, but it is not applicable to companies already reporting to the SEC (subject to the 1934 act) or investment companies.

The total offering amount under Rule 504 can be up to $1 million in a 12-month period less the aggregate offering of all securities sold within 12 months before the start of a 504 offering. Thus, if a company has raised $100,000 in preprivate money in the previous 12 months, it can still raise up to $900,000 without being accused of breaking the rules, or engaging in "integration." Generally speaking, there are *no* specific disclosure requirements under Rule 504 (disclosing what the company is about, what it intends to do, or who is connected with it). This means that, theoretically, an issuer can have a purchaser sign a subscription agreement and purchase stock without any information about the company being disclosed. However, the rule is dependent on the blue-sky laws of each state in which the securities are offered, which means that disclosure must be provided regardless of Rule 504 if a state's blue-sky rules require it.

Rule 504 also provides that at least $500,000 of securities must be sold according to a registration under a state's securities law. Consequently, an offer must comply with the blue-sky laws of the individual states in which it is offered. In many states, this requirement negates the effective simplicity of Rule 504 and the federal government's intent because many states' blue-sky laws are more restrictive than Reg D.

A word of caution to the entrepreneur—regardless of the amount of disclosure the issuer is willing to provide, Rule 504 does not dismiss the issuer from federal requirements nor is there an exemption from fraud provisions, including the areas of material omissions or misstatements. The penalties for noncompliance are severe, including monetary fines and mandatory jail sentences.

Commissions. One interesting aspect of Rule 504 is its provision for payment of commissions. It was reasoned by securities regulators that broker-dealers' involvement with selling 504s would provide an extra safeguard for investors. In addition, it was felt that removing the ban on commissions, which can be as high as the market will bear (generally 15 to 20 percent), would bring the expertise and sales organization of brokerage firms and investment bankers to the aid of small businesses. Unfortunately, the measure hasn't had the desired effect except for a few smaller brokerage firms. It seems the medium-sized and large Wall Street firms simply can't justify the expense required to merchandise offerings under $1 million.

The one area in which Rule 504 has helped is in allowing the issuer to "generally solicit," or advertise, for subscribers to an offering. Some states have been quite lenient in allowing it. In practice, however, few issuers have advertised their offerings in newspapers or through other common media as was expected. And finally, many states have approved offering Reg D by using the paper work used with SCOR/U-7 (more information follows).

Number of investors. With its limited disclosure requirements, Rule 504 also allows an issuer to sell securities to an unlimited number of investors. Theoretically, a company could raise $1 million by selling its stock at a penny a share to 100 million different investors. Obviously, the economics are not too attractive, but there's no rule that stops an issuer from selling $500 blocks of stock to 2,000 investors. Rule 504 is the only rule under Reg D that permits an unlimited number of investors.

One last note on Rule 504 is that the exemption provides for sales of securities of either debt or equity, thus opening the door for combinations of both via convertible debentures. A convertible debenture is a debt issue (debenture) that is convertible to a preferred or, most commonly, common stock at some future date, usually at a predetermined price.

Rule 505

Rule 505 is comparatively hassle-free.

- It exempts offers and sales of issuers other than investment companies.
- The offering in total cannot exceed $5 million during a 12-month period less what has been raised by preprivate money, as mentioned in the discussion of Rule 504, plus inclusion of any future offerings contemplated during the 12 months following the last sale under Rule 505.
- The sales cannot be made to more than 35 nonaccredited investors and they must be accompanied by the same kind of disclosure information required in Part I of the filing for an SB-1 registration (see Chapter 23).
- Sales can be made to an unlimited number of accredited investors.

- No general solicitation (advertising) is allowed.
- Rule 505 carries the same filing notification requirements as Rule 504.
- Rule 505 carries a disqualification from using the exemption if the issuer, defined as just about anybody connected with the company (including its officers, directors, principals, or underwriters) is a "bad boy," as defined in Rule 252(c)-(f) of Regulation A. Loosely, a bad boy is a person who has incurred the wrath of the SEC for the potential (without necessarily having been convicted) of having committed a securities violation, although the SEC can waive the misconduct disqualification. The issuer should seek advice of counsel if anyone connected with the company has had previous problems with the SEC.
- The same fraud, misstatement, and material omissions compliance apply as for Rule 504.
- Audited financials are required.

Obviously, the largest drawback to selling stock under Rule 505 is the limited number of nonaccredited investors allowed, which naturally means that the average investment per investor has to be considerably more than under Rule 504.

Rule 506

This is the last rule under Regulation D.

- Rule 506 exempts offers and sales of issuers, including sales by investment and reporting companies.
- The offering amount must be for offerings over $5 million with no time restrictions.
- Sales cannot be made to more than 35 nonaccredited investors. The nonaccredited investors must be capable of evaluating the merits and risks of the investment, and it is up to the issuer to verify that the investors are knowledgeable enough to make that evaluation.
- Sales can be made to an unlimited number of accredited investors.
- No general solicitation (advertising) is allowed.
- Rule 506 carries the same notification requirements as Rules 504 and 505 with primary emphasis on filing every six months.
- Audited financials are required.
- Rule 506 does not contain "bad boy" disqualifications, but as in all Reg D rules, the SEC's antifraud provisions apply, leading most issu-

ers to voluntarily make relevant disclosures to safeguard against later charges by disgruntled investors that they were not informed of all material facts.

Regulation D may be the answer to many an entrepreneur's dreams. But because of the contradictory nature of some of the rules, well-versed legal counsel should be considered a necessity.

Alternate Methods of Private Financing

The enactment of Regulation D in 1982 simplified and facilitated the registration process for selling securities. Actually, a number of rules and exemptions are worth looking into for the same reason and, as pointed out under the Reg D discussion, the principal advantage of an exemption from registration is that the buy and sell transaction can take place as soon as the parties decide to proceed. This eliminates the necessity of preparing and filing a prospectus, and it saves legal costs as well as accounting and registration fees.

Exemptions under the 1933 act are listed as exempted securities and exempted transactions. But since the whole area of exemptions is so complex, the entrepreneur should not proceed without first seeking the advice of qualified legal counsel to determine the best form of exemption to apply for. What the exemptions do is explored next.

Exempted Securities

Section 3(a) of the 1933 act exempts a number of securities because of the particulars of the issuer. Federal, state, and local governments are exempted, for example, so as not to hamper their ability to secure financing. Religious, charitable, educational, and nonprofit organizations are also exempted as are securities that don't present a substantial risk to the investor, such as short-term notes, drafts, bills of exchange, and insurance policies (except variable annuities).

Exempted Transactions

Section 4 exempts certain transactions from the provisions of Section 5, which provides, in effect, that a registration with the SEC must take place every time a security is sold. Exempted are transactions by any person other than an issuer (company), underwriter, or dealer and are aimed at ordinary daily stock sales by the shareholder. If Mr. Jones owns 100 shares of IBM, for example, he does not have to register the transaction of selling it to his broker.

Section 4 exempts transactions by an issuer not involving any public offering (the private sale exemption). An extremely complex area, it is meant to exempt the owner of a business who is selling the business to another person or a small number of persons (fewer than 25).

Section 4 permits broker-dealers to trade for their own account or as brokers for others (retail customers) without registration.

Some transactions are allowable for brokers to make without going through the registration process, such as those covered in Rule 144, which allows a broker to sell privately held securities of a public company after they have been held for the required holding period. This covers the sale of restricted stock without the requirement of registration.

Now, we'll look at some additional exemptions.

Intrastate Offerings

This exemption falls under Section 3(a) (11) and Rule 147. It exempts certain offerings from the registration requirements of the 1933 act and refers to "any security which is a part of an issue offered and sold only to persons resident within a single State or Territory, where the issuer of such security is a person resident and doing business within, or if a corporation, incorporated by and doing business within, such State or territory."

The SEC makes clear that the intrastate exemption is "intended to apply only to issues genuinely local in character, which represent local financing by local industries, carried out through local investment." It puts complete responsibility on the company to ascertain the residency of every purchaser. It's specific in that the selling of a single share out of the state during the distribution periods may result in the entire issue being considered a violation of the 1933 act. Good faith on the issuer's part that the purchaser is a resident is no defense when it comes to the company's liability.

The intrastate exemptions specify in brief that

- the offerings are allowed in only one state,
- the issuer must be a resident of the state,
- the issuer does the majority of its business in the state,
- there are no dollar amount restrictions,

- financial sophistication of investors is not required, and
- there are no SEC filing requirements.

Lest there be any confusion, the issuer, if a person (sole proprietorship, partnership) or if a company (incorporated), must be resident in the state in which the securities are being offered, which means that the principal office *must* be located in the state.

To further clarify, *doing business* in the state is interpreted as deriving at least 80 percent of the company's consolidated gross revenues within the state, with at least 80 percent of its consolidated assets located within the state and intending, and in fact using, 80 percent of the net proceeds derived from its offering in the state.

There are also no restrictions on the total dollar amount of monies that can be raised or the individual amounts that can be subscribed for. And there are no restrictions on the number of investors that can subscribe to the offering, but it must be stressed that the rules are strict that every investor *must* be a resident of, and maintain his or her principal residence in, the state.

The original purchaser-resident investor must also be made aware that he or she may not resell the securities until the distribution is complete, and the securities, according to the SEC, "come to rest in the hands of the resident investors." What's more, a precedent has been established in the courts that all of the stock must stay in the original state for as long as one to two years—depending on the court. That means if Ms. Smith, the purchaser-resident of the stock, decides to move out of the state before the waiting period has passed, she legally cannot take the stock out of the state, as that would be construed as an *interstate* purchase rather than an intrastate purchase.

It is the responsibility of the issuer to (1) obtain a written statement from each purchaser confirming the purchaser's residence and (2) place a legend on the certificate or other document attesting that the securities have not been registered under the 1933 act. The legend must also set forth the limitations on resale (as presented in the above paragraphs). If the issuer transfers his or her own securities, stop-transfer instructions must be issued to the transfer agent or the issuer must make proper notations to that effect in its own records.

It is most important that the issuer disclose in writing the limitations on resale and include the legend and notation requirements in connection with any offer (prospectus) or sales of the securities in question. Substitute certificates must carry the same information.

A word of assurance: if the issuer can prove he or she acted with diligence on the above matters, it's unlikely that the 1933 act would be interpreted harshly by the courts.

As far as financial sophistication is concerned, there is no requirement; the company (issuer) has no responsibility to ascertain that the purchaser of its securities is a savvy investor. There are no accredited or nonaccredited investor rules. Furthermore, the disclosure requirements are nonrestrictive, and the amount of disclosure is strictly left up to the individual issuer. Naturally, the standard provisions for fraud, misstatements, and the omission of material information *do* apply. An SEC filing is not required; the issuer must only comply with the individual state's securities rules and regulations.

Finally, because of the leniency for intrastate offerings, some financial promoters create intrastate "shells." They then sit on them for a year or two, after which they try to sell them to entrepreneurs as public company shells. That could spell trouble! These shells, although they are public, are only public in one state. If the purchaser (entrepreneur) intends to broaden the securities shareholder base to other states or intends to conduct business in other states, a registration will have to be made with the SEC, which is time consuming and can be very expensive. (See Chapter 31.)

Regulation A Offerings

An early 1990's federal revision has brought Regulation A back to new life, although complying with it doesn't exempt a company from having to comply with various state securities laws.

Regulation A is available to all issuers except

- investment companies,
- issuers of fractional undivided oil and gas interests,
- other mineral rights,
- so-called blank-check companies,
- companies not incorporated in the United States or Canada, and
- companies reporting under the 1934 act.

Under the revitalized Regulation A, the SEC has raised the limit of fundraising to $5 million in any 12-month period (of which $1.5 million can be from sales by selling security holders—assuming that the company has had some net income in at least one of the last two years).

In addition, the issuer can now "test the waters" before filing the offering statement with the SEC. What this means is that a company can generally circulate information to the public about the company to test the waters for determining if there would be an interest among potential investors in investing in the company should the company decide to actually register to sell its securities. In general, the contents of these materials to "solicit indications of interest" are unregulated, except that these preliminary materials must include a brief general description of the company's business, the experience of the executive team, and—very important—a statement that no money is being solicited or accepted until the qualification and delivery of an offering circular. These tcst-the-waters materials must be filed with the SEC on the date they are first used and they must be discontinued once the preliminary offering statement is filed and 20 days before the first securities are actually sold.

Why all this filing and refiling? This is the SEC's attempt to save the entrepreneur "large" sums of money by letting them test the waters before incurring the expenses of filing a formal document.

The issuer can also choose to use the optional user-friendly question-and-answer form (the SCOR form—see below) as well as a newly revised Form 1-A.

Reg A also contains bad boy provisions, which prohibit "use of the exemption if the issuer, its underwriters, or any of the directors, officers, or principals have engaged in certain specified acts of misconduct."

Reg A has no restrictions on the qualifications of the investor (accredited or nonaccredited) or on the number of investors. Nor are there restrictions on the resale of the securities, and an issuer can do some forms of advertising and general solicitation. An offering circular is required unless the total offering is less than $100,000, and the offering must be filed with the regional office of the SEC. This registration requires submission of two years of financial statements, but the statements do not need to be audited, although most states require audited financials under blue-sky laws.

One of the reasons Reg A has been used infrequently is that one of its sections refers to "sterilized" stock. The section deals primarily with the issuer (company) that has been in existence for less than one year prior to the offering but has not realized a net income from the operation. It also concerns an issuer that was organized for more than one year but has had no net income for at least one of the last two fiscal years. It says, in effect, that all securities issued to promoters, directors, officers, underwriters, dealers, and securities salespeople must be counted as part of the monies that constitute the offering. Otherwise the stock must be placed in "captivity" (sterilized and not usable), and this makes for too much unhappiness among the principal performers. A final Reg A note: be sure you check with your legal counsel and state securities commission before using Reg A. (Reg A has become the user's choice for Internet direct public offerings; see Chapter 34.)

SCOR and ULOR and U-7

Don't you just love the government's use of acronyms? It seems they can't conceive of a single program, rule, or regulation without also conceiving some cute set of letters or words to describe it. SCOR is the abbreviation for Small Corporate Offering Registration, and ULOR stands for Uniform Limited Offering Registration (and is the name used by some states instead of SCOR), whereas U-7 (sometimes referred to as Registration Form U-7) is the form you can use to file a SCOR or a ULOR. More confusion is yet to come.

Both of these programs are a result of the SBI (Small Business Initiatives) which stemmed from the SEC's Government-Business Task Force on Small Business Capital Formation. SCOR was adopted by the American Bankers Association (ABA) in 1987, and the North American Securities Administrators Association (NASAA) in 1989. Despite the fact that all these august bodies have endorsed it, that doesn't mean you can use it in your state. Other forms of SCOR may apply, so please check with your legal counsel or state security commission before undertaking any of these alternative fundraising programs.

Simply put, SCOR is a program under which you can raise up to $1 million a year with a minimum stock price of $5 per share. The stock is freely tradable and there are no SEC reporting requirements. The paper vehicle you use for this is the U-7 Form. If SCOR is approved in your state, your state's security commission or regional SEC office can furnish you with the form, instructions, and advice on filing out the form. Some states even furnish a total SCOR package for computers; all you have to do is fill in the blanks as they pertain to your project.

The concept for SCOR is great. Make it simple, inexpensive, and quick for a company to raise money. No high-priced attorneys or accountants. In practice, however, SCOR has proven to be a trap for entrepreneurs who may not have the sophistication needed to fill out many of the really tricky questions. My advice? Check it out, but use a lot of caution, and once more you should consult with your legal counsel.

Avoiding Integration

Entrepreneurs (issuers) using Regulation D or one of the alternate methods of private financing are exempted from many SEC rules, but they can't have their cake and eat it too. Some proposed public companies have attempted to use a private exemption *intrastate* and then made another public offering *interstate*. If the offerings are found to be a part of the same transaction, that's a definite no-no. They must be completely separate transactions. You have to be very careful in observing the 12-month rules and types of offerings.

An offering may be considered exempt in isolation, but it becomes non-exempt if integration is determined as a result of its being connected with other offerings. The SEC knows all the tricks. If there is the remotest possibility that an exemption may be misconstrued because of an offering made at a later date, the transactions could be considered integrated. The best way to avoid a problem is to secure the advice of qualified legal counsel regarding integration and multistep financing plans, or a lot of time, effort, and money could be down the drain.

FREQUENTLY ASKED QUESTIONS

All these exemptions have me confused. How do I determine which one is right for me?

It's tough. There are a lot of subtleties involved as well as state rules and applications. Talk with others who have used one, chat with an IPO specialist, and, bottom line, consult with your legal counsel.

My company is a rank start-up. Can I use an exemption?

You better. When all is said and done, using an exemption is the only way to go. Don't, I repeat, DON'T, try to raise money without using some legal exemption form/vehicle to take in dollars into your company checking account. The laws prohibit this and you *will* receive stiff fines and penalties if found out. And the more successful you are (and I assume you're planing on being successful), the greater the chances of your being found out!

I just don't have the money to hire an attorney; what do you advise?

Use what we call "sweat equity." You'll have to spend a lot of time delving into the SEC and your state's securities rules and regulations to discover all the fine points. When you have determined which exemption you feel best fits your situation, then take your business plan in hand and see an attorney. Explain your reasoning and have the attorney confirm your succinct legal findings.

Can I get assistance from my state securities department?

Sure can. Just march right in and ask questions. For the most part, you'll find the personnel a little reserved but glad to help explain the intricacies of the rules and regulations.

20

Due Diligence

*D*ue diligence refers to the process that must be complied with prior to an offering being made to the public. The purpose is to ensure that the company has complied with all the legal requirements established by the SEC, which includes examining and confirming that the corporate records, financial statements, and background information about the company preparing to go public are honest, correct, and in order.

Part of the due diligence process includes what has often been referred to as *corporate cleanup*—somewhat like kicking the tires of a car you're thinking of buying. It amounts to the underwriter-broker-dealer checking out the background of the entrepreneur, the company, and the people who will be running the company. This is also the time when the underwriter makes sure that the company is ready to go public and is a good investment prospect for customers. A lot of the due diligence and corporate cleanup processes are interrelated.

Legal Responsibility

The burden of complying with the due diligence process usually falls on the company's securities lawyer, whose responsibility it is to list, gather, and authenticate such things as articles of incorporation, bylaws, patents, the completeness and correctness of corporate minutes, and other information related to corporate documents. And strange as it may sound, the securities lawyer must also verify that the company exists!

In the early 1980s an IPO was handled by a major New York underwriter and backed by a major accounting firm and a prestigious Wall Street law firm. The offering raised over $20 million through a series of private and public financings. But as it turned out, the company never existed. It seems that the small group of corporate officers of the "company" (primarily a husband-and-wife team) completely fabricated this nonexistent company, including a brief and illustrious historical and operating track record, and for a year or so created a continuing operations record. The officers invented financials and sales from an office that was never visited by any of the underwriters, accountants, or attorneys. After the completion of the public offering, the company supposedly showed revenues in the millions of dollars, but in fact the business was strictly a paper company. The experts were very embarrassed, their insurance companies were quite disappointed, the public shareholders were outraged, and the operating principals were incarcerated.

Many stories abound of "black boxes" that were figments of the imagination of enterprising entrepreneurs. There are also hundreds of stories about precious mineral or oil and gas claims, and shopping-center sites on swampland that were plain and simple scams.

Part of the due diligence activity of legal counsel must be to make a "familiarization visit" to the company's offices or plant site (and, of course, charge travel time). More practically, competent legal counsel will assemble a due diligence file that will be maintained for review by the underwriter's counsel, audit accountants, and in some cases the SEC. It should contain the following information:

- Articles of incorporation (amendments) for the company and for subsidiaries
- Bylaws for the company and subsidiaries
- Annual reports up to five years
- Proxy statements and proxies up to five years
- Letters from auditors up to five years
- Legal counsel letters to auditors up to five years
- Distributor and sales representative agreements
- Listing of representatives by name and original contract date
- Sales agreements and standard contracts
- Stock option plans
- Employment agreements
- List of materials contracts, names, dates, terms
- Officer and director questionnaires
- Any other information management believes would be pertinent

Access must be provided to the following:

- Minute books of the company and subsidiaries
- Terms of short-term financing agreements
- Records of long-term debt
- Copies of debentures and agreements
- Leases
- All material contracts
- Patents and licenses
- Selling materials for last five years
- Any other terms, agreements, contracts, or purchases that management may deem pertinent to its business

Legal counsel may also take it upon itself to perform due diligence in other areas, such as notation of phone calls and written requests in an attempt to substantiate personal résumés and references of the management team. It may perform credit investigations and other background checks on management, and may contact key customers and suppliers to request copies of purchase orders sent to, or received by, the company.

Most of the above information sought by legal counsel may never be included in counsel's findings because its main purpose is to be available if requested by the SEC.

Corporate Cleanup

Corporate cleanup could actually be considered an extension of due diligence. Its purpose is to clarify, for the record, corporate transactions that are common in a privately held company. Another objective is to assure that the management team remains operative—that it will continue to be in control of the company and work together for its future success.

The process of cleaning up the corporate structure may necessitate the consolidation of several of the company's operations, partnerships, or various corporations that are under the company's ownership and control, which may mean merging them into one corporation. Merging could become a considerable undertaking—especially for an existing company with a lengthy operating history. Corporate cleanup could also encompass real estate purchases, mergers, acquisitions, liquidations, and capital contributions.

Another area that commonly falls under corporate cleanup is employment agreements with employees, management, and company officers, which may require dissolving some existing agreements, entering into new or revised ones, changing some compensation terms, and even issuing replacement of stock or new stock options.

Cleanup might also involve restructuring loans to or from officers and directors. It could also amount to no more than executing formal promissory notes where none existed before or establishing interest payments that are more in line with present common market rates. If such existing loans were to show bias, they could be found in violation of state laws; hence, they cannot be carried into a public company.

Occasionally, it becomes appropriate to remove some personal assets that are deemed not legitimate enough to be carried on the company's books, such as resort properties, autos, planes, or the CEO's favorite yacht. Making this information public can pose unwanted tax problems to the principals involved and may require a reissuing of the financial statements. However, eliminating these items from the company books not only saves the company money but prevents shareholders from making charges of corporate waste.

Other important areas that need cleaning up before the company becomes public are the adoption of defenses against hostile takeover attempts ("shark repellents") and clauses limiting liability. These actions would more than likely require changes in the corporate charter (bylaws) or articles in order to comply with SEC rules. In a private company, a simple phone call, a letter, or a lunch meeting is usually all that's necessary to make a change in the bylaws. Once the company is public, however, these actions require shareholder approval, which could not only take months to accomplish but mean considerable extra cost to comply with the stringent SEC public company proxy rules. Obviously, this process would be less expensively accomplished when there are only a few private shareholders as opposed to hundreds of public shareholders after the company has gone public.

Back to the ever-present concern about hostile takeovers: one way to deter or defeat unwelcome tender offers is to adopt staggered multiyear terms for directors. This assures that the key directors are continued over extended periods by electing, for example, two directors for three years, two for two years, and three for one year at *each* annual election, an approach considered a pretty safe shark repellant.

Instituting golden parachute provisions can also serve to protect employment benefits. They typically include favorable severance settlements for key management in case of an unfriendly takeover or an abrupt change of control by merger or acquisition.

More and more states are approving or revising laws that limit officers' and directors' liabilities. And it is mandatory that the company adopt the most current state laws. A word of advice: A company incorporated in a very conservative state should consider reincorporating in a state with more liberal laws.

Another thing that bears considering is the fact that too many defensive bylaws, such as golden parachutes, turn away some underwriters, especially on larger offerings. Their attitude is that these bylaws can make the issue more difficult to sell as they create suspicion and therefore make the issue unattractive to public investors. Also, there are a few states that may disqualify the offering for noncompliance with the blue-sky laws. Although smaller companies are not bothered as much by these issues as are larger companies, management should be aware of them and should consider the pros and cons with legal counsel vis-à-vis its particular circumstances.

As a safeguard against possible litigation, legal counsel must also be expected to review all contracts for unusual provisions; inspect loan agreements for restrictive clauses; review IRS audits; and examine employee benefits and pension plans for compliance with the Employee Retirement Income Security Act (ERISA), which sets standards for retirement and pension accounts. Counsel should also be responsible for checking federal, state, and local compliance on anything from hazardous wastes to zoning.

Accounting Due Diligence

As mentioned in Chapter 9, strict adherence to due diligence procedures is required on the part of the accountants for a public company. The accountant is responsible for reviewing all purchases, invoices, and canceled checks, and must provide assurances that the company's financial statements are fair and correct. The audit accountants must follow the guidelines of Regulation S-X, which deals with the form and content of financial statements, GAAP, and ultimate certification. They must also comply with the generally accepted accounting principles (see Chapter 9 for details) for presenting audit information. The accountant must then make certain that the company complies with the Foreign Corrupt Practices Act (FCPA), which helped to strengthen accounting standards.

If the accountant concludes that management's internal accounting controls are noticeably weak, due diligence must be intensified or the *accountant* can be held accountable under the Securities Act of 1933.

The SEC must rely on the validity and authenticity of the accountant's audited financial statements that are included in the registration statement. This puts the responsibility on the accountant to perform a "reasonable" investigation, and ultimately to provide assuring "comfort" letters to the SEC and underwriters that very specific accounting procedures have been complied with.

Dual Responsibility

Because a number of areas of due diligence and corporate cleanup can be designated the responsibility of either legal counsel or accounting, a company's management usually has to make a decision as to who does what. For example, both legal and accounting can become involved in pension plans. Lawsuits, warranty disputes, and employee-union relations could also involve legal as well as accounting issues.

FREQUENTLY ASKED QUESTIONS

When does the due diligence take place?

The legal aspects of due diligence start when a management team engages a securities lawyer. The accounting part of due diligence begins when the audit accountants are retained.

Does this mean that I don't have to be concerned about it until I begin the IPO process?

Technically yes, but it's good advice to talk with both legal counsel and an audit accountant well in advance about the basics of due diligence.

Why is that?

For a lot of reasons pertaining to the proper operations of a public company versus a privately held concern. As an example, a privately held company frequently leases real estate from the officers of the company with lease terms most likely designed for the best tax advantage. These leases will probably have to be redone and, in more extreme cases, the property sold and new leases written.

21

Underwriters

The primary goals when going public are to have a successful offering, to receive a fair price for the stock, and to have a stable, liquid aftermarket trading in the stock. The underwriter's responsibility is to assure that these goals are achieved.

Nothing prevents a company from acting as its own underwriter; there are no set rules or regulations (see Chapter 22). However, the business of selling securities is so specialized that it's best left to the acknowledged specialists in the field.

Underwriters are sometimes referred to as *investment bankers.* In fact, on their calling cards almost all are listed as investment bankers. But for our purposes and from a practical point of view, they are underwriters. Their main function is to underwrite stock issues, whereas conventional investment bankers are known to perform a variety of services involving the raising of capital. Underwriters usually represent a firm, a broker-dealer who specializes in underwriting securities. In simple terms, that means they buy a company's stock from the company, or take it and sell it to other dealers or the investing public.

Choosing an underwriter has occasionally been likened to choosing a spouse. Management is attempting to establish a relationship of mutual confidence, respect, and trust with a little bit of love/hate involved. Nonetheless, during the IPO process the two teams invariably build a close personal relationship that, it is to be hoped, will flourish for years to come.

The underwriter who leads or heads an IPO is given the title of *managing underwriter.* It's the responsibility of the managing underwriter to form a selling syndicate or group of other investment bankers (usually broker-dealers) to participate in the distribution of the securities. Consequently, the selection of the right managing underwriter is critical from the start. The company's reputation will ultimately ride on the managing underwriter. In turn, his or her reputation on the Street and successes and failures reflect on the company.

Types of Underwriters

The types and nature of underwriters have varied over the course of financial history. From the market's inception through the mid-1950s, underwriting represented the principal source of income for securities companies. Since then, because of the unsteadiness of the stock market, the majority of underwriters have come to operate as broker-dealers and enjoy a mix of income from underwriting fees and stock commissions. No longer is a distinction drawn between wholesale, retail, or a combination of the two. The only distinction shows itself in larger firms that have departmentalized separate divisions for wholesale and retail. In either case, the game is the same.

Wholesale

Traditionally, the wholesale investment banking firm was a separate entity from a retail investment banking firm. It did not cater to the general public or individual investor but concentrated its efforts on distributing large blocks of stock to retail firms. Those wholesale investment bankers that exist today are specialized underwriters who make large financial commitments to place large blocks of stock with institutional investors. They also put together large selling syndicates among broker-dealers.

Retail

Retail broker-dealer firms traditionally relied on wholesalers to put together IPOs, and they functioned primarily as participants in selling syndicates. Their retail brokers sold and distributed stocks to their individual private retail investors.

In the past, the size of an underwriter's firm was thought to be related to the affiliation with the issuer. The larger the firm, the more committed the relationship. Because of that general feeling, the National Association of Securities Dealers (NASD) conducted a study that attempted to determine if being associated with a larger underwriter's firm was more beneficial to the new IPO. The study questioned whether a directorship or continuing advisory position was part of the underwriting agreement. The results are presented below.

Large firms. These are national firms, often with hundreds of brokerage offices located across the country and thousands of individual retail brokers with millions of individual personal accounts. Their IPO interests are exclusively underwritings totaling $20 million and over. Many of the underwriting clients are *Fortune* 1000 companies, with an emphasis on the top 500. Their main involvement is the issuing of secondary financings. These large firms usually have extensive investment banking departments that can supply help and expertise on anything from initial financing through large institutional private placements for both debt and equity to mergers, acquisitions, leveraged buyouts, and sophisticated merchant banking functions. They can operate on a local, national, or international level. The NASD survey found that 43 percent of these large firms had financial advisory relationships with their public offering clients and were on a retainer basis with many of them.

Medium-size firms. For the most part, these are regional firms, serving a limited geographical area, often with a dozen or so branches and a few hundred brokers. Many operate in a single state or in a group of states that are defined as a region. They are primarily interested in IPOs in the $10 million to $20 million range from established companies with a profitable operating history. Their investment banking departments usually offer full services but with less depth in personnel and experience than the large firms. The NASD study revealed that only 14 percent of the medium-size firms had a financial advisory relationship with their IPOs.

Small firms. There are fewer small firms operating today than in the past. The economics of operating a small firm with a full back office to serve retail customer needs is simply not financially justifiable. Consequently, many have merged or been acquired and integrated into one of the medium-size firms. Those that remain are boutique-type firms that usually specialize in particular areas of business or low-priced OTC stocks. Most small firms do not have specific investment banking departments or personnel other than multiple-skilled owners. Their IPOs are usually smaller in size (up to $7 to $10 million). The NASD survey showed that less than 8 percent of the small firms had any continuing financial advisory relationship with their IPOs.

Industrial Classification

Many underwriting firms that specialize in offerings, often for specific industries, are scattered throughout the country. They usually work with established selling syndicates that share their interest in a particular industry. Although they don't limit themselves to a particular size offering, most of them tend to concentrate on regional and smaller firms. They know the territory and they know the industries. For example, in the Midwest, agriculturally oriented IPOs receive the greatest interest; in California, high-tech industries are in favor; the Northeast has a long-standing love affair with medical issues.

For the entrepreneur, there are definite advantages in establishing a relationship with an underwriter that has a proven track record in a particular industry. For one thing, the company's management doesn't have to spend a lot of time educating the underwriters or brokers about its industry. In addition, the selling syndicates know how to reach the investors who are inclined to purchase stocks in a particular industry. Drawbacks, however, must be considered. Because these underwriters specialize in particular industries, there is always a possibility of a conflict of interest, so entrepreneurs need to use their best business judgment in deciding with whom to go. It pays to do a little research into the IPOs the underwriter has handled in the past five years. Nevertheless, the underwriter's base knowledge and understanding of the industry can save a great deal of time and educational effort.

Types of Underwritings

As mentioned earlier, the two basic types of underwritings are *firm commitment* and *best effort,* and both can have an option variable.

Firm Commitment

Firm commitments are the most desirable kind of underwriting. As the term implies, the underwriter agrees to make a firm commitment to purchase the entire amount of the company's stock issue regardless of its ability to resell the securities to the public. In actuality, the selling of the stock to the public by the syndicate members is a foregone conclusion. The stocks are usually presold before any final signing takes place with the company. However, if the underwriter or syndicate members misjudged and can't resell the securities, they simply buy them in their own account and sell them at a later date, thus assuring the issuing company that it will receive a set amount of dollars at a set date, usually five to seven days after the effective date of registration. Of course, a high level of risk is involved for the underwriter, but this type of underwriting is normal for most large and regional firms, and has become standard procedure for the smaller firms.

Often, underwriters issuing a firm commitment agreement will request an overallotment option, known as a "green shoe" (see Chapter 27). This is the variable option for firm commitments. The green shoe allows the underwriter to purchase a specific number of additional shares of the company's stock, usually 10 to 15 percent of the total issue.

Best Effort

This type of agreement states that the underwriter will extend its best efforts to sell the company's stock but does not agree to purchase the unsold securities for its own account. In effect, the underwriter is acting as an agent of the issuer or company. A best efforts is not as desirable as a firm commitment, but it's an agreement commonly used for low-priced IPO issues. Large underwriters don't do best efforts agreements, and they are seldom done by regional underwriters.

Options

Some best efforts agreements come with a variable option referred to as "all or none," which specifies that the underwriter must sell the whole transaction or the entire amount of the issue will be canceled. There can be no partial sales. Today, all or none is being replaced in many agreements with a mini/max, or minimum/maximum, clause that allows the company to determine a medium dollar amount of an offering. Let's say the offering is for $4 million. The minimum is then set at $3 million with a maximum set at $4 million. That means if the underwriter raises $3.2 million in a best effort, the company will accept it as it's above the minimum. Obviously, the goal is to achieve the full amount of $4 million. But accepting the medium amount prevents a lot of time and effort being wasted on an unsuccessful all-or-none underwriting.

Finders

Finders are individuals who serve as intermediaries in bringing together underwriters with companies that wish to go public. Most often, finders are lawyers, accountants, and management consultants. They play an important role for both sides in introducing clients to underwriters and investment bankers, which doesn't mean the entrepreneur or prospective IPO management team can't seek out an underwriter directly. It's just that reputable finders can be a major time-saver because they command the respect of underwriters. They usually are familiar with underwriters' calendars and schedules as well as knowing how best to approach the underwriting investment banking community. Many smaller underwriters will not even consider an IPO without a finder's recommendation as they don't have the staff to prequalify a project.

The ideal finder not only knows how to present the prospective underwriting to the underwriter/investment banker but is familiar with the form of corporate structure needed to make the project appealing. An underwriter also expects that the finder will have performed due diligence on the company by investigating its business history, the current condition of all aspects of the company, and the company's future projections and prospects as well as the background of the management team.

The finder also serves as a bridge between the company and the underwriter. This may come as a surprise, but because of the nature of the financing, few of the smaller underwriters have highly qualified people who can really understand the technical aspects of a company and work closely with the company throughout the underwriting process. Although all underwriters may understand the registration and selling process, they don't always comprehend the inner workings of the company and depend on the finder to bridge the gap. What's more, some underwriters don't have a continuing interest in the success of the company after the public funding is completed. This is especially true of low-priced issues, and for that reason alone, all companies with low-priced issues should strongly consider the retention of a qualified IPO consultant to act as a finder.

Finders' compensation depends on the deal that is cut. Some finders work exclusively for underwriters and could receive a flat fee, a percentage, warrants, or all of these. If compensation comes from the issuer, it could also be in the form of stock plus consulting fees. It depends on the role played by the finder and the involvement. But whether fee or percentage—which has been known to range from 1 to 15 percent—it should all be in writing as full disclosure is required in the prospectus by the SEC and the NASD.

Shopping

Shopping a deal can often do a company more harm than good. A company planning to go public may put out feelers to a number of prospective underwriters/investment bankers to see if there would be any interest in underwriting the offering—in other words, "shopping" for the best deal. But there are advantages and disadvantages to this practice.

On the one hand, shopping can assist the company in gaining a better understanding of how much the market values the company. If a company shows merit, underwriters are willing to take the time and effort for a preliminary investigation, which will determine whether they would be interested in proceeding and proposing a deal.

If a company is determined to shop, it is best to select three to five prospective underwriters and hold preliminary discussions. The company should deal openly with the underwriters and inform them, without revealing names, that it is also talking with other firms. It should be made very clear that the company is exploring the possibility of going public. Be forewarned that underwriters are competitive, but they don't care to get into a bidding war with each other. However, if underwriters feel positive about the company, they will advise the management of their interest and pursue the matter from there.

Now for the bad part. Underwriters hesitate to expend the time and effort required to investigate a proposed project if they don't feel they would be seriously in the running. They may require an exclusivity. Also, if the company shops over an extended period of time and is turned down or receives just moderate indications of interest, word can spread around the street and cause irreparable damage to the company's plans. Underwriters have a habit of talking to each other about their business, especially about syndication. When a company exposes itself to an underwriter, chances are the underwriter will test the waters with peers to see if there is any interest in syndication. If prospective selling syndication members have turned down participation in the offering previously, it is very difficult to regain their interest. In addition, underwriters/investment bankers don't care to take on a project if they know it has been rejected by some of their peers. The fact that it has been shopped around may force the company to revalue the deal, most likely downward.

Generally speaking, simultaneous shopping should only be considered by major companies when pursuing larger underwriters. It should be very carefully considered by companies pursuing underwritings for smaller, lower-priced issues. Then again, there are times when entrepreneurs need to rely on their gut feelings.

Underwriter Selection

There are, essentially, four important areas to be considered when selecting an underwriter: performance, experience, distribution, and aftermarket (aftermarket is terminology used to show how the issue—the price of the stock—has performed following its going public). Each is important and each requires special attention. In the final analysis, however, *compatibility* may rank above them all. The company management team and the underwriting team have to get along if the process is to succeed. All through the underwriting-IPO relationship, each team will be testing the other's patience. As mentioned earlier in the book, a lot of paperwork must be cleaned up, and this invariably results in creating one roadblock after another. What it really boils down to is that the company wants its money and the underwriter wants to sell stock. It takes a lot of doing on the part of the entrepreneur-CEO to make sure that the underwriter is completely comfortable with the IPO's progress and doesn't slack off.

Performance

The entrepreneur has a personal obligation and one to the company to select an underwriter with a good reputation on the Street and credibility for putting together strong-selling syndicates. It also pays to inquire about the firm's basic philosophy: Is it aggressive or conservative, and does that stand fit in with the company's goals?

Asking Questions

The process of evaluating and selecting an underwriter should include contacting principals of other IPOs and questioning them regarding their experience and feelings regarding the underwriters being considered. Some questions to ask include these:

- Were there any last-minute surprises?
- Were you satisfied with the interest your underwriter showed in your company and with its knowledge of your industry?
- How do you feel about its syndication abilities?
- Has your underwriter maintained an adequate aftermarket interest in your stock?
- Are you satisfied with the aftermarket performance, and how much do you attribute the price movement to your underwriter's support?

- Is your underwriter continuing to support your stock through research reports and by soliciting additional market makers?
- In retrospect, would you use the firm again?
- Would you recommend it?

Also to be considered in the underwriter selection process is the possibility that the company may, in the future, require additional rounds of financing in the form of debt, equity, or a combination of them. Management should be satisfied that the potential underwriter can provide this service as well as offer continuing financial advice that might also encompass mergers and acquisitions.

Before a final decision is made on the choice of an underwriter, the management team should take the time to research the underwriter's performance on previous offerings. This information can be found in the publication *Going Public: The IPO Reporter* (Investment Dealers Digest, Inc., New York, NY), which provides information on all the new IPOs and tracks their performance in the aftermarket.

Good underwriters are particular, too. They must protect *their* reputations, which can be a significant factor in attracting new investors. A top firm very often has underwriting standards that exceed those set by the SEC, the NASD, and states.

Distribution

A broad distribution of an IPO's stock is the goal of any company because it means the stock has been sold to many individual investors in smaller amounts, which usually results in a larger and more stable aftermarket for the securities. Fewer shareholders holding large blocks of stock can adversely affect a stock's selling price should they all decide, for whatever reason, to sell their holdings at the same time.

Most underwriters of larger issues traditionally attract institutional investors. But institutional investors are seldom attracted to low-priccd issues, and some institutional investors, by policy, don't invest in certain industries. So the company should know in advance if the proposed underwriter's particular institutional investors have any interest in its type of company.

Some underwriters are more sophisticated in assembling selling syndicates than others. They know how to assess their investors' makeup and then seek out selling syndicate members that will complement the issue.

If international exposure is important to the company, or if the company plans to sell its product or service to an international market in the future, the company should be sure to make the managing underwriter aware of its plans. If the company has particularly strong geographical areas where its customers or clients are located, the managing underwriter should try to get selling syndicate members who are located in these communities.

Throughout this process, the company ought to have an idea of the makeup of clients that are trading with the underwriter. Do they have a reputation for quick turnovers—anxious to dump their stock and move on to the next hot deal—or are they interested in purchasing the stock for long-term investment?

Aftermarket

Once the initial securities are sold, stock movement is important. A strong aftermarket performance and perceivable trading activity in the stock are needed. This requires the managing underwriter and, it is to be hoped, all selling syndicate members to expend all their efforts toward making a market in the stock. It means they keep the trading activity of buying and selling the stock going by maintaining inventory in the stock and buying and selling from their own accounts as opposed to just functioning as agents. (See Chapter 27.) In addition, the underwriter needs to continue to sell the company to new market makers.

A large part of the aftermarket activity is devoted to maintaining existing shareholders' interest and attracting new shareholders. This can be achieved through cooperation between the market makers and the lead underwriter, which is expected to be able to furnish syndicate members with analysts' research reports about the company. (See Chapter 27.) It's the company's responsibility to provide a continuing flow of information to the market maker's analysts. If the underwriter has a reputation for supporting stocks in a particular industry, it's reasonable to assume that the firm's analysts also have a respected reputation on the Street for their expertise in that industry.

The Underwriter's Dilemma

The underwriter must make critical judgments on the ability of a company to provide a product or service that profitably fills the needs of its own customers, the investment community. If its judgment is wrong, it can fail, too. Testifying to that are the many defunct companies that were taken public by underwriters that are also now defunct, largely because of misjudgments in this crucial area and especially true of low-priced issues.

In many cases entrepreneurs have put together companies that they hoped would fill a product or service void in what was expected to be the next hot industry. The computer industry for both software and hardware is a good example as is biotech and, more recently, Internet industries. The general public becomes primed to look for "hot investments." They look for opportunities to get in on the ground floor of what are felt to be the IBMs or Microsofts of a whole new industry. Underwriters are quick to recognize investors' product demand and are very receptive to looking at prospective IPOs with a hot word like *Internet* attached. The outcome is predictable. Many of the new companies are not able to fill the customer need economically or efficiently, and in reality the customers' needs may never truly materialize. Consequently, companies fail and underwriters are left with egg on their faces. Industry trends generally stem from news stories about problems looking for solutions, specifically something that could solve a need in our society.

Underwriters are more comfortable when they are interested in a particular product or service for which they would like to do an IPO. An overriding factor is the enthusiasm an underwriter shows for the basic business of a company. The underwriter also wants to feel philosophically in tune with the company. If these factors are met, the underwriter will proceed to qualify the company in four essential areas: management, product or service, finances, and business plan.

Management

Management is probably the most important factor in evaluating a company. An assessment is made about capability, integrity, intelligence, and desire to achieve. The management team members' past performance will be checked, individually and jointly, if they have worked together before. Their successes as well as their failures will be taken into consideration. The underwriter will want answers to such questions as: Does management have personal capital at risk? Are the key management positions filled, that is, chief operating officer, marketing director, chief financial officer, and technical and production personnel? Can they inspire and lead the company's employees? Do they have good management capability?

Product or Service

The underwriter must assess the industry in general. Is it in a fast-growth posture? What is the quality of the product or service and its relationship to the competition? Are the competitors larger or smaller, and is there a defined market niche? How long is the life of the product or service and has a second generation been identified and determined feasible? Can a corporate identity be established? Are there copyright, trademark, patent, or proprietary issues involved? What type of research and development is planned? Is a solid market plan in place? Has the product or service been market proven?

Finances

The underwriter will conduct a financial review to ascertain how effectively capital has been spent to date. Is the company using financial resources and alternatives to best advantage? What is the current asset, equity, and debt structure? Are there past earnings, and how do they compare with the industry norm? Is the projected growth reasonable? At what level of sales will the breakeven point be reached? When will additional capital be needed? Is the financial valuation supported by net earnings projections?

Business Plan

The underwriter will review the business plan to gain insight into the company's business history, products or services, manufacturing or production operations, market analysis, competition, and management. Of course, of primary interest in the business plan is the use of proceeds. A heads-up underwriter will try to make sure the funds received from the proposed IPO will be sufficient to accomplish the company's growth goals and will not be used to fill the pockets of the management team or to bail out key shareholders.

The main purpose for these reviews are to give the issue the best possible chance for success by eliminating all the negative factors. The entrepreneur and the management team should look on this interrelating and investigative process by the prospective underwriter as a positive approach toward building the confidence and trust so necessary for both sides.

Indirect Costs

Underwriters' warrants come under the heading of indirect costs and are often issued to the underwriter by the company for little or, in some cases, no cost. It frequently amounts to 10 percent of the total of the new issue of securities being sold to the public. For example, the underwriter will be given 200,000 warrants that carry the rights to purchase 200,000 shares of stock if the public issue is for 2 million shares. The underwriter is usually given the rights to purchase these additional shares at a 20 percent premium over the initial offering price. On an $8.00 new issue, the underwriter would agree to pay $9.60. The warrants are normally exercisable 12 months after the initial effective date. But the exercise period has been known to be extended to as much as five years.

Another form of indirect compensation comes from an agreement to give the underwriter a continuing input into the company's operations, which can be by way of a board of director's seat, as a member of the board of advisers, a salaried position, or consultation under a continuing agreement.

Negotiations

For the edification of the entrepreneur, the terms of an underwriting agreement are always negotiable, including the fees, the type and price of the securities being offered, the total size of the offering, the timing, rights for future financings, the states in which the issue will be offered, the composition of the selling syndicates, and even the corporate structure of the company and the makeup of the board of directors. It's not unusual for the actual negotiation process to begin the moment the IPO is presented to the underwriter, and it could continue until the final agreement is signed, which could be the same day, or the day before, the issue is declared effective.

Although there are no set rules or even official guidelines regarding the underwriter's compensation, each individual offering is reviewed by the NASD and state securities authorities for fairness to all sides, including the investor. The NASD in particular will scrutinize the total amount of compensation and expenses received by the underwriter, reviewing commissions, accountable and nonaccountable expenses, warrants, advisory fees, finders' fees, consulting agreements, and stocks or securities received. As a rule, it will question compensation that equals or exceeds a value of 15 percent of the total amount of the offering. If it concludes, for whatever reason, that the compensation is excessive, it has the power to bring the proposed underwriting to a complete halt.

The NASD is especially cautious about the purchase of a company's securities by officers, partners, managers, and brokers who are affiliated with the underwriting firm. Although these purchases are not illegal, the NASD may require the owners to agree to restrictions on the resale of their stock. If there is any difference between the amount paid by these individuals and the price set for issuance to the public, the NASD may declare the difference as additional underwriting compensation, which could become another negotiating point in reaching an agreement with the underwriter.

Letter of Intent

At some point in the discussions with the underwriter, the company and the underwriter must come to some form of agreement that justifies proceeding. This agreement comes about in the form of a letter of intent, which is simply an agreement to agree. In practice, it attempts to eliminate as much ground for misunderstanding as possible, especially as to what the parties will eventually agree upon.

With a few exceptions, the letter of intent is a nonbinding agreement. As soon as an underwriter agrees to enter a firm deal, it must set aside a certain amount of its capital to assure that it is financially capable of completing the project. This does not apply to best efforts underwritings. Despite the rules, a final agreement is seldom signed until the day before (after the close of the market) or the day of the offering.

The binding part of the letter of intent is that the entrepreneur is responsible for the payment of certain costs—any expenses incurred by the underwriter in preparation of the underwriting—regardless of whether the underwriting is ultimately completed.

The contents of the letter of intent are extensive. It covers many points that are agreed upon in the final definitive agreement as evidenced by the sample sections in a letter of intent presented below.

Sections Included in a Letter of Intent

- The *introduction* attests to the fact that preliminary discussions have been held between the company and the underwriter. Based on these discussions, the underwriter agrees in principle to underwrite the proposed public offering in accordance with the terms set forth in the letter of intent.
- *Representing counsel* identifies the legal counsel for both the underwriter and the company.
- The *registration statement* specifies the particular form of the statement to be submitted (S-1, SB-2, etc.) along with covering informa-

tion and establishes the time frame for each aspect of submission and the responsibilities of each party (company and underwriter).

- *Underwriter's counsel* sets forth areas of responsibility of counsel, such as NASD or state blue-sky filings, the number of registration statements that are required, and the filing fees.
- The *public offering* affirms decisions reached in the preliminary agreement as to a minimum/maximum amount or range of shares, the type of security to be offered, and the price range. This section also discloses the type of offering—best efforts or firm commitment and indicates the date the offering is expected to be released, extension clauses, escrow agent, and designation of the transfer agent.
- *Percentage of ownership* specifies the number of shares to be offered to the public and what the minimum/maximum ranges of percentage of stock ownership will be.
- *Commencement of offering* usually declares that a bona fide public offering will be made by the underwriter within three business days of the effective date of the registration.
- *Future sales* states that the company pledges not to make any additional sales of its securities without the underwriter's permission for a certain period of time, usually 12 to 24 months from the effective date. This clause will also contain certain restrictive covenants regarding the sale of stock by existing shareholders.
- *Reciprocal indemnification* states that the final agreement will provide for reciprocal indemnification by both the underwriter and the company regarding liabilities under the 1933 act.
- *Questionnaire information* notes specific information that must be supplied by the company to the underwriter.
- The *litigation* section declares that either party will inform the other of any litigation or suspension actions by regulatory agencies.
- *Blue-sky laws* disclose states in which the proposed offering will be registered and who is to handle the registration.
- *Adverse change* is the underwriter's "backing-out" clause, which says in effect that it can pull out of the deal "solely on its own judgment" and is usually invoked in cases where there are material adverse changes in the company's financial or business conditions, or adverse stock market conditions.
- *Underwriter's commission* sets forth the commission percentage/range the underwriter is to receive.

- *Expense allowance* determines the nonaccountable and accountable expense reimbursement from the company to the underwriter, including the nonrefundable amounts from deposit.
- *Underwriter warrants* specify the intended warrants to be issued to the underwriter and the terms of exercise.
- *Rights of refusal* affirm the terms regarding the rights of refusal on the part of the underwriter for representing the company in future financings.
- *1934 act registration* declares that the company will file the required Form 10, which specifies that it must become fully reporting after the completion of the initial offering. (This may not be applicable depending on the company's or the underwriter's wishes.)
- *Additional points* can cover any agreed-upon understandings, such as conflict with the law; agreements to consolidate, merge, or sell certain subsidiaries or divisions or assets; board of directors positions; ongoing consulting agreements; exemptions in certain states; net worth; debt reduction or limitation; and sales figures to be met before or maintained until the underwriting is effective.
- *Formal agreement contemplated* is a statement to the effect that this is a letter of intent and a definitive agreement will be executed immediately prior to the effective date of the proposed offering.

Note that this generalized outline for a letter of intent is to assist the reader in gaining a fuller understanding of the process and should not be considered all-inclusive.

Underwriting Agreement

The definitive underwriting agreement is almost redundant except for the final stock pricing and the amount of stock to be issued. All of the points have already been thoroughly discussed and agreed upon. The document is usually a formality whose signing takes place after the market has closed on the day before the effective date of the offering. At this last moment, the company still has a legal right to back out of the deal, but it becomes responsible for all of the accrued expenses of the offering if it does.

The managing underwriter will also have met previously with all the selling syndicate members, and they will have concluded an *agreement among the underwriters,* a document designating the number of shares each has committed to and authorizing the managing underwriter to sign the underwriting agreement with the company on behalf of the syndicate members. Among other items, the agreement among the underwriters sets forth the terms of the agreement between the managing underwriter and the selling syndicate members regarding commissions, expenses, and any warrant distributions.

The underwriting agreement itself is an extremely involved document with as many as 20 to 40 pages. While these agreements may vary in details, they generally follow a pattern containing numerous warranties, conditions, and covenants that establish the rights and obligations of all the parties as shown in the sections of a model agreement below.

Introduction and definitions. This section introduces and identifies the parties to the underwriter's agreement and acknowledges the selling syndicate. The security to be offered is defined as either debt or equity, common or preferred, and the number of shares to be sold are clearly specified.

Representations and warranties. This provision covers the guarantee by the company that the representations and warranties made by the company regarding the underwriting are true, correct, and complete as of the date the agreement is put into effect. In addition, the company warrants that it is properly incorporated and accredited. More specifically, the company avows that

- all outstanding stock is duly authorized, validly issued, fully paid, and nonassessable;
- it has conformed with the requirements of the 1933 act, including the registration statement (with names of the accountants and proof of their independence);
- the company has the power to issue the new stock;
- no material changes have taken place in the company's capital structure;
- there are no violations in the articles of incorporation, bylaws, or other documents of the company or its subsidiaries;
- the financial statements present a fair and truthful picture of the company;
- there are no legal actions pending (unless noted);
- the company has not attempted and will not attempt to manipulate the stock in any way;
- the company has not been involved in bribery or made any unlawful political contributions; and
- all trademarks, patents, and so forth are legitimate.

Terms of the offering. This portion of the underwriter's agreement will not include the offering price of the stock until the actual signing. But it will include the underwriter's pledge to buy and pay for the securities (firm commitment or best efforts). It will also verify the timing involved and any minimum/maximum or green shoe provisions (mentioned earlier in this chapter).

Covenants. In this section the underwriter spells out the company's responsibilities as follows:

- The company is responsible for paying all fees, including stock transfer and registration.
- The company is responsible for keeping the registration statement up to date. This is most critical. If changes are necessary in the registration statement, the company is required to inform the underwriter and then make the appropriate filings with the SEC, the NASD, and the appropriate states. Those changes will necessitate *stickering* the prospectus (pasting in changes), which is time consuming and expensive. For that reason alone, the entrepreneur and company should be cautioned not to enter into any new negotiations, bring out new products, lose major customers, make any significant management changes, or make any other consequential changes while the registration is in effect.
- The company agrees to file for registration in the necessary states.
- The company agrees to furnish quarterly and annual reports.
- The company agrees to abide by the uses of proceeds set forth in the prospectus.
- The company promises not to buy or sell any other securities without the underwriter's written permission (with qualifiers for the selling shareholders).

Conditions. Three basic conditions must be complied with: one that seems to work for the benefit of the company, one that seems to benefit the underwriter, and one that benefits both the company and the underwriter. Usually attested to by an accountant's comfort letter, they are as follows:

1. The underwriter relies upon the accuracy of the company's representations and warranties.
2. The company must furnish the underwriter with letters from the company's legal counsel that assure the accuracy, truthfulness, and completeness of the company's representations and warranties.

3. Neither party can sell stock until the offering has been declared effective by the SEC.

Indemnification. Under the 1933 act, an investor can file suit against officers of the company, principal shareholders (10 percent or more ownership), directors, underwriters, or any person or organization voluntarily named in the registration statement. The indemnification provisions excuse liability for material misstatements or omissions by the company in the registration statement and are applicable to both the underwriter and the company—indemnifying one from the other. What they imply, in essence, is that if all parties concerned perform their individual due diligence activities adequately and can prove that they have done so, the courts may not hold them liable.

Cancellation. This section contains a clause that allows the underwriter to cancel the offering after the effective date but before the closing, providing the underwriter can show cause and justification. Examples of justification are natural catastrophes affecting the company (flood, fire, etc.); a declaration of war; a national banking moratorium; and national or international general economic, political, or financial problems.

The balance of the agreement contains the normal boilerplate provisions that are part of most agreements. To repeat, the definitive agreement is very lengthy and involved. In an effort to be thorough, no stone is left unturned. Pro forma copies are furnished to all parties before the signing meeting so that relevant details can be reworked before the actual signing takes place. Actually, as a rule the agreement has been thoroughly gone over and approved long before the signing, which is the culmination of what seems like months of blood, sweat, and, occasionally, a few tears.

FREQUENTLY ASKED QUESTIONS

Can I use my stockbroker as an introduction source to an underwriter?

Certainly. Talk with your broker to determine his or her ability to introduce you to his or her firm's corporate finance department. Most firms have well-defined procedures for this action and are pleased to at least listen to your story. In some cases, your broker may also receive some financial incentive.

Is it difficult to sign up underwriters?

Sometimes, but remember that they are just like your friendly retail store. They need product to sell to stay in business and you have that product in the form of stock. Underwriter selection should be accomplished carefully. Don't necessarily sign up with the first one that comes along. Be sure it is experienced in your type of industry and excited about doing your deal.

What is the timing involved in signing up an underwriter?

It's difficult to set forth definitive timetables. Underwriters maintain what they call "calendars" that list their underwriting schedules for months in advance. Calendars change because an underwriting might be signed up as far as two years in advance, and a lot can change in that period. A company may not be able to obtain interim financing or its whole product/service, and consequently its market, may shift. If an underwriter drops out, you might be just the deal to slide into an open spot.

Do I have to know about all the parts in an underwriting agreement?

Not in this lifetime. Your securities counsel will go over all the little details and their various implications with you. But it is helpful if you have some familiarity with the documents.

Self-Underwriting

Can a company go public without an underwriter? No rules or regulations prohibit it, but the tradition of a company going public successfully without an underwriter has not been favorable. This doesn't mean it hasn't been done or is not being done. Hundreds of small companies have done it. But few have ever gotten beyond "small."

The fact is that a self-underwriting IPO over $5 million is rare. Small offerings priced around $1 per share and under $500,000, however, are not uncommon and are especially true of the early Internet direct public offerings (see Part Six). Traditionally, self-underwritings are more popular when a "hot new-issue" market exists. Investors tend to get caught up in speculative new-issue fever and throw normal IPO caution to the wind. It happened in the mid-1980s when hundreds of self-underwritings popped out from under the woodwork, and the Internet is reopening the possibilities.

The Big Fallacy

Supposedly, the big benefit of doing a self-underwriting is to save the underwriter's fee. The entrepreneur should look at these figures: Discount or selling commission savings amount to approximately 10 percent of the total underwriting plus the possible savings of unaccountable expense allowances of 2 to 5 percent. Most companies, however, provide for the underwriter's commission in their registration statement. They do that because if they intend to do any kind of selling, they will be coming to underwriters to participate in a selling syndicate, which means that the company will be paying the underwriter commissions on part of the issue.

The problem is that underwriters, as a rule, will not subscribe for more than 10 percent of a deal without having their name on the cover of the prospectus. If they do the work, they want to share in the credit. That leaves the company desperately seeking participation for the other 90 percent of the offering. Another problem is that underwriters want warrants, and if the market is tough, the company will have to make deals with underwriters to entice them to sell its new issue. Expense allowances and warrants are part of the cost of doing business with underwriters.

There's more to consider. Even if a company finds a broker who expresses interest in soliciting sales for the company, the broker's firm must first approve the broker's participation (unless the broker is working individually). Unless the individual broker carries a great deal of clout, his or her firm will likely deny participation. Creditable brokerage firms are reluctant to expose themselves to liability connected with selling stock in a new IPO unless they have conducted due diligence, or unless another firm is leading the IPO. What's more, selling small amounts of stock can't justify the cost of conducting the due diligence, especially without reimbursement or warrants. Considering that the broker-dealer commission of 10 percent is split, usually 3 percent to the firm and 7 percent to the broker, and considering the deals and aggravation the entrepreneur-company must go through as a self-underwriter, one has to ask, where's the savings?

The Carrot

Directed stock will perk up the ears of any broker. It's a list of names, addresses, and phone numbers of friends, family, and business associates of the company—people who are likely to purchase stock in the IPO because they know the entrepreneur and management team and want to participate. What makes this list so desirable is that it gives underwriters and brokers an opportunity to open new accounts and sell additional product. Naturally, the company that attempts a self-underwriting wants to keep this list to itself, thus saving the commission, but the list may be impressive enough to make the individual broker or broker-dealer want to work out a compromise.

Market Makers

In order to trade the stock in the aftermarket after the offering has been completed, the company needs market makers. They are the specialists who help to create aftermarket interest and make regular trades in the stock. Unless there is a broad distribution of the stock and a lot of seeming interest in its trading plus continuing efforts to keep up that interest, it is difficult to achieve broker-dealer trading participation. Such participation requires additional time, effort, and expertise on the part of the company, whereas if an underwriter is used, it is his or her responsibility to line up other market makers and assist the company in expanding aftermarket interest.

"Blue-Skying"

Every state has rules and regulations governing the selling of securities, particularly new issues, and they are another roadblock the self-underwriter must be prepared to face. Regulations were enacted to protect gullible investors from purchasing stock from unscrupulous promoters. Getting such stocks approved by state security departments is called "blue-skying." Blue-sky laws also require the registration of broker-dealers. Because self-underwriting requires blue-skying the company's issue, the company must wait until the market makers tell it in which states they plan to trade. Unfortunately, this can cause delays in trading. Applications must be submitted and approved before trading can commence, and if the company arbitrarily does its own blue-skying without foreknowledge of which states it will trade in, unnecessary expenditures of legal and filing fees can result.

Pros and Cons

The fact: self-underwriting does not carry the prestige of a project that receives the acceptance of the brokerage community. Underwriters tend to look at self-underwritings as issues that are substandard or that the issuing company is too cheap to retain a real underwriter. It also has a tendency to turn off new-issue investors.

The tragedy is that if the company fails to complete the offering, it becomes almost impossible to raise funds from other sources and highly improbable that an underwriter would consider taking on the issue.

Another thing that should be considered by the entrepreneur is that the SEC approval process always seems to take longer with self-underwritings. The general impression is that the SEC doesn't seem to attach as much urgency to self-underwriting as to those handled by professional underwriters. In addition, rumors are rampant that a greater number of amendments are being required by the SEC on self-underwritings.

So much for the cons. We're still trying to come up with something for the pros.

Whether justified or not, the financial community has put a stigma on self-underwriting. The general reaction is, "This deal must not be good enough to attract an underwriter." Another concern of the financial community is that the efforts expended by the company to do a self-underwriting can become a large distraction to the management team's real business of running the company—not only in dealing with the SEC and with state rules and regulations but in working with broker-dealers and market makers to keep the issue in the public eye.

It's very difficult to operate any kind of company and also devote time to making individual sales of stock. Unless there is a bona fide reason, such as the management team's having the whole issue sold, it is advisable to consider leaving the selling of securities to the pros.

FREQUENTLY ASKED QUESTIONS

What type of companies make for good self-underwriting candidates?

The successful self-underwritings are those in which the management team has the ability to sell the deal to investors they know. Another good self-underwriting prospect is a company that has a large, devoted customer base. Companies have been known to advertise that they are doing an IPO by placing information right on the boxes containing their product; a customer contacts the company, which then furnishes the customer with a copy of the prospectus and a subscription agreement. These are now more commonly known as direct public offerings (DPOs).

What effect is the Internet having on self-underwritings?

The Internet may significantly change the whole aspect of self-underwritings. The initial rush is on and the regulatory bodies are indicating cooperation with adopting rules to facilitate Internet public underwritings. Please see Part Six of this book on Internet DPOs for more information.

FOUR

The Public Offering Process

23

The Registration Statement

The Securities Act of 1933 requires the registration of any form of securities sold to the general public (see Chapter 18). Anyone who purchases unregistered securities has the absolute, unequivocal right to rescind that purchase, which means getting the purchase money back in *full*. If the stock is sold at a loss, the purchaser can sue for damages and the amount of the loss. This assurance is effective for one year from the date of the original purchase.

To avoid breaching the securities laws, the entrepreneur *must* prepare and file a registration statement with the Securities and Exchange Commission disclosing all the information pertaining to the stock offering. In the following pages, we will attempt to bring to light the full process of assembling these documents, including the different types of forms that are used, the various regulations that affect the registration, and a detailed explanation of each part of the documents.

The registration statement is composed of two parts: The first part is the prospectus; the second part is the registration statement itself. The prospectus is printed in booklet form. The first printing is the preliminary prospectus, the red herring noted previously that contains certain caveats (warnings) printed in red ink to inform the reader that the prospectus is not in its final form. The purpose of the prospectus is to elicit interest from prospective investors in the underwriting and to solicit "indications of interest" from the selling syndicate. Participating broker-dealers commonly distribute the red herring to their retail customers and then report to the lead underwriter the amount of stock they feel they can sell based on the indications of interest. The final prospectus includes the offering date, the price of the stock, and other pertinent information. Copies of the final version are sent to all the people who received the red herring. They contain the effective date of the registration statement from the SEC.

The following are headings that require disclosures in Part I of the registration statement:

- Covers
- Summary
- The Company
- Use of Proceeds
- Dividend Policy
- Dilution
- Capitalization
- Select Financial Data
- Management's Discussion
- The Business
- Management and Certain Shareholders
- Legal Proceedings
- Description of the Securities
- Financial Statements

The following subjects are addressed in Part II of the registration statement:

- Expenses of distribution
- Indemnification of directors and officers
- Recent sales of unregistered securities
- Exhibits and financial statement schedules

The Regulations

Information concerning SEC regulations that require specific forms and formats must be included in the company's disclosures. Of particular concern in this regard are regulations S-K, S-X, and C. (The government seems to be continually changing the filing details, but accounting professionals and legal counsel can keep up to date through releases and bulletins that are available.)

Regulation S-K

The full name of this regulation is S-K Standard Instructions for Filing Forms under Securities Act of 1933, Securities Exchange Act of 1934, and

Energy Policy and Conservation Act of 1975. This regulation specifies the requirements for the nonfinancial portions of the registration statement. All areas of the S-K will be addressed later in this chapter.

Regulation S-X

The full title of this regulation is Form and Content of and Requirements for Financial Statements, Securities Act of 1933, Securities Exchange Act of 1934, Public Utility Holding Company Act of 1935, Investment Company Act of 1940, and Energy Policy and Conservation Act of 1975. This regulation specifies the financial statement requirements and denotes the form, content, and time periods for submissions. It is primarily the responsibility of the audit accountants to follow through on the requirements of the articles of this regulation listed below. It should be noted that not all articles are relevant to IPOs.

Article 1	Application of Regulation S-X
Article 2	Qualifications and Reports of Accountants
Article 3	General Instructions as to Financial Statements
Article 3A	Consolidated and Combined Financial Statements
Article 4	Rules of General Application
Article 5	Commercial and Industrial Companies
Article 6	Registered Investment Companies
Article 6A	Employee Stock Purchase, Savings, and Similar Plans
Article 7	Insurance Companies
No Article 8	
Article 9	Bank Holding Companies
Article 10	Interim Financial Statements
Article 11	Pro Forma Financial Information
Article 12	Form and Content of Schedules

The information requirements are lengthy and complex. More complete information can be found in a booklet available from the SEC titled *Small Business Informational Package.*

Regulation C

This regulation denotes the proper procedures to be followed in the actual preparation and filing of the registration statement itself. It deals with

the mechanics of paper size, number of copies, size of type, and other detailed filing requirements. Regulation C also addresses the following areas:

- Definition of terms
- Confidentiality of information
- Incorporation by reference
- Delayed and continuous offering and sale of securities
- Written consents
- Acceleration of effective date
- Amendments and withdrawals

Financial Reporting Releases (FRRs)

Financial reporting releases (FRRs) expand on the financial statement
disclosure requirements of Regulation S-X. They also report on current accounting practices and changes that have been instituted. FRRs have the
status of a regulation.

Staff Accounting Bulletins (SABs)

Staff Accounting Bulletins (SABs) are additional information sources
that are published; they include interpretations and practices that are currently being followed by the SEC staff. The information pertains to financial
statement disclosures.

Filing Process

The filing process begins with the submission of the registration statement to the SEC. The registration statement requirements are detailed in SEC
forms that are designated S-1 through S-18. Actually, some of the S-numbers
between 1 and 18 don't exist; that's simply the way the government numbered them. S-1 is the most complete form, but most IPOs use the simplified
forms, which are SB-1(for offerings under $10 million) and SB-2.

Filing Types and Descriptions

I will concentrate on the requirements mentioned in forms S-1, SB-1,
and SB-2. The other forms contain information requirements for specific
businesses (oil and gas, real estate companies, investment trusts, etc.) and spe-

cial situations. For example, forms S-2 and S-3 are commonly used for secondary offerings of a company that has already completed an initial public offering, is now an existing public company under the 1934 act, and has been fully reporting to the SEC for three or more years.

Form S-4 is used for a registration statement with the SEC for a company that is involved in a merger or acquisition.

Form S-6 is used for registering unit investment trusts.

Form S-8 is primarily directed to securities that are used for employee stock option plans or other employee benefit plans and trusts.

Form S-11 is the form used when registering securities for real estate companies and investment trusts.

Since 1933, Form S-1 has been the securities registration statement for all issuers. The SEC has also adopted several more simplified forms—SB-1 (offerings under $10 million) and SB-2 (unlimited amount)—that have now become the more frequently used forms. Neither SB-1 or SB-2 can be used by existing companies reporting under the 1934 act, investment companies, or insurance companies.

Advantages of SB-1 and SB-2 over S-1 are as follows: SB-1 requires a balance sheet only for the last fiscal year (SB-2 for two years), whereas S-1 requires one covering the last three years. SB-1 requires statements of income, changes in financial condition, and shareholders' equity positions to cover the last two years; SB-2 requires three years, and S-1 requires three years' coverage. SB-1 and SB-2 do not require that financials be prepared in compliance with the SEC's accounting rules of Reg S-X as required by S-1 but rather according to generally accepted accounting standards (GAAP). SB-1 and SB-2 do not require the company to produce five years of selected financial data, reports on management's discussions, analysis of individual manager's financial condition, or the support schedules and backup documents required by S-1. Finally, SB-1 and SB-2 do not require the company to produce as detailed a description of the business, its properties, and management remuneration and transactions as S-1 requires.

The Registration Statement Part I (the Prospectus)

Although no special sequence is required for the contents of the prospectus and registration statement, over time an order has evolved as described below.

Outside Front Cover

The current commonly accepted size format for a prospectus is 8½ by 11 inches. Some underwriters use the smaller format of 7½-by-9-inch size. The cover paper ranges from high gloss with two-color to four-color printing to conventional prospectus paper stock, which is almost tissue thin. The final decision in this area usually depends on the underwriter's preference and particular marketing format.

The cover page highlights key points about the underwriting. These include the following:

- Name of issuer (company)
- Company logo (optional)
- Title of offering
- Dollar amount of securities offered
- Number of securities offered
- A distribution table showing price to the public
- Underwriter's discount and commissions
- Proceeds to the issuer
- Net proceeds to selling shareholders
- Date of prospectus
- Name of underwriter (may also include logo)

Regularly required statements are normally printed in boldface roman 10-point type. The distribution table will include the maximum and minimum number of shares and also dollars offered in a mini/max offering. A preliminary prospectus will show statements that are subject to change printed in red ink (red herring).

The following statement, customarily set in 10-point caps, must also appear:

THESE SECURITIES HAVE NOT BEEN APPROVED OR DISAPPROVED BY THE SECURITIES AND EXCHANGE COMMISSION NOR HAS THE COMMISSION PASSED UPON THE ACCURACY OF THIS PROSPECTUS. ANY REPRESENTATION TO THE CONTRARY IS A CRIMINAL OFFENSE.

Inside Front and Outside Back Cover Pages

The outside back cover typically contains the table of contents, notices pertaining to information about price stabilization, and details about distributing the prospectus. The front and back inside covers are commonly used to display illustrations or photos of the company's products, the purpose being to improve the issue's marketing. There are, however, negatives to showing pictures or illustrations that should be considered. They result in increased costs for reproduction and printing, and, more important, there's a possibility of legal risk as the illustrations can imply more than the intent of the product. Today this is becoming less of a problem as the average prospectus reader's visual interpretations are more sophisticated. Nevertheless, attention still should be paid to what the illustrations depict and to the captions that accompany them.

Prospectus Summary

The first page usually contains a brief description of the company's business and products or services. It may include use of proceeds, risk factors, select financial data, and a description of the securities being offered. *Because this summary sheet is often what stock analysts and financial publications quote when describing the company and its offering, great care should be exercised to write a succinct and favorable summary.*

The Company

This section is intended to provide more detailed information about the company, including its name, address, phone numbers, and locations of branches or subsidiaries. The section will note historical information, such as when the company was incorporated, and, if appropriate, a brief history and brief description of its business, products, or services.

Risk Factors

The more speculative the company, the greater the number of risk factors. By laying its cards on the table and disclosing the potential risks for the investor, the company protects itself against nondisclosure accusations. Examples of risks could include dependence on a single supplier or a large customer (such as the U.S. government or a major department store chain); uncertainty in the size of the market; lack of experience on the part of the management team; lack of, or a deficit in, operations or earnings history; operating losses; and any number of other things that could possibly point to a potential risk. It is not unusual to find a list of 15 to 25 risk factors on a new IPO.

Use of Proceeds

A great deal of thought needs to be given to the drafting of this section because after the completion of the offering, the company must file continuing reports with the SEC explaining and substantiating that the money was spent as described (see Form SR).

This section essentially explains the purpose of the offering, and explicitly discloses what the money will be used for. Uses must be listed in their order of priority. Contingencies for any possible change in use must be explained. If, for example, the proceeds were to be used primarily to pay off an existing debt, the proposal would be easy to describe or explain to the SEC, underwriters, analysts, and prospective shareholders. However, if there are specific areas where the money is to be spent—which is usually the case—a detailed listing of each use and the amount to be spent must be noted and justified. Should the amount seem unjustified in the eyes of the SEC and investors, it is likely to raise eyebrows—and questions.

Dividend Policy

This section reports on the company's dividend record and plans for future dividends. Most often, new companies' plans call for holding on to future earnings in order to enhance growth, so the decision is not to pay dividends in the immediate future. If that's the case, the decision must be disclosed. This section also contains restrictions that may exist on dividend payments, such as existing restrictive loans or provisions covering preferred stock.

Dilution

This section discloses the difference between what the existing shareholders paid for their stock and the price the prospective new shareholders will have to pay. It is generally exhibited in chart or tabular form. Also disclosed in this section are the prices paid for the stock by the officers, directors, and major original inside shareholders. The purpose for presenting the figures graphically is to show

- the new intangible book value per share before and after the offering;
- the book value increase per share as a result of purchases from new shareholders; and
- the amount of immediate dilution per share to new purchasers.

Usuallly, the existing shareholders, especially the original founders, paid a significantly lower price for their stock, and there is often also a substantial dilution as far as new purchasers are concerned. Dilution ranging from 70 to 90 percent is not uncommon in small public company offerings.

Capitalization

This section, which is usually presented in a table format, sets forth the capital structure (showing both debt and equity) of the company's financial position prior to the offering and its pro forma structure after the offering.

Selected Financial Data

The section on selected financial data applies only to S-1; it is not applicable for SB-1 and SB-2 registrations. All S-1 registrations are required to supply financial data for the five years prior to registration. The data must cover net sales or operating revenue, income (or loss) from continuing operations, total assets, long-term debt, redeemable preferred stock, and cash dividends. In addition, if the fiscal annual financial statement is more than 135 days old on the date the registration becomes effective, an interim statement called an *unaudited stub report* must be included. The stub report must cover the additional quarters and should also compare the equivalent periods for the previous year of operation. All of these data are noted in gross amounts per share and adjusted to reflect the designated number of outstanding shares.

While stub periods are unaudited, the information should be presented with the same close scrutiny administered by audit accountants. Companies are usually allowed to include additional data that they feel will enhance the picture of their financial progress—so long as they don't go overboard in their assessment.

Management's Discussion and Analysis

This section also applies only to S-1 registrations. It is customarily written for or by the company's management team and covers information about, and an analysis of, the financial condition and the effectiveness of the company's operations. Its purpose is to promote investors' understanding of the company from a financial point of view. The report is required to cover the past three fiscal/annual years or go back five years if that can improve the company's financial picture. Any stub period should also be included. The report should cover specific information on the following points:

- The company's liquidity and capital resources, including both short-term and long-term commitments
- Expected sources of capital and plans for future capital needs or commitments, as well as pro forma cash flows
- Discussion about significant facts resulting in unusual or infrequent things or situations affecting prior years or anticipated in the future, such as capital gains from the sale of real estate, a patent, subsidiary, a onetime sale, or whatever else seems pertinent
- Discussion of anything that could possibly affect the future cash flow of the company's operations, such as a potential lawsuit, a product "going bad" and requiring recall, or machines breaking down

The Business

This section is included to give the potential investor information for evaluating the strengths and weaknesses of the company, its products or services, and its industry. The following are subjects that are applicable to most companies and require thoughtful explanations and responses:

- Historical development of the company (five years for S-1)
- An anticipated operating plan for the next year if the company has not had any operating revenue during the last three years
- Financial information along with comparisons for the industry
- A description of the company's primary product or service
- A description of the principal markets and methods of distribution being used and broken down, if possible, by the type of industry, geographical areas, and foreign markets
- A complete listing and description of any patents, trademarks, licenses, franchises, or concessions held by the company, including an evaluation of their importance and the effort taken to secure them
- A status report on any new products (publicly announced), product development, and industry areas being entered or contemplated
- A report on the sources and availability of raw materials from a sole source or multisource suppliers
- Disclosure of the seasonality of the business, if applicable

- Disclosure of working capital practices, such as the need to maintain a significant inventory to satisfy rapid delivery requirements, or procedures for allowing extensions of customer payments and terms
- Disclosure of the extent of reliance on one or a few major customers
- A listing of contract backlogs by dollar amount
- A statement on government contracts, if any, that are subject to renegotiation or termination
- An analysis of the competitive conditions in the company's industry
- The number of company employees
- The effects and costs associated with the company's compliance with environmental protection laws (if that is a consideration)

Properties

This section requires a disclosure of the location, and description, of the physical properties owned or leased by the company, including all major plants, mines, branch offices, and so forth.

Legal Proceedings

This section requires a description of any ongoing or pending legal actions involving the company as either plaintiff or defendant. It does not apply to routine litigation having to do with the company's ongoing business, such as routine collection matters.

Management

Because the management section is of paramount importance, it has been broken down into specific headings that follow.

Directors and executive officers. This part lists the name, age, and position of each director and officer of the company. Wherever relevant, their names are to be footnoted to point out their relationship to the company, such as founders or promoters. Also to be included are the terms of office for the directors and at which annual meeting their respective terms expire. An explanation of how the bylaws handle vacancies on the board also belongs under this heading.

Résumés. The full name of the person, executive position and/or directorship, and the date of involvement with the company must be declared. The person's prior employment for a minimum of five years, including dates, should be covered as should family interrelationships—spouse, parents, relatives through first cousins and by marriage—and any past negative encounters with governmental regulating bodies.

There is no special style or procedure that must be adhered to in the presentation of a résumé. Some prospectuses show resumes of only four or five lines; others are a full page or more.

Significant employees. This section is devoted to employees who are not officers or directors but whose expertise makes a significant contribution to the company and its operation. Formal résumés or disclosures about their backgrounds are not necessary.

Advisory board. As a general rule, résumés of advisory board members are not required, nor are there any formal disclosure requirements. Because they are selected on the basis of their special expertise, however, including their résumés could be a definite advantage and should be considered.

Consultants. Including consultants is not a mandatory requirement. It is strictly the entrepreneur's or the company's decision to include consultants involved with the company. If their names are impressive, they are often included. Advertising agencies and marketing, financial public relations, or public relations people or business consultants can lend a special prestige to the company because of their technical expertise.

Remuneration. This section discloses pertinent information about all the officers and directors of the company, such as the following:

- Compensation, including salaries, stock options, royalty agreements, direct fees, incentive fees, and incentive options
- Benefit compensation, such as auto allowances or autos furnished, insurance benefits or payments, housing, country club fees, major entertainment benefits, and other perks
- Loans to officers, directors, or their families
- Remuneration to principal shareholders (This part is often presented in chart form, listing the name, address, shares owned [direct, beneficially, and owner of record] by all officers and directors; also listed

are persons who hold 5 percent or more of the company's stock. This chart usually contains a heading that shows the percentages held by those listed before and after the offering.)

Special transactions. This section identifies special transactions with the management, officers, directors, and major shareholders (5 percent or more). If the company is less than five years old, it also includes promoters associated with the company. It will declare future transactions, such as golden parachutes (mentioned previously) covering compensatory arrangements with officers or directors that are contingent on their resignation or termination or as a result of a change in control of the company from leveraged buyouts, mergers, or acquisitions.

Description of Securities to be Registered

This section of the prospectus, also referred to as "Description of Capital Stock," describes the particular securities being offered. It spells out all the particulars on the total authorized capital stock in both common and preferred shares, including par or stated values, dividend rights, conversion or redemption provisions, voting rights, liquidation, and preemption rights. It explains the transferability of each class of stock and any restrictions that apply to the various classes of securities. It also discloses pertinent information on all outstanding warrants, options, and incentive stock option plans and describes the rights they carry in addition to revealing plans for the stock. Special voting requirements are also noted in this section, and information is usually provided about the company's transfer agent.

Underwriting

In some prospectuses, this section has been called the "Plan of Distribution." It contains information about the principal underwriter(s), the selling syndicate members, the underwriter's method (firm commitment or best efforts), and the number of shares subscribed to by each underwriter or selling group member. It describes the agreement between the company and the underwriter, the terms agreed upon—including commissions, warrants, commissions reallowed to syndicate members, and unaccountable expense allowances—as set forth by the NASD under its Rules of Fair Practice.

This section should also include the name of the escrow agent and a brief description of the terms of the escrow agreement. It will note which exchanges the company's stock will be listed or traded on. In addition, any material relationship between the company and the underwriters will be disclosed, such as the underwriter's right to arrange for a designee to the company's board of directors. It will also reaffirm the indemnification of the underwriter from any liability under the securities acts.

Legal Matters

This part identifies the company's legal counsel and its opinion as to the validity of the securities being offered. Mention should be made if legal counsel owns any of the company's stock. The counsel to the underwriter is typically also identified in this section.

Experts

This area recognizes any experts whose counsel and help have been sought in the preparation of the registration statement, generally the audit accountant. It includes an indemnification statement that refers to the audit report regarding the company's financial statements.

Additional Information

This section is just what the heading implies. It is only included if there is additional information that must be dealt with according to Part II of the registration statement or that has been called for by the SEC.

Financial Statements

This section discloses all the company's financial statements and includes a confirming report from the auditing accountants. There are differences between the requirements of an S-1 on one hand and SB-1 and SB-2 filings on the other. You are advised to consult with your accounting firm for the latest details. Generally speaking, S-1 requirements are tougher and extend for longer periods.

Remember, unaudited stub period reports are needed if the audited statements are over 134 days old. And they must be accompanied by a comparison with the preceding year's report.

The first page of this section should be the accountant's report or audit opinion. It generally runs two paragraphs in length. Sophisticated investors would simply glance at this page, but if it is longer than the expected two pages, they usually suspect that the company's financial health is not normal. If they are still interested, they will review the opinion to find out what the problem is. (See Chapter 9.)

The accountant's report is followed by the actual financial statements, which include the following:

- Balance sheet
- Income statement
- Changes in financial position
- Shareholders' equity
- Notes to the financial statements

Generally speaking, financial statements need to be consolidated (combined) within subsidiary or multiple operations. Subsidiaries can be excluded from consolidation only if the consolidation does not result in a meaningful disclosure.

According to the rules, separate financial statements are required for unconsolidated subsidiaries that represent more than 20 percent of the consolidated assets or accounts (company and subsidiary) or greater than 20 percent of the consolidated income. Further, if there is more than one unconsolidated subsidiary and the aggregate total of the assets *or* income exceeds 10 percent, then summary or separate financial statements must be included.

The rules are also specific regarding disclosure of businesses recently acquired or to be acquired. For example, Company A is going public and has agreed to buy Company B for $1 million with monies derived from the offering. However, that will leave the principals with two companies, each having its own financial statement. The rules state they must have only *one* financial statement even if the purchase is made after the offering has been completed. That requires the pro forma (projected) financial information to be recast to assume on paper that the transaction has taken place prior to the offering.

Pro forma financial information is generally required for significant business acquisitions and dispositions as well as for reorganizations, unusual asset exchanges, and debt restructurings.

Bear in mind, disclosure is required for any information considered material. Materiality can be determined by asking the question, "Would a reasonable investor consider it important in deciding whether to buy the security at the price offered?"

The Registration Statement Part II

Part II of the registration statement contains information that is not included in the prospectus. However, because it is filed with the SEC, it is available for public scrutiny. It is prepared in an item-and-answer format. The following subjects and information are typically included:

- Miscellaneous expenses of issuance and distribution
- Insurance documents or indemnification for the liability of officers and directors
- Listing of the sales of unregistered securities for the last three years (Mentioned earlier was that the sale of unregistered stock was illegal, but the specific type of transaction noted here is not necessarily illegal. It could concern money raised privately prior to any thought of pursuing an IPO; in such a case, the entrepreneur or company did not use Regulation 504 (mentioned earlier). Or it could concern a combination of Rule 504 that was ultimately ruled integration, and therefore disallowed, by the SEC. There could be serious consequences if it is discovered that the past issuance of stock violated the 1933 act, so the company is advised to make a rescission (abrogation) of the money by going back to the original investor and redoing the investment according to SEC rules.)
- Various subjects, including a list of all subsidiaries, the underwriting agreement, corporate charter (articles of incorporation), bylaws, financial statement schedules, and copies of material contracts

Misstatements

Everything in the registration statement must be true. There cannot be any omissions that could result in half-truths. The ultimate liability for misstatements lies with the issuer or, more directly, the officers and directors of the company.

If this truth standard is not met by the effective date of the offering, the security buyer has a right to sue the issuer up to the statute of limitations period of three years from the effective date. Please note: This holds true for all purchasers of the securities, including those purchased in the aftermarket, whether the buyer ever saw the prospectus or not. That's three years! Obviously, officers and directors are especially careful not to allow mistatements to occur.

Officers' and Directors' Questionnaire

All directors and officers of a public company are required by the SEC to provide what seems to be an overwhelming amount of personal data for possible inclusion in a registration statement, prospectus, or proxy statement, as noted in Chapter 7. This information is usually obtained by the company's counsel through a questionnaire. It is time consuming, extensive in its request for detailed factual data, and frequently requires an affidavit to confirm its veracity and correctness. The document has been known to be 20 to 30 pages in length, covering 30 to 50 specific bits of information. It covers the following points, not necessarily in this order:

- History of employment (past ten years with contact names for verification)
- Statements regarding any family relationships within the company
- Listing of offices or directorships in other companies (especially public companies)
- Complete education history with dates and degrees
- Listing of all business and professional memberships, past and present
- Listing of all lawyers or accountants engaged in the past five years
- Extensive inquiry into all litigation or regulatory actions in the past ten years
- Listing of all associations with security offerings during the past ten years
- Listing of present and past fiduciary relationships
- Complete disclosure of compensation by the company, including salaries, options, incentives, royalties, insurance, and any special benefits accrued or contemplated
- Complete disclosure of the company's securities owned, including those controlled directly and those controlled by a beneficiary, plus disclaimers
- Disclosure of all past and contemplated transactions with the company

Overview of the Process

The process of preparing a prospectus and registration statement for a proposed public offering often requires the skill of a magician and an adeptness at walking a tightrope. The prospectus is the selling tool used by the company, the underwriter, and individual brokers to influence investors. The underwriter expects the company to come up with a clean, beautiful, salable picture of the offering and still disclose all the material facts without hype, without the hindrance of negatives, but complying with the SEC's strict rules and regulations.

The burden for carrying this off usually falls on the shoulders of the company's lawyers. They carry the principal responsibility for the assembly and preparation of all the nonfinancial parts of the registration statement. They have to make them look good—and be legal. It requires complete co-operation and coordination between the company, underwriters, accountants, printers, public relations specialists, advertising firms, and, on occasion, postal and delivery services. The lawyers tread a thin line in covering all points of possible contention to provide the company with a registration statement that becomes an insurance policy against potential shareholders' lawsuits. This is not to imply that legal counsel would, or is expected to, do anything that is not aboveboard. It's just that at times they must use all the intricate legal language at their disposal to make the company look good.

In effect, the lawyers assist the company and its management in preparing the registration statement and in performing due diligence. Legal counsel, as the principal drafters, solicit information in both oral presentations and written form, and exercise judgment as to the accuracy and consistency of the information supplied.

In the final analysis, however, legal counsel only volunteer an opinion that the securities being offered are legally issued, fully paid, and nonassessable. The company and its management must assume the final responsibility. Management must make sure that the information presented is accurate, complete, and verified and that the registration statement is prepared properly. It's a dirty job, but somebody's got to take the responsibility.

FREQUENTLY ASKED QUESTIONS

Can the management team prepare most of the registration statement?

Possibly, but not probably. What usually occurs is that the attorneys take the business plan prepared by the management team and redo a considerable portion for many parts of the registration statement. There are a lot of parts, the risk factors being one example, which almost have to be prepared by legal counsel because of the legalese of the wording.

Is the officers' and directors' questionnaire reproduced in the registration statement?

No. However, legal counsel will use this document to prepare the bios used in the registration statement. They take particular note of the actual dates and references supplied. The questionnaire is kept on file in the event either the underwriter or the regulatory bodies request it—all part of the due diligence process.

What is the true purpose of the registration statement?

Twofold. First, it is a disclosure document meant to furnish both the good and bad about the company. Second, it is a selling document meant to furnish concise information about the company and its business, management, and finances.

What is management's primary responsibility regarding the registration statement?

Management can't take a passive role in the preparation of the company's registration statement. To do the job right, management must become involved throughout the preparation process. Remember, the officers and directors will be signing the final documents, which confirms they agree with and understand all that it contains.

24

Filing and Review

The process and procedures for a filing often require prefiling conferences. These are simply meetings with the SEC staff to discuss the proposed offering and to make certain that the relevant forms and regulations are complied with and that adequate disclosures are made.

The SEC reviewers do not pass judgment on or evaluate the quality of a proposed public company or offering. They do try to keep the offering on the right track, offer information on how to handle any technicalities that may crop up, and, most important, do their best to prevent the defrauding of public investors.

All of these topics are examined in the following pages as are the actual filing, preliminary prospectuses, filing stickers, filings with other regulatory offices, and the different types of reviews and amendments. And, finally, SEC comment letters—letters from the SEC on how to properly complete the prospectus and registration statement—are discussed.

A reminder to the reader: this book attempts to cover a lot of ground and present an overall perspective on the going-public process. Because the process is very complicated, you are well advised to seek advice from your attorney in the filing process.

Prefiling Conferences

Some companies, especially those with newly developed or highly technical products, would be well advised to schedule a prefiling conference with the staff at their regional branch of the SEC. It is there to help—not hinder. The SEC staff is adept at pinpointing problem areas that may arise during the process of assembling information for the registration statement. For example, a company may want to know how it can justify setting aside 25 percent of the offering for research and development; how to handle a legal or accounting problem in a filing, such as a partnership litigation; or how to deal with a questionable regulation compliance.

Any question about the prospectus or registration statement is open for discussion. Many questions about the filing can be handled at the regional level over the phone. If the matter is more complicated, the SEC staff may wish to arrange a meeting in its regional offices with the appropriate specialty advisers from its staff to assist the company in determining appropriate actions or disclosures. More difficult questions could even be referred to the SEC head office in Washington. If a response is urgent, a phone call instead of a letter is not out of order. If a phone call determines that a prefiling conference is necessary, it's usually the responsibility of the company's legal counsel to verify the appointment by letter, stating all the facts.

The company's legal counsel as well as the company's management team should come fully prepared with their bagful of questions for SEC staff conferences. If the questions are specialized, the appropriate company expert, such as the accountant or production chief, should also be present. Generally, the SEC replies in writing. But bear in mind, the SEC does not suggest language nor put into words any of the specifics of a registration statement. The primary reason for prefiling calls or conferences is to assist in clarifying details that could affect a registration and to avoid costly delays once a registration has been submitted.

The SEC, by the way, will accept limited questions without the company's name being discussed or revealed during the inquiry. A lawyer could tell the SEC that his or her client is contemplating a takeover of General Motors and wants to know what the SEC's response would be to something like that; the client's name need not be mentioned. A term that describes such a situation is questioning on a "no-name" basis.

Filing Technicalities

After a thorough review by all the involved parties, the completed registration statement must be signed by those who are a party to it. That could include the principal executive officers, the principal financial officer, and members of the board of directors. Each signature must be accompanied by the name typed or printed beneath it. If the person signing holds more than one executive position, the position being signed for must be indicated. To avoid any inconvenient delays, it is possible to use a power of attorney for absent signers. The powers of attorney must be attached as exhibits along with a certified copy of a resolution by the board of directors authorizing such signatures.

The experts (attorneys, accountants, etc.) involved in preparing the registration statement must attest to the validity of the statement and furnish consents for the use of their names on the statement. The consents, which also must be hand-signed, are filed with the registration statement. Three copies of the complete registration statement must be filed and one copy must be hand-signed (original signatures, not copies). In addition, ten copies must be available for public inspection.

Unless all documents are complete, the SEC will not review the filing. Therefore, it is necessary to attach a cover letter stating that all filings under the statute have been filed and the submission is complete. The registrant is required to pay the SEC filing fee at the time of filing.

Initial Filing

When a registration statement is received by the SEC, it is assigned to an examiner, who is backed up by an attorney, an accountant, an analyst, and, when necessary, an expert in the company's particular field. The SEC, for example, maintains oil, gas, and mining experts on staff who review all filings in their respective domains. The examiners, in turn, are overseen by a chief examiner.

Examiners are responsible for reviewing the statement. They check for any inconsistencies and make sure that the statement complies with all the SEC's requirements. But the SEC seldom makes an independent investigation on the specifics of a particular type of business, although they have the right to. If the company will be doing business with branches of the government, however, especially the military, everything referring to those declarations will be thoroughly checked out.

If the company is involved in a new industry or one that is highly technical or complicated, the SEC will usually perform an extended review of the registration statement to give its staff an opportunity to familiarize itself with the product. Generally speaking, the easier a document is to read and comprehend, the less the scrutiny.

Timing

By statute a registration automatically becomes effective 20 days after it is filed, but with the ever-present backlog of filings, the rules have a clause in which the 20-day automatic effectiveness provision is voluntarily suspended. For the most part, a registrant can expect to receive an initial comment letter from the SEC four to six weeks after its initial submission.

Comment/Deficiency Letter

The SEC reviews the registration statement that has been filed and then sends out a deficiency letter, better known as a letter of comment. The comment letter represents the staff's views about what steps should be taken to make the prospectus complete and accurate.

It should be understood that "complete and accurate" is a subjective opinion by the SEC staff. Unfortunately, a proposed IPO has to be very careful in its review of the SEC's comments and should temper its initial reaction. Justified or not, it's hard to find a filing that does not receive at least one comment letter. The comment on one submission requested that the company review the use and spelling of *principal* versus *principle*. The SEC request, in this situation, was justified. The company corrected the spelling as well as several other small items, and the offering was successfully undertaken with no more comments from either side.

One frequent subject of comment letters is accounting. The SEC habitually requests additional information or requires further accounting footnotes to clarify such matters as policies and practices, related-party transactions, unusual compensation agreements (with both management and outside consultants), methods of off-balance-sheet financing, relationships between divisions or subsidiaries, and other components of the financial statements. Accounting comments are routinely clarified, as the rules and regulations for SEC accounting are fairly well defined.

Other areas for comments regarding the registration statement may not be as clearly defined. The staff's suggestions or notes to problems can be limited to such items as failure to comply with instructions on the registration form or a request to stress a risk factor more fully.

If the company believes that the commission staff's suggestions are inappropriate or that the criticisms are not well founded, the better part of valor is to "cool it." It's best to simply comply with the request if the problem is minor. This will save a lot of valuable underwriting time in spite of a small loss of ego.

If staff objections are major, on the other hand, or you don't understand them, an attempt should be made to discuss them with the SEC staff. It's possible that the staff missed a point or asked for some information the company considers privileged and does not want to disclose. Many times the problem can best be handled by complying. If the company does not wish to comply, it can request informal conferences. You will always find the SEC staff to be most generous with its time. Remember, the SEC's livelihood does not depend on getting the issue completed. But management will have the opportunity to convince it. If members of the SEC staff decide to be obstinate, the company can argue the point until the IPO window closes. In other words, the SEC has the ability to delay an offering for as long as it likes. If it is obvious that the company is acting in good faith, it will get full cooperation from the SEC. It may take some modification and compliance on the company's part, but it should eventually succeed in having the registration become effective.

Commission staff members can be unyielding when something does not smell right to them. They have a way of delaying the offering by issuing additional comment letters, often for obscure reasons, with the end result of delaying the offering. Eventually someone has to give, and it usually is the company by modifying or withdrawing the offering. Those are the choices.

Common Comments

Noted below are the most frequent comment letter questions and observations from SEC staff:

- What is the current status of the company, its business, and its products or services?
- Are all known problems of a new product disclosed regarding development, production, marketing, and customer satisfaction?
- Is management's background and experience misstated or not fully disclosed, and were there any prior business failures?
- Are there any company-related transactions that are not fully disclosed?
- Note additional detailed financial statement disclosures, primarily by footnotes or added risk factors.
- The management's discussion and analysis is insufficient, primarily in its description of the business.

Types of Review

The following are four basic types of review by the SEC. All are aimed at determining the adequacies of the disclosure, and all are usually followed through with a letter and phone calls. The staff's job is to find deficiencies. It almost always does although not with any malicious intent.

Deferred review. In the event that an initial review by the staff shows that a registration is so poorly put together that it is not even worth the time to comment on it, the SEC will write what is called a "bedbug letter" advising the registrant to withdraw the registration statement under threat of a stop order.

Cursory review. Cursory review is not often used. The comment letter will indicate that the staff has performed a cursory review and has not found any glowing deficiencies and that no written or oral comments will be forthcoming. It usually requests that all persons connected with the underwriting—company counsel, accountants, and underwriters—write letters to the SEC indicating that they are aware of the statutory responsibilities under the 1933 act.

Summary review. Almost identical to the cursory review, summary review also is not often used. The staff simply furnishes a few comments based upon a limited review.

Customary review. This preferred review includes a full review by the branch examiner with input by the accountants, attorneys, analysts, and all needed experts and a detailed comment letter signed by the branch chief.

Amendments

A company's replies to the SEC's comment letters are called amendments (to the registration statement). Several different types are used as described below.

Delaying amendment. This amendment is designed to delay the 20-day effective date of a registration. If a company has received a comment letter, the registration technically becomes effective 20 days later. If the company has not had enough time to reply or to make up the deficiencies listed in the comment letter, it replies to the SEC with a delaying amendment requesting a new effective date. Failure to do so can result in a defective registration and/or the possibility that the SEC may feel compelled to issue a stop order against the company. Such action can result in civil liabilities against the company and its principals as well as the underwriter. As a rule, each time the company replies to the SEC with further amendments, in whole or in part, its action automatically restarts the 20-day period.

Substantive amendment. This amendment is commonly filed to correct the deficiencies in a registration statement. Usually it is in reply to the SEC's comment letter. But it can also be instigated by the company to update events in the company that took place after the original filing. The registration statement must be correct and current when it becomes effective. If a company allows a registration to lapse without its becoming effective or by not filing any amendments, the SEC will allow a time period of nine months to expire before giving the company 30 days' notice and declaring the registration abandoned.

Price amendment. This amendment is commonly used on larger registrations where the actual offering price and the total amount of stock to be offered are not determined until the day of the offering or the day before the offering. The purpose of the amendment is to insert this last-minute information. The SEC will then declare the offering effective immediately and is usually done by phone followed by a confirming telegram.

Filing the Substantive Amendment

The substantive amendment can be employed for all amendments filed after the initial comment letter. It is not unusual to follow the comment letter with as many as three or four substantive amendments. Each must comply with certain formal requirements, and each must be filed with a facing cover sheet. Substantive amendments must also be consecutively numbered in the order in which they are filed.

On first registration, the SEC will issue a filing number that has to be used on all further correspondence and filings. Each amendment must be filed in triplicate with one copy hand-signed, and eight additional copies must be filed to be made available to the public. If any of the amendments contain revised financial statements, a new hand-signed certificate is also required from the accountants.

Each amendment's cover letter must clearly indicate the SEC's reference number and the particular SEC comment number from the respective comment letters. The company's comments have to reflect the action taken by the company regarding each SEC comment—for example, the withdrawal of a section, a word change, the changing of parts (any part or word), or the addition of new parts or language should be noted in the cover letter.

As a registration proceeds through the SEC bureaucracy, it is not uncommon that at each review step someone at a higher level on the SEC staff reviews the statement. This can become disconcerting for those in the company involved in the process. New comments or questions often come from the final reviewers, and a final reviewer will very often reverse a subordinate on a point that had been thought resolved.

Because certain comments include requests for additional information, the SEC staff may have further comments on receipt of this additional information. Therefore, an appropriate period of time should be allowed for staff review of the amendment before any requested date of effectiveness.

The registrant company had better take care not to do what it would normally do with a response of this type, which would be to go over the head of the assigned reviewer. Diplomacy is the best policy. If a significant issue is involved, counsel should respectfully request a further review at the next higher level. The better part of valor is to allow the SEC staff to have the final word on whether the company has adequately responded to its comments. Also remember that the goal is to obtain the registration's effectiveness, not to prove who has the better legal mind.

Finally, because of the large number of filings and the constant heavy workload of SEC staff members, the company should photocopy all amendments and all correspondence to staff members involved in the filings as a protection.

Preliminary Prospectus (Red Herring)

As mentioned earlier, the preliminary prospectus comes by its nickname *red herring* because portions that are subject to change are printed in red ink. A preliminary prospectus is distributed by the company, its underwriters, and the selling syndicate members to prospective investors to assess investor interest. As a means of informing the reader that it is not the final prospectus, the following statement is printed in red ink on the cover:

> A registration statement relating to these securities has been filed with the Securities and Exchange Commission but has not become effective. Information contained herein is subject to completion or amendment. These securities may not be sold nor may offers to buy be accepted

prior to the time the registration statement becomes effective. This prospectus shall not constitute an offer to sell or the solicitation of an offer to buy nor shall there be any sale of these securities in any State in which such offer, solicitation, or sale would be unlawful prior to registration or qualification under the securities laws of any such State.

On larger offerings, the red herring is distributed at the time the initial registration statement is filed. For smaller offerings it may be wise to hold off on the printing and distribution of this document until after the initial comment letter has been received from the SEC and reviewed and the first amendment filed. The main reason is the expense involved in a required new printing when changes must be made. According to the SEC, each person considering purchase of the company's stock is supposed to receive a copy of the final prospectus and should also receive copies of amendments as they are filed. It's pretty obvious that this can involve a tremendous amount of time and money so that it is better not to distribute the red herring until the initial comment letter is replied to and the company has a sense of the extent of the SEC's comments and how many more changes may be needed.

Current red herring printing costs and expenses for distribution can easily come to $3 each ($2 for printing and $1 for mailing). Consequently, it is desirable to distribute a red herring and a final prospectus to prospective investors just once. Unfortunately, this intention often falls by the wayside along with the best-laid plans.

The registrant should also make a point of keeping track of the name of each person who receives information on a new issue, including the red herring. Although the primary responsibility for this lies with the underwriter and, by extension, the members of the selling syndicate, it's good to have a record of where the interest lies.

Stop Order

Mentioned earlier in this chapter under the heading "Deferred Review" is the SEC's ultimate hammer called a *stop order*—an order from the commission suspending the effectiveness of a registration statement. Once the order is issued, it is unlawful to mail or commence to offer, sell, or deliver a prospectus or securities connected with the offering. The effect of a stop order is to warn the public that the SEC has found the registration untrue, misleading, unreliable, or lacking material facts. The stop order can be issued only after a notice has been sent to the registrant granting a 14-day period to request a hearing. If the company corrects the deficiencies, a declaration will be issued by the SEC and the stop order will cease to be effective.

Obviously, a company wants to prevent this action from ever taking place. A stop order has an ugly way of tainting an offering and making the chances of its ever being sold very slim. After all this, you should know a stop order is rarely, if ever, employed.

Stickers

Section 10 of the 1933 act states that a prospectus must contain all the pertinent information about the previous history of the company up to the effective date of the registration. It also requires that information about the company be noted in the prospectus after the effective date of the registration (when the prospectus is already in the hands of the investor), and it must be kept current. It is possible to do this without having to do a posteffective amendment by adding a prospectus supplement known as a *sticker.* The information is printed on a sheet of paper, glued to the cover page of the prospectus, and referred to as "stickering" a prospectus.

Stickering is usually done for a period of 90 days after the effective date of registration. But in reality it goes on for longer than 90 days. Stickering is often done until the offering is sold out and continued until it is very clear that a posteffective amendment is not called for.

Stickers (prospectus supplements) do not require SEC review. They are used to add such information as the company's receiving a sizable contract (especially if the contract was noted as pending in the prospectus) or to inform investors of the hiring of a key officer or director that was noted as a possibility in the prospectus.

The cost and follow-up of using stickers can be expensive. Not only must the underwriter and members of the selling syndicate be supplied with stickers to be attached to the prospectuses, but stickers must also be sent to individual prospectus recipients. Therefore, it may be advisable for the company to delay the announcement of any important information until the *quiet period* is over. The quiet period is the 90 days after the effective date of registration, during which the company cannot make any additional comments beyond those referred to in the registration statement. The reason is that the new information could be considered a hype, which is not looked upon favorably by the SEC. New information, for example, might refer to the signing of a contract or the completion of an acquisition or merger, which could push up the stock's selling price.

Acceleration Letter

An acceleration letter is a request to waive the normal 20-day waiting period before an offering's being declared effective by the SEC. It is a letter from the company's legal counsel to the SEC to the effect that the company has completed its amendment filings and has complied with all the points in the SEC's comment letter.

The request to accelerate the effective date is very common and is filed simultaneously with the pricing amendment, which discloses the offering price of the security, the total number of securities to be offered, the underwriter's commission, and the net proceeds to the company. This final, pricing amendment, along with the acceleration letter, is important because it requests that the stock be placed *now* with the investment public. The reason is that most larger offerings are firm commitment underwritings. The underwriter has its money at risk and doesn't want to risk a change in market conditions, which may seem right at the moment. The SEC knows the importance of timing and makes every effort to oblige.

State Filings (Blue-Sky Laws)

The 1933 and 1934 securities acts and the Securities and Exchange Commission regulate the issuance of securities. But each state also has its own securities laws and the final authority over which securities can be sold in its jurisdiction. These state securities laws are referred to as blue-sky laws, as discussed earlier.

It is usually the responsibility of the managing underwriter, after determining in which states it will offer the securities, to ensure that the company files with those states at the time the initial filing with the SEC takes place. Many states will not allow a security to be sold or permit the distribution of a preliminary prospectus until the state filing is done. The blue-sky laws also require the registration of broker-dealers and investment companies doing business in the state. These laws were first drawn up to protect "gullible" investors from "unscrupulous" promoters trying to sell them the "blue sky"—how the law got its name.

Background

In 1911 Kansas was the first state to adopt the first omnibus securities law. By 1929 about half the states adopted similar laws, but each state had its own variations, which caused nationwide registration problems. Because of that, in 1929 a Uniform State Securities Act was approved by the Conference of Commissioners on Uniform State Laws and the American Bar Association. In 1948 the Investment Bankers Association began working on versions of blue-sky laws modeled after the federal law. Finally, in 1956 a new Uniform State Securities Act was approved by many of the states.

Since 1956 there has been a continuing effort to adopt a nationwide standard that would be tied into the federal law. Most of the states have adopted the Uniform State Securities Act, but some states are still doing it their own way. Of interest is that Delaware and the District of Columbia are the only jurisdictions that do not yet have a local securities law. Some states have extremely tough blue-sky laws, whereas others are content to rely on an effective federal SEC registration statement. Each state also conducts its own style of review as there is no set pattern for state review.

Types of State Review

Merit review. Some of the "tough" states employ merit review, which means that if the state's securities commission or review board doesn't like the offering on its merits, it can deny it. Period! No questions asked! No appeal! Merit review states have an approval statute as opposed to the federal SEC disclosure rules.

Most of the states with merit review want satisfactory answers to questions such as the following:

- What percentage of the company is offered to the public?
- Are the promoters reaping all the benefits while the new investors are putting up all the money?
- Is the company an operating company with a product or service?
- Are the underwriter's fees—that is, commissions, warrants, unaccountable expenses—too high?
- Is there a holding period for insiders' stock (similar to Rule 144)?
- Have there been any criminal convictions of officers, directors, or insiders?

If the answers they receive are satisfactory, the state's commissions can be quite reasonable.

Qualification review. The statutes providing qualification review are basically the same as those providing merit review. The securities must qualify according to the state's standards or the registration can be denied or suspended. No sales can take place until the securities are approved.

Coordination review. This review is a form of qualification, but most of the states that use it simply have a rule that no sales are allowed until the issue is declared effective by the SEC.

Notification review. This procedure requires the filing of a Notice of Intention to sell. After the filing is reviewed, sales of the stock can take place immediately unless the administrator/reviewer takes action to hold up the offering. In this type of review, the underwriter must be careful not to assume that approval is automatic.

Violations

Violation of state statutes in the sale of securities can result in civil liability, and in some states criminal action is taken. All states have provisions prohibiting fraud that include penalties. These provisions enable the state agency to investigate principals, give public notice and warning, and obtain injunctions, often coupled with the power to subpoena and to examine witnesses as well as business records. Violations, at minimum, will cause sales to be rescinded and may also call for investor restitution.

Filing

Filing of the actual registration statement is up to the company's counsel or underwriter's counsel. The state's filing fees are usually paid by the company. The filing should be coordinated with the underwriters as they are the ones who decide in which states to file. Their decision is usually predicated on which states their brokers are registered in, the location of their client-investors, and the preference of the members of the selling syndicate. Some states require that the company retain local legal counsel to handle the filing, especially if there are proceedings before the state's securities commission.

Blue-Sky List

The company's securities counsel should furnish a preliminary blue-sky memorandum for distribution to various brokers that includes a list of the intended blue-sky states. It should also make note of any restrictions or other limitations, such as the number of securities that can be sold in a particular state. When all the blue-sky paperwork is completed and the offering is effective with the SEC, a final memorandum must be submitted.

Blue-skying can be a complicated process that requires a lot of coordination between the company, the underwriter, and state authorities to meet all the deadlines and keep the timing in place for an effective offering.

The good news is that after a stock is publicly traded, most states automatically allow it to be traded in their jurisdiction, especially if the company is listed in Moody's or Standard & Poor's. Stocks that are traded in the Nasdaq market are also looked upon with favor by most states.

NASD Review

The National Association of Securities Dealers (NASD) must also put its stamp of approval on the offering. It is mainly concerned with Regulation S-K, which deals with the contents of the registration statement, and the underwriter's compensation. It reviews the selling commission of the underwriter, the reselling commission (or pass-through) to the selling syndicate members, and other items that come under the umbrella of the underwriter's compensation. These include such items as the amount and uses of the accountable and nonaccountable expenses and the number, type, cost, and exercise price of warrants or options granted to the underwriter. The NASD also reviews finders' fees and the possible association of any of the people involved in the underwriting with a NASD member.

For what they may be worth, the following are some typical concerns that have been culled from various NASD comments following its opening statement, "On the basis of our review, we have decided to defer an opinion with respect to the fairness and reasonableness of the proposed terms and arrangements until we have received and reviewed the following":

- The NASD association, affiliation, or relation of all officers, directors, and principal shareholders (5 percent or greater) of the registrant
- The acquisition of the registrant's unregistered securities by any NASD-affiliated person, including the security holder's name, date of acquisition, amount acquired, consideration rendered, and whether such NASD affiliate will participate in any capacity in the offering
- Whether the issuer intends to register as a broker-dealer or otherwise become a member of the NASD
- Confirmation that the proceeds of the offering will not be commingled with the proceeds of any other public distribution

To reiterate, NASD's concern is to determine whether the underwriter arrangements are fair and reasonable for protecting the public investor. The interesting part of this process is that the NASD does not have published rules as to what it considers fair and reasonable. It has issued some guidelines, but the NASD has caused considerable delay in proposed underwritings in numerous cases while everyone concerned tried to figure out what it considers fair and reasonable.

Therefore, it behooves the underwriter's counsel to apply for a NASD review as soon as possible after the registration statement is filed with the SEC. The review may require a renegotiation of the underwriter's agreement.

FREQUENTLY ASKED QUESTIONS

How long does the filing process take?

Typically, 45 to 60 days. However, it can be much longer with complicated filings that involve many comment letters.

How much does the company get involved in the filing process?

Not a lot. Filing is completed by legal counsel and it's really a major paper-shuffling process. If some of the comments get technical, the company may get further involved with educating legal counsel on some fine points to be incorporated into the replies.

What if some of the filing "hoops" are missed?

The offering gets delayed. Obviously, this means more dollar expenditures and the chance that the market window could close and the whole offering abandoned.

It sounds like there is some mystery about SEC comments; is that correct?

That's correct. And it's also why it is so important to retain legal counsel that is experienced with SEC filings. Experience has proven that attorneys who know individual SEC examiners have an easier time relating to the comment process and keeping it on a timely track.

25

Selling the Issue

The difference between selling large and small IPOs is the way the selling is handled. The dealings also depend on whether the issue is a firm commitment or a best efforts offering. As always, timing plays a critical role. On larger offerings (almost always firm commitments), for example, in which the underwriter has guaranteed the entire offering, the selling is usually done behind the scenes before the effective date—that is, commitments have already been solicited on the issue before it comes out. It's a foregone conclusion that the underwriter has put out feelers about the issue and is reasonably certain it will be sold out. On best efforts offerings, the underwriters don't have to put their money where their mouth is. They make no guarantees, but the underwriters and their selling syndicates will be pushing the issue before and after the effective date. Remember, they don't make money on it unless they sell it.

While the underwriters are doing their thing, management will be doing its thing, which is complying with SEC regulations. These include the preparation of presentation materials and the presentation itself, completing the required materials (red herrings and final prospectuses), and, of critical importance, scheduling its efforts. Management must be keenly aware of SEC requirements (restrictions) that directly affect the selling process.

Management must also work within the framework of the quiet period we mentioned briefly in a previous chapter. Loosely defined, the quiet period is that time from the moment the company's management entertains its first thoughts of going public until 90 days after the effective date of the registration statement. During those 90 days, according to the SEC, the company can only discuss or distribute information about itself and its activities that is disclosed in the prospectus.

A great difference of opinion in both legal and financial public relations circles exists over what is legal and appropriate to communicate and to whom during this preregistration and registration period called the quiet period.

Despite SEC efforts to clarify the rules, the question remains a gray area in which legal counsel is usually consulted. The rules governing various segments of the registration process can be as confusing to the well informed as to those studying them for the first time. I'll try to shed some light on the subject.

As for preregistration, it's always difficult to know exactly when a company has entered its quiet period. Generally, it is some time before the company submits materials to the SEC. One common rule of thumb is to assume that the SEC's registration publicity limitation begins about 60 days before any anticipated SEC filing date. This entire 60-day period prior to actual filing with the SEC is considered the preregistration period. The filing date is the date on which the company submits a registration statement to the SEC.

Barred Publicity during Registration

The registration period is generally assumed to extend from the date a tentative agreement or letter of intent regarding an offering has been reached with an underwriter until the conclusion of the postoffering period. It definitely includes the period from entering registration until the effective date and 90 days after. The effective date is the date on which the registration statement becomes effective on SEC approval and shares are available for the first time for public sale. In most cases the effective date will be the date on which the final documents in connection with the registration procedure have been filed. SEC rules limiting publicity usually apply throughout this period.

During the registration period, any release, speech, or publication not normally produced by the corporation should be carefully scrutinized by public relations and legal counsel for possible violations of the rules. In case of doubt, the SEC recommends that companies and their legal counsel consult with the staff of the SEC, usually at the regional level.

Under the 1933 act, it is unlawful to offer to sell a security during the registration period. Therefore, any type of extraordinary corporate publicity during registration may well be judged by the SEC as a selling effort on behalf of the security. In the eyes of the SEC, this holds true for any form of publicity that might tend to project an optimistic future for the issuing corporation in the minds of the investing public. The rules specifically state that after the filing date and before the effective date of the registration statement, no written communication offering to sell a security may be made except for the preliminary prospectus (red herring).

To further emphasize its concern about publicity for a selling effort, the SEC has said, "The release of publicity and the publication of information between the filing date and the effective date of the registration statement may . . . raise a question whether the publicity is not in fact a selling effort by an illegal means (other than the prospectus)." The SEC is also concerned that similar problems will arise "from publicity and the release of information after the effective date, but before a distribution is completed (before the stock is trading)."

Allowed Publicity during Registration

The SEC does encourage normal corporate publicity during registration. In a policy statement, the SEC made clear that during registration companies may do the following:

- They may continue to advertise products and services; materials such as sales promotion leaflets, displays, and general product or service publications may also be issued.
- Companies may continue to send out their customary quarterly, annual, and other periodic reports to stockholders. News releases disclosing financial results for these periods may also be issued, but must not include short-term or long-term growth estimates (other than a properly prepared forecast that conforms to current SEC forecasting guidelines).
- Companies may continue to make announcements to the press about factual business and financial developments, such as receipt of a contract, the settlement of a strike, the opening of a plant, or similar events of interest to the community in which the business operates. News releases about personnel appointments and new products or research developments also fall within this category, but such announcements must contain no estimates of how the new developments will affect earnings or sales, either in broad or specific terms, unless they conform with specific SEC forecasting guidelines that are outlined in the rules and regulations.
- Companies may answer unsolicited telephone inquiries from shareholders, financial analysts, the press, and other sources about financial and business operations published in the registration statement.

- Companies may respond to unsolicited inquiries about factual matters from securities analysts, securities holders, and participants in the communications field who have a legitimate interest in a particular corporation's affairs.
- Companies may continue to hold shareholders' meetings as scheduled and to answer shareholders' inquiries at these meetings relating to factual matters. Activities that are also allowed include speeches before trade and professional groups that were scheduled before the decision to register providing they don't contain projections other than those mentioned in the registration statement.

The SEC wants to make it clear that in spite of the allowed activities noted above, the prohibition against publicity, which might serve as a selling effort for a security in registration, still applies to corporate disclosure during registration. Disclosure of factual information in response to inquiries or resulting from a duty to make prompt disclosure under the antifraud provisions of the securities acts or the timely disclosure policies of self-regulatory organizations when a registered offering of securities is contemplated or in process can and should be effected in a manner that will not unduly influence the proposed offering. Regarding publicity during registration, the SEC stresses: "Neither a company in registration nor its representatives should instigate publicity for the purpose of facilitating the sale of securities in a proposed offering."

The best guideline in the delicate area of publicity during registration is to refrain entirely from publishing any material during the preeffective (quiet) period that is not a part of the registration statement. That includes any release, speech, or publication not normally produced by the company. Again, the SEC recommends consultation by companies and their PR and legal counsel with SEC staff in case of doubt or possible violation.

Brokers' Due Diligence Meetings

When first conceived, due diligence meetings (now commonly referred to as "road shows") were held within a few days of a company's stock effectiveness or trading date. The purpose was to assure all participating parties in an underwriting that the issue was about to be launched. These meetings were originally held at the company; invited participants were the management and directors of the company, the company's legal counsel, the audit accountants, the underwriter, key syndicate members and their respective legal counsel, the escrow agent, and representatives from the transfer agent.

Part of the road show ritual included the reading, word by word, sentence by sentence, and page by page, of the entire prospectus. The idea was to make sure that nothing was printed incorrectly and that there were no last-minute changes, especially financial, in addition to acquainting the selling parties with the details of the company and its offering.

Eventually, these boardroom rituals became shows and moved to grand ballrooms of hotels. The meetings were complete with dancing girls, theatrical spotlights, hors d'oeuvres fit for royalty, hundreds of guests, and elaborate presentations by the company's management team. It got to the point that each subsequent meeting outdid the last meeting. Finally, in the early 1980s the SEC stepped in and put a halt to these fabulous festivities, implying they had lost their purpose. So back the meetings went to small rooms. Invited brokers had to be registered to get in. The hors d'oeuvres were not as tempting and the atmosphere strictly business.

Today, when the underwriter decides it's time to introduce the company and the offering to the brokerage community, it does a road show. Both are formal and still somewhat elaborate meetings to which the selling group of individual brokers is invited. They are complete with such things as videotapes, charts, products, and everything else it takes to tell the company's story—the complete "dog-and-pony" show to which all the important people are invited. The company usually covers the cost with occasional help from the underwriter. The reading of a condensed version of the prospectus takes place and questions are answered.

Attendance at a brokers' due diligence meeting can range from one to hundreds depending on the selling job before the show. The company can spend a lot of time, trouble, and money to put on one or more of these affairs. But it must be done and, more important, done well because today's road shows are very important politically. And it is important that the IPO entrepreneur-CEO understand the politics involved. He or she will be dealing with brokers who come to these meetings because they are interested in deals, so management must impress upon them that this is the deal they've been waiting for. Remember, brokers need product to sell, and the company is the product; management's job is to get the brokers on its side.

To make the most of a road show, the company needs to involve its financial public relations firm. The company's part of the meeting should be rehearsed over and over and over again. And the players should listen to all the constructive criticism that's offered. Consider what's at stake. The end result can be very rewarding, and the deal will get done!

Timing. Road shows can be scheduled from as early as the printing of the red herring to as late as after the effectiveness of the issue—there are no set rules. They are best held within a week of the effective date depending on the number of cities in which they will be held. Plenty of time should be allowed for planning; it's not unusual to start working on plans months ahead of the actual meeting dates. The meetings are team efforts that call for the services of the underwriter and financial public relations firm to help coordinate them.

If the company is holding meetings in a number of cities, it should allow at least one day on either side of the meeting date. Figure a total of three days in each city. It will take that much time to make personal calls on individual firms, brokers, and potential investors. Breakfasts, lunches, coffees, drinks, dinners, and more drinks are the norm. Allowing enough time can save the company people and underwriters from frantically trying to accomplish last-minute arrangements as the actual date draws near.

Location. Choose a hotel or meeting place that has catered road shows in the past, one that brokers are familiar with.

Scheduling. Again, there are no set days. Experience shows brokers seem to prefer Tuesdays, Wednesdays, and Thursdays. If possible, avoid conflicts with socially significant events like the World Series, NBA play-offs, the Olympics, and the day before or after a brokers' holiday.

The Presentation

The whole purpose of the presentation is to sell the company to the people who will, it is hoped, sell the company to the investing public. Every effort should be made to impress upon the invited guests the ability and depth of the management team. It's important also to set aside time for questions and answers about the offering.

Although those in attendance know why they are there, the presentation should be paced to hold their attention. And it should be formatted in an orderly fashion. The following is an example of what could be included in the presentation and the sequence in which it could be presented:

- Introduction by the underwriter or designee
- Introduction of the cast: underwriter's name, company name, number of shares being offered, blue-sky states, effective date, billing date, closing date, trading date, and other things that will be covered

- Brief description of the company
- Introduction of the president/CEO of the company preceded by a brief bio
- President/CEO thanks presenter and shares information about the company—details and history
- Presenter or designated person presents audiovisual aids (if part of the program)
- Presentation of management team speakers (as appropriate) or otherwise, each team member introduced with a brief bio
- President/CEO or chairman of the board introduces the board of directors with brief bios
- President/CEO introduces board of advisers with brief bios
- Appropriate participant conducts question-and-answer session
- Closing remarks by the underwriter

There are many options in the audiovisual area. Video can be very exciting for a formal meeting presentation, but it can be very expensive depending on the budget. A 15-minute video can easily cost $10,000 for taping and editing; $20,000 is not out of the question. The same applies for "Power-Point" presentations. But amortized over all the cities in which it will be shown, it may be a bargain in time and effort that would otherwise be expended. Also to be considered is the need for a large room and expensive rental equipment such as projection screens and sound systems. Slide presentations can also be very effective. Production and presentation costs would not be as high, and slides offer the advantage of flexibility. They can be stopped at any time to encourage discussion. Many brokerage firms already have slide material about themselves that can be easily updated; and script changes can be easily made. Stand-up charts and transparencies are another option, but they can be awkward because of the size needed for an effective presentation. Handouts of executive portfolios, including product brochures, offering circulars, broker fact sheets, and samples are also always appropriate. (This can be part of the presentation even when an audiovisual presentation is used.)

Remember, whoever is a presenter during the presentation must make frequent caveats regarding what is being discussed. Nothing can be presented that hasn't been printed in the prospectus. If something should happen to come up during the question-and-answer period about the competition a product would face and it is not stated in the prospectus, the presenter should say no more than "It is management's opinion that the competition is limited," or something can be "anticipated." To be completely safe, technically one can only discuss what is in the prospectus.

Postmeeting

Much of the company's work begins after the due diligence meetings have been completed. Management should make it a point to keep in contact with the brokers who attended the meetings and keep them appraised of the progress being made by the company. By establishing communication lines with the brokers, the company will be keeping the pressure on, and the brokers will be more inclined to talk up the offering.

Tombstones

The company can help to create public familiarity with the offering and also give a hand to the brokers who will become involved by preconditioning the investing public with *tombstone ads,* which were discussed in an earlier chapter.

Tombstone ads, or tombstones, are more in the nature of announcements than advertisements. A tombstone is a "boxed-in" ad (that's why it is called a tombstone) that appears in financial papers and the financial and business sections of newspapers and magazines to announce the particulars of a new issue. It mentions the name of the company going public, the underwriter, and the total dollar amount of the offering, and it makes reference to the prospectus. Most important, it includes the names of the brokerage firms from whom a prospectus may be obtained. It can run during and after the registration period and is not considered by the SEC to be an improper selling effort. A disclaimer also appears at the top of the ad, which typically says in effect: "This announcement is neither an offer to sell nor a solicitation of an offer to buy these securities. The offer is made only by prospectus."

The company will place tombstones on the advice or encouragement from the underwriter and its financial public relations group. Some companies run them at the time the red herring is printed, at the time of the effectiveness of the offering, and at the completion and trading of the issue. They can be run once or on multiple occasions, usually depending on current stock market trends and the demand for a particular type of issue.

Tombstones should be considered an essential ingredient in selling an issue. The benefits easily outweigh the costs, so not running a tombstone can prove to be a grave error.

Escrow

Generally, from the effective date of an offering to the day the offering is completed (when all the monies have been received), the money goes into an escrow account. At that time it is turned over to the underwriter, who then turns the funds over to the company.

The selection process of choosing a bank or an escrow company to escrow the funds of an offering is a decision made by the IPO company and/or the underwriter. Distinct advantages and leverage accrue in deciding which financial institution should be chosen to handle an IPO escrow. The financial institution stands to earn considerable interest from investing the money held in the escrow account in short-term investments, which in turn offers the company an opportunity to improve its relationship with the financial institution it designates as its escrow agent.

Escrow experience counts too. Whoever is chosen must be able to perform all the complicated escrow requirements for a public company offering. Many banks and escrow companies out there can do the job. The question—which one will offer the company the best fringe benefits?

Closing

The closing of an offering is that time when all the transactions pertaining to the offering have been completed and all the monies, stocks, and commissions have been received and are dispensed. It is possible to have more than one closing on an offering. Let's say, for example, that we have a $12 million offering. We can designate the first closing at $10 million minimum, and a second closing will be for $2 million.

Closings differ considerably between small offerings on a best efforts basis and the larger offerings that are firm commitments. The one thing they have in common is that both mark the conclusion of a combined effort on the part of a lot of dedicated people culminating in the payoff.

Closing Meeting

The attendance at a closing meeting can be rather large. It will include all the key players involved in the underwriting. The meeting is usually held in the conference room of the escrow company or bank that handled the escrow. Those in attendance will include the following:

For the company

- The president (CEO) usually
- The secretary and treasurer (CFO)
- The company's legal counsel
- The company's accountants—with final comfort letter in hand

For the underwriter

- A managing executive
- A syndicate broker representative
- The underwriter's legal counsel
- The backroom office manager—the person who supervised the office responsible for stock transfers, securities going out, tracking stock confirmations, stock certificates coming in, money going out, and all the people who work in the office

Also in attendance are the transfer agent's representatives with stock certificates in hand and the escrow company representatives with checks in hand.

Best-Effort Closing

For the small, best-effort offering, the closing takes place after the selling period has been completed. The selling period is usually 60 to 120 days from the effective date with an extension allowance of 60 to 90 days by mutual consent of the company and the underwriter. The selling period is the time between the effective date and the date the actual trading of the stock begins. To make certain there is no confusion, the closing period for a best efforts underwriting is noted in the prospectus, usually on the cover, and further noted in the section on underwriting. Also by that time the selling syndicate members will have collected their money from the individual investors, and all the monies will have been deposited in and cleared the escrow account.

On the closing date the *big* meeting takes place, coordinated by the company's legal counsel, who brings along a closing memorandum. The memorandum simply states the actual closing process, informing those present who will receive specific original documents and who will receive copies of the documents. All the necessary documents are signed by the various parties, including an incumbency certificate that states that the officers listed in the registration statement are still with the company. A second comfort letter from the auditing accounts is also normally presented, assuring everyone that everything is financially correct.

The final order of business consists of an exchange of stock certificates or evidence of their transfer to the underwriter by the company via its transfer agent. (The underwriter will transfer the stock to the individual purchasers of the stock.) The order described here is occasionally reversed, with the underwriter giving the transfer agent a distribution list of the shareholders. Last, checks are passed out by the escrow agent, usually to the underwriter for its commissions and nonaccountable expenses, and then the company is given its money. Disbersed receipts are common practice for all the transactions—the end result being writer's cramp. If there are selling shareholders present, they will receive separate checks individually made out. And with no more business to conduct—the closing celebration party begins.

Firm-Commitment Closing

A firm-commitment closing is more complicated and hectic than one for a best-effort offering. The principal reason is that the actual selling price of the stock and the total number of shares being offered are not determined (committed) until the day before, or sometimes on, the actual day that the stock starts trading. Naturally, this creates a great deal of anxiety among all involved, but the paperwork and documentation for both types of closings are similar.

Because the selling price and the shares offered in a firm-commitment offering are not determined until the day of effectiveness, the preparation for the closing starts before the effective date, and an actual closing is usually scheduled a week or two later. As a result, a grace period is granted to gather funds and the needed closing documentation. The documents, which by the way also apply to best efforts offerings, include

- a letter to the transfer agent from the underwriters specifying shareholders' names and stock denominations;
- verified certificates of incorporation and of good standing of the company and its subsidiaries;
- an assertion by the company that it has complied with all legal requirements, that it has received approval of all actions leading to the closing, and that no publicity or events occurred that materially affected the offering;

- certification by selling shareholders (if any);
- a stock disposition letter to the transfer agent from the company;
- a final opinion to the underwriter from the company's counsel;
- a stock issue validity letter to the transfer agent from the company's counsel;
- a final opinion letter by the underwriter's counsel to the underwriter;
- an exchange of a list of receipts; and
- disbursement of official bank checks to the respective parties.

The Difference

It is important to recognize the principal difference between a best-effort and a firm-commitment underwriting. When the registration is declared effective under a best-effort underwriting, the underwriter proceeds to sell the stock. The monies received are escrowed until the underwriters have given their best effort and at least a minimum amount of stock has been sold to investors. As mentioned earlier, this could take 60 to 90 days, and a closing cannot take place until the money is in hand.

Under a firm-commitment underwriting, the underwriter is committing the money to the company, saying in essence that it commits its dollars to the company before selling the stock to the public. In actuality, the underwriter has lined up buyers of the stock through syndicate members and broker-dealers. The underwriter's money is usually at risk only briefly—maybe a week or two—but the risk is really only a bookkeeping function as the company doesn't receive the committed funds until the actual closing. In any event, the closing celebration usually makes up for all the stress and anxiety both sides have been put through.

FREQUENTLY ASKED QUESTIONS

How do you control publicity during a quiet period?

The top management of a company has to be well informed about what can and cannot be said. Then there have to be continual updates to be sure that everyone is singing from the same songbook. The most important point is that nothing can be talked about or disclosed that isn't referred to in the prospectus.

Should only one person be appointed to deal with all company publicity?

This is a good idea. Some companies use an internal PR person while others use their outside PR firm. Then again, many companies prefer to use only their top management, the president, or the chief financial officer. It's best to have this predetermined to give the person an opportunity to become familiar with his or her public spokesperson's role.

Do road shows have to be held?

Very few IPOs today can get by without a road show. Most CEOs and their management teams would prefer not to do road shows because they are very physically demanding and require immense amounts of concentration. But the brokerage community expects them because that's where they get a chance to "size up" management and the deal.

26

Listings

The primary securities trading markets where a majority of the stocks sold in the United States are listed are the New York Stock Exchange, the American Stock Exchange, the regional exchanges, and the over-the-counter (OTC) markets.

Although I'll address all of these markets, in this book I'll concentrate on the OTC market because almost all initial public offerings are traded there.

Since the early 1980s, the OTC market has gained overwhelming investor acceptance as a bona fide, legitimate marketplace. In fact, many members of the financial community consider the OTC market as a leader in trading innovations that will go well into the 21st century. It's the exchange where many of the nation's newest and most exciting issues got their start and where most remain, among them Microsoft, Apple, Intel, and Netscape.

What follows is a brief look at the markets that I hope will promote a better understanding of all the trading markets.

The New York Stock Exchange

In the past, the listing dream and final destination for all public companies was the New York Stock Exchange (NYSE). It carried the prestige of being the world's largest and oldest trading place for stocks. This august body is self-ruled by a board made up of members who own a seat on the exchange; owners may be corporations, partnerships, or individuals. Membership is obtained by purchasing a seat on the exchange. The seats are limited in number, and in recent years, depending on the profitability of the market (based on investor interest and market volume), the seat prices have fluctuated from $750,000 to $1.8 million.

The NYSE, the American Stock Exchange, and the regional exchanges use an auction method of trading (as opposed to the OTC method of telecommunications), which means that an individual, known as a specialist, physically conducts trading activities at a trading post in one particular floor location (exchange). The specialists, or their firms, make a market in one or a group of assigned stocks. Their primary function is to bring buyers and sellers together, and their responsibility is to maintain a fair and orderly market. Specialists match buy and sell orders in their trading books. Only if there is an imbalance in the buys and sells do they trade out of their own account—this is done to preserve the orderly market in a particular stock and to make certain there is continued supervision of the process by the exchanges. During times of large or extreme market fluctuations, such as happened on Black Monday 1987, the specialists' trading system is put to the test and the value of the auction method of market trading is often questioned.

The listing requirements for a company on the NYSE are extensive as is the process. The minimum requirements for listing on the NYSE are

- two thousand shareholders,
- publicly held shares with a market value of $18 million,
- one million publicly held shares,
- income before taxes of $2.5 million, and
- net assets of $18 million.

In addition, the NYSE requires "substantial representation" of outside members on the board of directors and usually an audit committee on the board that is made up entirely of independent, outside directors to maintain financial integrity.

The American Stock Exchange

The American Stock Exchange (AMEX) is the second largest exchange in the United States. It is the world's largest trader of foreign stocks, but the companies listed on the AMEX are generally smaller in size than those on the NYSE. The AMEX is also considered a specialist trading market very much like the NYSE. Traditionally, however, its competitive advantage is that it offers more assistance to its listed companies in the areas of arranging investor conferences, meetings, and research programs.

All of its listing, disclosure, filing, and voting rights rules and requirements are similar to those of the NYSE—except that its minimum listing requirements are less demanding. The minimum listing requirements for AMEX companies are

- eight hundred shareholders, 600 of which must own at least 100 shares;
- three hundred thousand publicly held shares;
- publicly held shares with a market value of $3 million;
- income before taxes of $750,000;
- net assets of $4 million; and
- a bid price of $3.

The Regional Exchanges

Regional stock exchanges serve distinct regions. They are involved with the trading of stocks nationally, but their emphasis is on stocks that have a particular regional interest. Stocks on regional exchanges can also be traded on the OTC market.

Today's regional exchanges are essentially option trading markets, the most notable being the Chicago Board of Trade. The remaining exchanges have consolidated further into the Pacific, Midwest, Philadelphia, and Boston exchanges. The listing requirements vary for each exchange, but the minimum requirements generally range as follows:

- Net worth of $1 million to $2.5 million
- Earnings from minimal to $100,000
- Market float from none to $500,000
- Number of shareholders from 500 to 1,000

The Over-the-Counter Market

The over-the-counter (OTC) market is subdivided into Pink Sheets, the Bulletin Board, the National Association of Securities Dealers Automated Quotations (Nasdaq), and the National Market System (NMS). Its daily trading function and mechanism differ from the exchanges in that its business is conducted via telecommunications through broker-dealers across the country as opposed to the procedures used by the NYSE and the AMEX. The interconnect is via phones and computers, and each broker-dealer provides a bid and ask price for each of the individual stocks he or she chooses to make a market in. There are no specialists along the lines of the NYSE, which creates a true negotiated marketplace.

The broker-dealers buy and sell on an inventory basis. Their governing body, the National Association of Securities Dealers (NASD) is composed of broker-dealers themselves. They have a paid administrative staff numbering in the hundreds that are located around the country. The NASD, as a non-profit organization, establishes and enforces the regulations for the OTC market. Its chief concerns are

- to protect investors from illegal actions by the listed companies and broker-dealers,
- to establish and implement rules of fair practice for the broker-dealers,
- to ensure that all broker-dealers comply with federal and state securities regulations, and
- to arbitrate grievances or disputes between broker-dealers and investors.

Pink Sheets

The *Pink Sheets* are so named because they are printed on pink paper on over 300 pages measuring 6 by 14 inches. They are printed daily and are available by subscription from the National Quotations Bureau, a subsidiary of Commerce Clearing House. Each trading day's list, which is compiled the previous afternoon from all the market makers across the country, will show the bid and ask price quoted from the market makers.

Pink Sheets are considered the OTC trader's bible. By looking up a company by name, the stock, warrant, or bond and the firm that makes the market in each security can be identified. Each market maker's trading line phone number is listed. If the company is on the Nasdaq system, its symbol is also shown.

The first level of the OTC markets are the companies that trade in "The Pinks." Approximately two-thirds of these companies have either chosen not to, or are unable to, meet the requirements to trade on the Nasdaq system.

There are actually no listing requirements for the Pink Sheets. If the company is publicly traded with two market makers, it is automatically listed. It is the responsibility of the company's management to secure the market makers and broker-dealers to trade its stock. A broker or trader that wants to trade the stock for an investor would look up the company in the

Pink Sheets, identify the market makers, call them on the phone, request quotes, and then execute the trade to the customer's best advantage. Confirming paperwork is processed through the broker-dealer clearing system.

The OTC Bulletin Board

The SEC also has a program called the OTC Bulletin Board, which is an "electronic computerized" Pink Sheet trading report. Although the Bulletin Board is a successful stock quotation system of almost 6,000 stocks, which includes some substantial companies and about 1,000 community banks, the brokerage community does not like to trade Bulletin Board stocks because of the large amount of paperwork required with each trade.

During market trading hours, this computerized system displays the *firm* and *nonfirm* quotations, and indications of interest in eligible OTC stocks that are not listed on the Nasdaq market.

The initial eligibility of all Pink Sheet stocks that were listed when the Bulletin Board went into effect are "grandfathered"—that is, exempt from current requirements. The decision for determining initial tradability lies with the market makers/broker-dealers. A new listing can be instigated or reinstatement can be made by complying with SEC Rule 15c2-II.

The Bulletin Board functions very much like the existing Nasdaq system but is not part of the Nasdaq market; rather, it is an electronic quotation medium for securities traded outside the Nasdaq. Each company has a designated symbol on the screen that is updated every 90 seconds. Firm quotes (bid or ask) are shown as are nonfirm bids and wanted and unpriced entries. There is no trading on this system but each listing has the name and phone number of the market maker who is trading the stock being quoted. The cost for listing is paid by the market makers and is free to the companies. Because of the complications and restrictions in the system, quotes will be shown on the screens only at trading desks as opposed to screens normally found in a brokerage office.

The Nasdaq System

In 1971 the National Association of Securities Dealers (NASD) introduced the National Association of Securities Dealers Automated Quotations (Nasdaq) service and drastically changed OTC trading. The Nasdaq is a computer-based quotation trading system with terminals in broker-dealers' offices all over the country, and it is able to display up-to-the-minute firm quotations.

Today the system is divided into various levels of service. Terminals, subscribed to by Nasdaq broker-dealers, display quotes of the best bid and the lowest offer, and the more complex terminals display all the market makers in each stock, their quotes, last trades in price and amount, and continuous volume.

Over 500 stock brokerage firms are listed market makers on the Nasdaq, and the average company trading on its system has eight market makers versus one specialist on the exchanges. What's more, the services of the market makers are voluntary, whereas the specialists on the exchanges are assigned. This seems to suggest that the OTC may offer a company better trading advantages for its stock.

There are over 5,000 companies listed on the Nasdaq whose initial minimum listing requirements (approved August 1997) are

- net tangible assets (total assets less total liabilities and goodwill) of $4 million *or* a market capitalization of $50 million *or* a net income (last fiscal year or two of the last three fiscal years) of $750,000;
- three hundred shareholders (round-lot holders of 100 shares or more);
- one million publicly traded shares;
- a market value of $5 million for publicly traded shares;
- a bid price of $4;
- an operating history of one year *or* $50 million in market capitalization; and
- three market makers.

The minimum maintenance standards (approved August 1997) for remaining listed on the Nasdaq are

- net tangible assets of $2 million *or* a market capitalization of $35 million *or* a net income (last fiscal year or two of the last three fiscal years) of $500,000;
- three hundred shareholders (round-lot holders of 100 shares or more);
- a million and a half publicly traded shares;
- a market value of $1 million for publicly traded shares;
- a bid price of $1;
- an operating history = N/A or $50 million in market capitalization; and
- two market makers;

In addition to the above minimum initial listing and maintenance requirements, the Nasdaq has adopted corporate governance requirements that must be complied with by all Nasdaq small capitalization companies—the Nasdaq Small Cap Market. The requirements are summarized as follows:

- Distribution of annual and interim reports
- A minimum of two independent directors
- An audit committee, a majority of which are independent directors
- An annual shareholders meeting
- Quorum requirement
- Solicitation of proxies
- Review of conflicts of interest
- Shareholder approval for certain transactions
- Voting rights

Current listing and maintenance requirement details can be accessed from the Nasdaq Web site at www.nasdaq.com.

The NMS Market

The National Market System (NMS) functions through the Nasdaq computer system and is designed for larger OTC companies. Its trading activity is similar to the NYSE and the AMEX in that computers show continuous volume updates throughout the trading day.

Listing requirements for the NMS are divided into two categories—developing and operating companies. Developing companies are required to have a minimum of $4 million in net tangible assets, a net income of $400,000, pretax earnings of $750,000, a public float of 500,000 shares with a market value of $3 million, 400 shareholders, a bid price of $5, and two market makers. Operating companies are required to have a minimum of $12 million in net tangible assets, a public float of 1 million shares with a market value of $15 million, a bid price of $3, and two market makers.

NMS stocks have automatic margin status, which acknowledges full equality with the exchange-listed stocks. This marginable status indicates increased liquidity and therefore attracts more institutional trading. *Important note:* Current listing and maintenance requirements can be accessed from the Nasdaq Web site at www.nasdaq.com.

Public Listings

The company should take advantage of the services of its financial public relations firm to arrange for listings in as many publications as possible. Shareholders should also be informed on a continuing basis about the various publications in which they can find the company's stock quoted.

Most newspapers and financial publications list stocks on the OTC market in some form. *The Wall Street Journal* carries the Nasdaq "Additional List" and many regional daily newspapers also carry a supplemental list of companies that have a regional interest.

Standard & Poor's Index is a widely accepted index of market performance and trends that includes the price activity of a broad base of 500 leading listed and OTC stocks, including industrial, transportation, financial, and public utility stocks. Moody's is an investment rating service of corporate bond issues, preferred stocks, and selected common stocks.

As a point of information, all listed stocks and bonds must have identification numbers. They are provided by the Committee on Uniform Securities Identification Procedures (CUSIP), a NASD agency.

Broker-Dealers and Wholesale Market Makers

The difference between broker-dealers and market makers can be confusing to the layperson. Generally, a broker will execute a buy through a dealer for his or her client and sell a stock for a client through a dealer—who can also be a market maker (that is, establishes the price). The broker operates on a commission basis, purchasing or selling stock or other securities from a dealer. Dealers can also be the people who make markets on various stocks. Their money is made from the spread, such as on the OTC market, between the bid and the ask price. Although most firms operate in the capacity of broker-dealers, they seldom make a market in all the more than 15,000 OTC-listed stocks.

In addition to broker-dealers are wholesalers, who are primarily dealers. They make a market (dictate the price of a stock from available information on the stock) and keep an inventory in a number of securities (selling shares of stock that they themselves have purchased for sale). They function in the capacity of dealers to other broker-dealers or to those who are just brokers. As a rule, they have few retail accounts (as brokers).

Market makers are essentially securities firms that make markets (designates the price) by always being ready to buy and sell certain securities. They can be brokers or dealers and can operate retail or wholesale.

NASD market makers are bound by the rules enforced by the NASD, which require them to trade at the prices quoted in the Pink Sheets or displayed on the Nasdaq system. Their quotes must be "reasonably related" (an SEC term) to the prevailing price of the security.

It is usually the responsibility of the company to make certain there is a market maker for the company's stock. This often takes a certain amount of wining and dining on the company's part. Of course, the market maker prefers to handle a security that shows trading activity. The more trading activity, the more opportunity for the market-making firm to make money on the stock, and the less chance of keeping the firm's capital at risk. A good public relations effort by the company is also important to keep its stock in the public eye (see Chapter 12). If the price of the stock goes down and the market maker has a lot of it in inventory, the market maker could lose. By the same token, if the market maker has sold a security without having inventory, it must now go out and buy some. In the meantime, if the price has gone up, the market maker stands to lose. Some market makers prefer to stay flat (hold no inventory) on some securities. The names of market makers can be found in the Pink Sheets.

Because market makers wear several hats, it's important for the company to join forces with the market makers whose hats can make the company look good.

FREQUENTLY ASKED QUESTIONS

Can a company go public only on the OTC market?

No. However, very few companies are large enough at the time of an IPO to qualify for the NYSE or the AMEX. Even established companies usually choose to go public in the OTC market. Microsoft is a good example: It went public not because it needed financing but because the company had granted so many stock options that it had over 400 shareholders and thus was forced to go public. It chose the OTC.

Is it true that the NASD keeps raising its entry-level requirements for IPOs?

It sure seems that way. In the mid-1980s, the minimum net worth requirement went from $500,000 to $2 million. Now it has doubled to $4 million in net tangible assets.

Why is this?

Generally good economic times, inflation, and the desire to continue to legitimize the OTC verus the exchanges.

Then how are smaller companies going to have access to the public financing markets?

A good question. This has been a continuing problem since the mid-1980s. Some of it was partially resolved by the implementation of Reg D and the more recent SCOR programs. However, these have not solved the stock trading dilemma. A lot of hopes and dreams are now resting on the Internet to change this. (See Part Six.)

FIVE

Completing the Public Offering

27

Aftermarket Trading

Aftermarket trading begins after the new issue has been sold to the original purchasers, who bought the shares via the prospectus. The entrepreneur should be aware that the aftermarket trading of a small best-effort IPO is pursued differently from that for a large firm commitment IPO. In larger firm commitment issues, the underwriters have *their* dollars at initial risk as well as their reputations for pricing an issue (see Chapter 16). For the smaller best-effort offering, the *public investors'* dollars are at risk. On a larger issue, the underwriters are geared to "stabilize" the stock price—that is, they will support the market price of a new issue to keep it from falling below the initial offering price when the trading of the stock goes into the aftermarket. When a new issue discounts (stock price goes down) on first trading, for whatever reason, it reflects true supply and demand for the first time and could result in its being negatively branded for months, a possibility underwriters want to avoid. Discounting a new issue also adversely reflects on the pricing strategy judgment of the lead underwriter and the analysts in the selling group. So they turn to *stabilization,* a form of legal manipulation, which has the approval of the SEC.

When a stock starts trading, the underwriting group hopes for an even market—an equal number of buyers and sellers. The ideal is a gradual rise in the price of the stock. Stabilization is not put into effect unless there are too many sellers, which forces down the price of the stock. The market maker will then step in, buy the stock to stabilize the price, and hold the stock in inventory to keep the price from going down. For the smaller best efforts offerings, the new issue stands on its own. Stabilization is less frequent if used at all.

Although the SEC allows stabilization, the underwriter must furnish detailed reports to the SEC if it is undertaken. Furthermore, the stock purchased for stabilization cannot be resold at a higher price. It must be resold at the purchase price or below. If losses occur as a result, they are shared pro rata by the total selling syndicate. If the stock price continues to fall after stabilization has been put into effect, the underwriter may withdraw support at its own discretion without notice. In fact, the underwriter is not obligated to support the issue by stabilization.

Underwriters will make every attempt to place the stock in strong hands among syndicate members to avoid stabilization. Investors selling immediately after trading commences indicates that the syndicate member could not control its clients from selling out just because the stock price didn't go up and could thus cause the syndicate member to be eliminated or, at a minimum, offered reduced participation in future offerings.

Overallotment

Just as investment banker-underwriters don't relish a steep discount or the falling price of an IPO, they find it hard to deal with a hot issue. Either extreme presents extenuating circumstances that call for legal manipulation. When an offering that discounts from the initial offering price requires stabilization, a hot offering with a large initial demand or a drastic increase in the initial offering price will usually see the use of an *overallotment*.

The purpose of an overallotment, like stabilization, is to ensure an orderly aftermarket. It allows the underwriter to sell up to 15 percent more of the stock than what was originally settled on. For example, if the underwriter had a $12 million underwriting at $6 a share (2 million shares total), it would be able to sell an additional 300,000 shares of stock—the green shoe option mentioned in an earlier chapter. The name for this option comes from the first company to ever use it, the Green Shoe Company, and is often used if the syndicate members' initial indications are that interest in the stock may be higher than anticipated. It is put into effect when there is a big demand for the stock and the stock becomes a hot issue. The additional monies raised by the green shoe go to the company less selling commissions. The purpose, as mentioned earlier, is that the extra shares reduce the upward pressure on the price of the stock and ensure an orderly aftermarket.

When the underwriter anticipates either overallotment or stabilization, it must disclose its expectation on the front cover of the prospectus as follows:

IN CONNECTION WITH THIS OFFERING, THE UNDERWRITERS MAY OVER-ALLOT OR EFFECT TRANSACTIONS WHICH STABILIZE OR MAINTAIN THE MARKET PRICE OF THE COMMON STOCK OF THE COMPANY AT A LEVEL ABOVE THAT WHICH MIGHT OTHERWISE PREVAIL IN THE OPEN MARKET. SUCH STABILIZING, IF COMMENCED, MAY BE DISCONTINUED AT ANY TIME.

Smaller Issues

It's not common for a smaller best-effort IPO to use a green shoe; rather, a minimum/maximum offering, which is the common overallotment method for best-effort underwritings, will be used. If the offering is for 2 million shares, for example, the underwriter may get an indication from syndicate members that they can probably move between 1.5 million to 2 million shares, in which case the minimum/maximum would be 1.5 million to 2 million.

Stabilization, as a rule, is also not used on smaller offerings. If the stock discounts—it discounts. The best that can be hoped for is that the primary market makers will purchase the stock for their own inventory if it goes down. Most market makers are usually capable of holding the position long enough to stabilize the discount or downward trend. If the market goes down, it is often because a weak syndicate member is cutting losses rather than an indication of the market reception to the new issue.

Trading activities are fairly predictable. A study was made of 21 new issues of at least $5 million that had price-earning multiples of 10. The average PE multiple on the Dow Jones at the time was 12 so a 10 was considered a good-quality issue. The study showed that during the first three days of trading, as much as 35 percent of the publicly held shares turned over, which is about the same average as that for smaller issues. Generally, the first month or so can see a high degree of volatility in the pricing and trading volume of a new issue. Unfortunately, the company is at a disadvantage in affecting this trading activity because the issue is still in its quiet period—the 90-day period during which there can be no form of public announcements and no hyping of the stock without stickering the prospectus. This is the time when speculators are still coming in and going out, so the company can depend only on the support of the underwriters and the selling syndicate to maintain its stock at a reasonable price and trading level.

During the quiet period, the entrepreneur should establish a strong rapport with individual brokers involved in the issue during the selling period. If the company's stock discounts, it's helpful to be able to reassure the brokers that the company is as strong as when the offering came to them. With money in the bank, the company is even stronger and its goals and projections are more likely to be met.

Ideally, the stock has been priced by the underwriter at a 10 to 20 percent discount below what the underwriter felt it was really worth, enticing investors to buy at the offering price. The inevitable speculators will usually get out during the first 30 days of trading, which allows the brokerage community time to find committed shareholders who will hold the stock for the long haul because the company shows promise and in hopes that the stock price will go up as anticipated. This is the ideal. Unfortunately, the ideal is not always attainable. But who's to say it can't happen?

Market Makers

Market makers are securities firms that make markets, continuously ready to buy certain securities for their own inventory or to sell securities from their own inventory.

To be more explicit: market makers are broker-dealers. They put their money at risk by buying or selling a stock with their own money as opposed to brokers who, without putting up their own money, will buy the stock from one source (the market maker) and sell it to another source (a client). Brokers won't buy a stock unless they have a selling transaction lined up, whereas market makers actually buy the stock and hold on to it until they find a buyer. Most brokerage firms are also market makers and may own stocks from hundreds of companies. Other firms only make a market in a few stocks and are always prepared to buy or sell shares of those stocks at the quoted price on the exchange.

Nasdaq market makers are bound by the rules enforced by the NASD, which require them to trade at the price displayed on the Nasdaq system or the quotes in the Pink Sheets or the Bulletin Board. In addition, they are forbidden to jump in and out of securities during the day. They must always be ready (at risk) to buy or sell the stock and hold it in inventory, a rule that also applies to market makers on the NYSE and all other exchanges. The Nasdaq system also requires that the quotations the market makers give or display must be reasonably related to the prevailing market in the security.

Market makers can be either wholesale or retail. Wholesale market makers may have just a few individuals that they make trades for, and, consequently, almost all their business is in trading between retail brokers, which is called wholesaling. Ideally, one would expect them to carry large amounts of a company's stock in inventory. On a practical basis, they maintain relatively flat inventories, playing the spreads when the stocks move up or down. Nobody likes getting caught with his or her stocks down.

A retail market maker is the trading department of a retail brokerage firm. Most often it carries inventory to accommodate the brokers in the firm, usually concentrating its positions in securities that were underwritten by the firm. Generally, a wholesaler will make a market in hundreds of stocks, whereas a retailer will make a market in only a couple of dozen.

A market maker actually does more than just hold on to inventory of a stock. Good market makers form a working partnership with the company whose stock they trade to provide the best possible market for the existing shareholders and prospective shareholders. The market-making firm will do this in a number of ways: (1) by assigning an able trader to the company's stock (one who has faith in the company); (2) by furnishing adequate capital to support the market in the company's stock (having enough money available to buy more stock if necessary and also to be able to hold the stock until buyers present themselves); (3) by taking risk positions in the stock and being long or short as appropriate (the market maker tries to equalize the market; if more stockholders are trying to sell, for example, the market maker will take a long position and hold the stock in inventory until the buyers come along; on short sales, the market maker must be able to transact a sell order and buy back later even if it means losing money on the transaction—what is called covering the short); (4) by providing liquidity for a strong and effective market in the stock (having money ready and at risk); and (5) by acting as a salesperson for the company when talking to securities firms throughout the country (when a retail brokerage firm solicits information about the company for a client, the market maker will provide the information and sell the stock to the brokerage firm). Incidentally, a company can have many market makers.

Why Firms Make Markets

The obvious reason for market making is that customers of a firm are interested in certain securities. Often, the decision to make a market will be sparked by a retail broker who has contact with the company that is attempting to create interest. Because the business is customer driven, the best reason for trading a stock is to sell it. If a stock is in demand, market makers want to trade it. And firms make a market in a stock if they have participated in the selling syndicates that distributed the company's shares in an IPO.

Firms also make markets in stocks that are recommended by their analysts who think well of the stock's potential for price appreciation. However, the stock must also be able to generate interest by the firm's customers. That's one reason why, as a rule, the analyst's recommendation has to be seconded by the firm's sales department—the brokers who work for the firm.

One of the biggest reasons why many firms make markets is primarily for the trading profits that can be realized. Their trading department could easily be their key profit center as they will always try to sell the stock to the buying broker for more than they paid for it. Some firms, however, believe the trading department should fulfill a service function, based not on making trading profits but on the retail sales activity that the trading department generates. They will sell the stock to the brokers for their cost plus reasonable expenses. They may be selling for less than other firms, but they do it to get the business. And some market makers will trade stocks for their arbitrage possibilities, simultaneously selling the same security in different markets. Arbitrage is a way of profiting from the differences in price on two exchanges.

Before the entrepreneur gets involved with a prospective market maker, he or she should have answers ready that will satisfy the market maker's concerns, such as the following:

- Are the company's prospects promising? If not yet, when are they expected to become promising?
- Is the company's stock an attractive product now or likely to turn into one soon?
- Does the company have a good overall investor relations program that can assist the market maker's efforts to promote it?
- Is management willing to keep the market makers informed and to keep an open line to the traders, the corporate people, and research departments?

Depending on what is required by the market makers, management must be ready with a complete package of basic information. It should include complete financial statements, business plans, details of the present stock ownership, and a favorable annual report (the company's most important sales tool).

After the deal is set, management needs to establish a communication line with the market maker's *very* key people. Every shareholder letter or mailing should be forwarded to the market maker and followed by personal contact. The market maker should be invited, in writing and by phone, to all corporate social functions, annual meetings, open houses, and product display presentations and should also be sent all 10-Q, 10-K, and 8-K mailings.

Maintaining a good relationship with market makers should be a number one priority for company management. A determination must also be made to continue to bring new market makers into the fold. Remember, they are the bread-and-butter people.

Analysts

Analysts are opinion leaders in the brokerage community. They are usually employed by brokerage firms, banks, and such institutional investors as universities, pension funds, insurance companies, and an increasing number of financial planners. In large NYSE ("Big Board") firms, analysts may specialize in just a few stocks or in a specific industry.

Analysts generally issue reports to the brokers in their firms, who then use them as a guide in advising their individual customers. Most analysts also write or contribute to market letters, which often have a great influence on customers. On New York's Wall Street securities analysts have been called Wall Street's "idea men . . . financial detectives" and "wizards of odds." They are billed as impartial judges of companies, but their employers increasingly judge them on the trading volume they generate from their recommendations to buy "favored" stocks. Around 15,000 analysts regularly chronicle the daily dramas of America's public companies. Nearly 4,000 work for brokerage houses, spewing out reams of research reports.

Analysts seem to feel compelled to lend their expertise to something that studies suggest they have never been good at—picking stocks that will enjoy immediate glory. They rarely use the word *sell* in a report, though they may utter it privately. They have a tendency to couch bad news in dazzling, creative phrases. For example, a stock does not collapse in price, it "underperforms the market." Part of their wizardry image stems from the fact that they are often put in a position of making value judgments to determine whether a stock is underpriced or overvalued at its present market price and its near-term to long-term investment prospects. It is because of this intuitive aspect of their work that most analysts consider their business to be both a science and an art.

Regardless of what the rest of the world may think, analysts are looked upon as friends by companies. Management must go out of its way to cultivate relationships with them, to let them know who the company is, what the company is about, and all the great things that are happening in the company. What's more, it should be done on a continuing basis. Out of sight, out of mind.

The Haves and Have Nots

One problem is that analysts in the low-priced OTC market are a rare commodity. Small brokerage firms (fewer than 10 brokers), most likely don't have a designated analyst. Medium-size firms (up to 50 brokers) will possibly have someone who functions in the capacity of a combination analyst-syndicate manager. The larger firms (more than 50 brokers) can be counted on to have a full-time analyst.

Unfortunately, analysts in the larger firms tend to concentrate only on the firm's own underwritings and are usually not interested in small companies. Medium-size firms, which as a rule don't have a preponderance of underwritings, are often open to working on outside stocks, and small brokerage firms can't afford to do much at all.

What Analysts Look For

A few items for management to consider and a few suggestions that analysts, brokers, and individual investors should look for in an IPO are listed below. The company must present convincing evidence that it meets or will meet the following criteria:

- High and sustainable levels of earnings growth
- High levels of profitability
- Low levels of debt as a percentage of capital
- Solid and improving balance sheets
- Positive cash flow dynamics
- Reasonable market valuations and price-to-book value relationships
- Dominant positions in small but rapidly growing markets; unique products; aggressive strategies in large, highly fragmented markets
- Management teams that are competent, understandable, and predictable

Analysts also study the management team to answer the following questions:

- Who are the members of management, and what are their professional histories and track records?
- Are the business plans and the corporate strategy simple to manage, understand, and evaluate?
- How well does management articulate the business plan and strategy?
- To what extent does management show its confidence in the company by owning stock in it?

- What incentives for good management performance (and penalties for poor performance) does the company provide?
- Does management really accept its responsibility as a public company and treat shareholders as partners?
- Does management scrupulously avoid any conflicts of interest?

Do's And Don'ts

Here are some do's and don'ts for dealing with analysts.

- Use direct mail.
- Participate in local, regional, and national securities industry conferences.
- Make presentations to analysts' societies.
- Keep the investment community continuously informed.
- Keep management accessible.
- Don't be overly aggressive in corporate strategy.
- Don't overemphasize minor events.
- Don't be overly optimistic in communications.

Group Presentations

Not a great many analysts are involved with low-priced OTC stocks. Consequently, the OTC entrepreneur should make every effort to cultivate the few that are available.

Occasionally, management is presented with an opportunity to address analysts' societies or social gatherings. These can prove invaluable ways to get the company story to the right ears. Financial PR firms are usually aware of such meetings and can assist in securing an invitation.

If invited, management must decide whether the CEO and/or president should make the company presentation alone or whether to involve other top executives who possess special expertise. Audiovisual presentations should be considered or a slide presentation of not more than 15 minutes. Another acceptable form of presentation would be for the CEO to simply extemporize for the time allotted. After all, who knows the company better? It can also be a more intimate presentation.

A common mistake made at analysts' meetings is rehashing volumes of information that is commonly known or easily obtainable by reading existing materials. It can be far more profitable to spend the time telling analysts about future strategies and projections, both short-term and long-term, and give them a feel for the philosophy of the company.

Just for the prestige, analysts prefer to meet the CEO or CFO of a company. Successful OTC companies that have participated in similar meetings know that. They consider it to be part of the strategy in building and maintaining a friendly relationship with analysts.

The meetings with analysts should also be followed up by a mailing that includes a financial public relations packet about the company. If the contact seems worthwhile, the mailings should continue. In some quarters, the feeling is that analysts can't do much for the little guys. Well, a lot of the little guys are now big guys because they didn't follow that advice.

FREQUENTLY ASKED QUESTIONS

What happens if the stock goes up even after an overallotment?

Just what the company owners want. The market is really pretty simple. If there are more buyers than sellers, the stock price goes up. It's the best of the free-market system.

Who should establish and keep up the continuing relationships with market makers?

Original contact is usually established by the underwriter (who is also a market maker) and the initial market makers come from the retail selling syndicate supplemented by the wholesale market makers. After an IPO, the company should consider continuing contact a company responsibility. It's best to designate one individual as the market maker contact; that person is frequently the CFO or the CEO.

Should a company offer analysts an on-site visit?

You bet. Many analysts like to get out and "kick the tires." Others feel the personal contact may influence their opinions, but they won't be offended if you ask.

28

Continual Reporting

Continual reporting is the one thing that public company officers complain about most. According to the consensus, it's one of the disadvantages of going public.

Once a company achieves public operating status, it's required to file on a continuing basis a stream of never-ending reports to federal regulators (SEC) and shareholders. We'll examine the various reports that are required by the government and attempt to shed some light on how a public company can take advantage of these reports by making them reader friendly for shareholders.

The reports fall into two general areas—legal and public. They must be filed on a timely basis in formats that don't leave much room for self-expression. They are time consuming and expensive to produce. The legal side is burdensome: it deals with the requirements that must be complied with according to the rules and regulations of the SEC, the exchanges, and the markets. The legally required reporting starts immediately after going public and continues at an unrelenting pace forever after.

The optional public reporting leaves room to lighten up and personalize the process, which is especially true for annual reports and shareholders' letters. Keeping the investment community interested in a company is no easy task, and it's also expensive. It is not unusual for the typical small public company to spend as much as $100,000 annually for printing reports and financial public relations. Continuing legal and accounting expenses could easily double that. The annual accounting audit is vitally important and must be reviewed and kept current throughout the year.

Continuing legal advice should also be figured into the budget, as all required reports must definitely be reviewed by legal counsel. Projects such as acquisitions, mergers, and divestitures all call for legal expertise to meet SEC requirements. Even press and shareholder releases should go through legal counsel's review.

The whole complex matter of shareholder relations, with the preparation of quarterly and annual reports, is best handled by professional financial public relations people. They are familiar with the proper distribution techniques and have established financial press relationships. And they know who the PR reports should be sent to, such as market makers, individual stock brokers, analysts, prospective investors, newspapers, magazines, and broadcasters. Successful public companies have recognized that continual reporting is an opportunity to maintain and enhance the value of their stock.

It is management's decision, of course, whether to hire a PR firm on a retainer or strictly on a project basis to produce the quarterly reports to shareholders, the annual report, shareholders' letters, and other specific PR information. The first year's expense for printing and mailing alone could easily run in excess of $10,000. Good financial public relations may seem expensive, but it's an important adjunct to continuing reporting (see Chapter 12). Now, on to the reports that must be filed.

Form SR: Application of Proceeds

Federal rules require disclosing information about the expenses of the offering and the use of the proceeds on a continuing basis. Once the company has received its IPO money from the underwriter (less the underwriter's commission), the company must report to the SEC how much money it received and what the money is going to be used for. Form SR is required to be filed every six months for as long as the company is using the proceeds as stated in the prospectus. The designated period is usually 12 months, but it could extend for years.

For firm commitment offerings, Form SR must be filed within 10 days after the proceeds were applied, and every six months thereafter. For best efforts offerings, an initial filing of Form SR must be made to the SEC within 10 days after the first three-month period following the effective date of the registration statement.

Form SR is the SEC's way of making sure that the company is using the proceeds in the time period prescribed and for the purposes it said they would be used. For example, a company may have stated in the prospectus that among its use of proceeds, it intended to spend $1.5 million for marketing, $2 million for equipment, and $3 million for operating capital. If, instead, the company spent $750,000 on an office building without declaring that in the prospectus, the SEC would consider it a fraudulent use of the proceeds.

The form can be confusing and tricky, requiring some creative financial accounting and help from legal counsel and auditing accountants. There is no consideration in the form for any type of interest from money on deposit until it's spent, for income derived by the company, or for profits earned. The SEC doesn't allow for that in the form. Hence, six months down the road when the next Form SR is filed, the company will have to sort out information that will show that the application of proceeds was as stated in the prospectus— with no accounting for the income realized.

The entrepreneur should be pleased to learn, however, that Form SR is not a public disclosure form. It is filed only with the SEC and is not sent to the media or shareholders.

Form 8-K: Current Reports

Form 8-K is a report that a company must file when a significant event— internal or external—occurs that could materially affect decisions on buying, selling, or holding stock in a company. The report must be filed no later than 5 to 15 days (depending upon the event) after the event occurs. Timely disclosure rules may also require companies to issue a press release before disclosing the particulars that are reported on Form 8-K. Legal counsel plays an important role when reporting on Form 8-K, especially on the interpretation of "other materially important events." Events that are considered significant are explained below.

Changes in control of the company. This refers principally to changes among persons who control or own big blocks of the stock. For example, a principal of a company could leave the company and his or her stocks would change hands; or the controller of a large block of stock dies. The public must be advised there is a change in a big block of stock and in the company's management. The requirements are very specific regarding the financial aspects. (See discussion of Forms 3 and 4 and Schedule 13-D later in this chapter; Forms 3 and 4 concern officers and directors of corporations holding 10 percent or more of the stock; Schedule 13-D refers to anyone who acquires 5 percent or more of a company.)

Acquisition or disposition of assets. This applies to majority-owned subsidiaries if the asset value is greater than 10 percent of the company's assets.

Bankruptcy. Not surprisingly, this is considered a very significant event. In the event of bankruptcy, instructions are specific that Form 8-K is to be filed immediately after receivership appointment. All the pertinent facts must be noted, including the court involved, the date of the event, name of the receiver, and date of the appointment of the receiver. An amendment is also required confirming the plans for reorganization or arrangements for liquidation.

Change of audit accounting firm. This requirement is aimed at determining whether a change in the auditing firm is the result of a policy dispute between the auditor and the company management. Management, for example, may want the auditor to take an unethical depreciation on a piece of equipment. The auditor informs management that it would not be proper, and management fires the audit accounting firm. The departing auditor files a letter of comment, noting that the departure was not amicable.

This section could also contain an accounting or format change made by a new audit accounting firm.

Directors. Resignations or the election of a new director is not required to be included in an 8-K report. However, if a director resigns and specifically requests the company to disclose the resignation along with the reasons for it, the company is obligated to do so on Form 8-K. A copy of the resignation letter should be attached as an exhibit, and management can include a statement regarding the resignation if it wants.

Optional. This is a catchall for other materially important events. If management and the board want to report a situation of material importance, they must file by the tenth of the month following the occurrence of the event. The company can report the event or distribute 8-K reports detailing the event to its shareholders. Actually, it seems to be better just to inform the shareholders by a friendly letter or by issuing a press release rather than mailing out copies of the 8-K.

Forms 10-K and 10-KSB: Annual Report

Forms 10-K and 10-KSB, the latter for smaller companies, are the annual reports that must be filed with the SEC by corporations with more than

500 shareholders and assets over $2 million. They provide an overview of the company's business and must be completed and filed with the SEC within 90 days after the end of the company's fiscal year.

Form 10-K is comprehensive in its reporting requirements. Divided into 4 parts with 13 subheadings, Form 10-K calls for audited financial statements with associated footnotes and thorough coverage of the company's operations during the past year. For instance, if the company leased a building, an explanation must be given for leasing the building and a complete description of the building must be included. Management must also explain what happened, historically, during the year—for example, the company introduced two new product lines, started a new subsidiary, signed a licensing agreement in Europe, sold a plant in Chicago, increased the truck fleet, sold off a product line—anything and everything having to do with the company's operations, including sales and marketing.

This report requires the signatures of all the officers and members of the board of directors, so they should all have ample time to add their input and to review it carefully. The SEC attaches a great deal of importance to the 10-K report.

The SEC also encourages inclusion of business projections, which could present a problem. The 10-K may be included in the annual report that goes to shareholders. If a projection is not met, it could result in a complaint from an irate shareholder, who may even threaten to sue the company. Therefore, the SEC provides the company a "safe harbor," which allows projections to not always be fulfilled. The company can make them but is protected so long as it states that these are just projections and may never reach fruition. Many companies refuse to use projections because of the problems they can cause. If projections are to be used, all aspects should first be thoroughly discussed with legal counsel and audit accountants.

Because the 10-K becomes the basis of the annual report, it should be considered a very important document and handled as an important piece of investment communication.

Forms 10-Q and 10-QSB: Quarterly Report

The 10-Q and the 10-QSB (for smaller issuers) are quarterly reports required by the SEC that contain information similar to that which is in Form 10-K. The report must be filed for each of the first three fiscal quarters and is due within 45 days of the close of the quarter. The main purpose of the quarterlies is to reduce the number of surprises during a company's fiscal year reporting.

Like the 10-K, the quarterly report has specific guidelines, and it is in the company's best interest to secure help from legal counsel and audit accountants in its preparation. Although audited financial statements are not required, there are substantial financial disclosures that must be made. Part I of the 10-Q requires disclosure of the following information:

- Income statement, balance sheet, and a statement of sources and application of funds
- A text analysis by management of the quarterly income statement (particularly in reference to material changes)
- Information about capitalization (and changes)
- Information about shareholders' equity (and changes)

The following information, as applicable, must be disclosed in Part II:

- Legal proceedings involving the company
- Changes in securities (For example, another company may step into the picture to purchase part of the company and could be issued preferred stock, which would change the basic securities structure. Issuance of warrants would also constitute a change.)
- Changes in security for registered securities (For example, the company may have received a large contract and decided to buy back some of the stock. It must declare in this form that it has made an offer to repurchase some stock.)
- Default on senior securities
- Increase or decrease in the amount of outstanding securities or indebtedness
- Submission of matters to a vote of shareholders
- Other materially important events
- Particulars and summary of 8-Ks filed during the reporting quarter (As stated earlier, an 8-K is a current report that provides information on certain specified material events that could affect a decision to buy, sell, or hold stock in the company; it must be filed within 15 days of the event.)

The SEC does not require the second part of the 10-Q report to be presented to the public shareholders. But the company should think of the 10-Q quarterly report as a natural opportunity to communicate with the investing public and shareholders. The fact that it contains financial statements should make the recipients inclined to read the quarterly report more carefully than if it were just a shareholders letter. It would also be worth taking a salutary approach to the report by making it reader friendly rather than simply presenting the cold, hard facts. And since the data are gathered for the report, management should consider including it in a warm, personal shareholders letter.

The Annual Report

After the company becomes public, *the annual report is the single most important document the company produces.*

Because so many publications deal with annual reports in detail (check your local library), I'll touch only on points I think are worth remembering. The annual report is standard reading in areas not considered strictly financial, such as customer relations and supplier relations. It is widely recognized as the voice of management reporting on the health and promise of the company. Naturally, it is a vital communication link between management and shareholders. Therefore, management should discuss the report thoroughly with legal counsel, the auditing accountants, and the PR firm before starting.

There are two distinct parts to the annual report. The first is the corporate message—information about the goals of the company and management, which can take up to half the total pages. The second part usually deals with the financial picture.

Preliminary planning should include an evaluation of other annual reports in the industry. Management should have an idea of what it likes to see and what it doesn't like. The input from other sources, such as underwriters, brokers, and analysts should be solicited. A brainstorming session with the PR firm, designers, and printers can be most helpful in determining the overall theme, the style of type, the pictures, the illustrations, and the number of pages that will be needed. Management should be open to suggestions and ideas from these people. (Remember, they have a lot of experience in this area.) A budget and timetable should be determined and adhered to. A decision should be made on the information that will accompany charts and illustrations, and a distribution list needs to be compiled.

As to the contents—the company, the people, the products, the programs, and the prospects should be well defined. The chief executive's opinions on important issues, such as strength, growth, profitability, and the promise of the company, should be thoughtfully placed and highlighted.

The final product should also fit the company's image. Generally, small companies tend to go all out in publishing annuals, especially their first one. A full-blown, four-color major production may not be the answer—just as simply sending out photocopies of the company's 10-K is not the answer. The underlying purpose of the annual report is to favorably influence the financial marketplace. Everything in the report requires careful planning—and easy reading.

The Corporate Message

The president's report usually leads off the corporate message portion, which is probably the most widely read section of the annual as readers particularly like to hear it from the horse's mouth. It's the one opportunity for top management to communicate directly with all the owners (shareholders) of the company. It should be composed in a personal, reflective, and intimate style. Here is the president discussing the company's current and future operations.

Here are some key ideas to include:

- History: the company's story, implying in a positive way that the future will be significant and monetarily rewarding
- Strategy: describing how the company is being run today in accordance with long-term strategies
- Markets: indicating how the company is competing better
- Governance: explaining how the company is being run by the board of directors to assure survival, profits, and ethicality
- Future: specifying corporate goals for the next five years

A photograph or a portrait-style picture of the president would be most appropriate.

Design

If a picture is really worth a thousand words, good layout and design for an annual report are essential and should be eye-catching. A good design visually holds readers and leads them further into the contents. Consider color, art, photos, illustrations, charts, maps, size, and typography; select a good paper stock and cover stock. Headlines and captions are the first things read. In case the reader goes no farther, these should encapsulate the whole story management has to tell.

The art director, working with the financial PR firm's creative team, can usually be depended upon to come up with good ideas on art and photographs—

whether they should be stock photos or shot on location; whether to use black-and-white, color, or shaded halftones. Before proceeding, there should be a combined decision on the charts and graphs that best depict the company's operations. The SEC requires specific type sizes and type styles for some parts of the financials. Other than that, allow the creative people an opportunity to suggest underlines, boldfaces, and line spacing. Obviously, there is always a concern for paper cost, but good-quality paper for an annual report must have top priority.

As a general rule, small companies print three to four times as many copies as they have shareholders. This policy makes sure there are enough reports to cover the fringe areas—brokers, analysts, requests, and the media. To further assure that these additional copies get into the appropriate hands, it's important that the mailing list be kept up-to-date.

A salable annual report requires a great deal of effort and attention to detail by all concerned, including top management. It is important to start planning early—as much as three to four months ahead. But the results can be far-reaching and well worth the effort.

Proxies

Webster's defines proxy as "authority to act for another." In the case of a public company management, proxies are a request for shareholders to allow management to vote their shares.

Under state corporate laws and stock exchange rules, most matters that materially affect shareholder rights must be submitted to the shareholders for approval, which is done through a special shareholders meeting. The proxy statement informs shareholders about the nature of the meeting and identifies the management soliciting the proxies.

Typically, proxies account for a large majority of the votes cast at a shareholders meeting. Shareholders may withdraw or revoke their proxy at any time before a final tabulation of the vote. The proxy, then, is a power of attorney granted by a shareholder for the special purpose of authorizing another individual to vote his or her stock. In most cases, this solicitation concerns the company's annual meeting, which includes the election of the board of directors. For these situations, the proxy package must contain the company's annual report, including the audited financial statements, the names of the directors to be elected, information about them and the management team, and a disclosure of management remuneration.

At various times, the company will need to inform its shareholders of other important matters pertaining to the operations of the company—a major acquisition, divestitures, or stock splits for example—usually by notices in nonvoting situations. The information contained in a notice must be a description of the matter to be considered or voted on and any pertinent information relating to the matter.

According to SEC proxy rules, derived from section 14(a) of the 1934 act, all proposed proxy materials must be submitted to the SEC ten days before being sent to shareholders and thus allowing time for the SEC to review the submitted materials for misstatements and omissions. If the SEC has no comments within the ten days, the proxy materials can be distributed to shareholders. Proxy materials should not be mailed until this clearance is obtained.

Mailing

Getting proxy materials to shareholders is no easy matter. Since the late 1970s, there has been an increase in the complexity of the mailing process. First, there has been a large increase in the number of shares held in a "street name" (in the name of a brokerage firm on behalf of the owner). In 1975 shares held in a street name were a small percentage; today the estimate is over 55 percent of shares. Second, there's an increasing layer of stock ownership by brokerage firms holding certificates in a street name through a depository trust company (DTC)—a computerized go-between for securities transfers that charges and credits each member's account. Third, over this period there has been a general decline in the U.S. mail service, which, coupled with the fact that the traditional proxy period coincides with the mailing of tax returns and refunds, usually results in the system's being overburdened.

Fortunately, most companies have found a way to relieve themselves of the headache of getting proxies to shareholders. Today, the actual process of mailing, receiving, and tabulating proxies is most frequently handled by the company's transfer agent. Its personnel also attend the annual meeting and, with the help of the secretary of the company, supervise counting and tabulating votes on the issues.

FCPA: The Foreign Corrupt Practices Act

The Foreign Corrupt Practices Act (FCPA) is a major post-Watergate piece of legislation that is deceptively named, especially as it pertains to IPOs. The IPO management team should not ignore this act just because it appears on the surface to deal only with foreign operations. In reality, it relates to recordkeeping and applies to all public companies. Failure to comply with its provisions could lead to serious problems.

The FCPA has nothing to do with foreign activities or corrupt practices. It was originally passed by Congress in 1977 because investigations revealed that a certain amount of questionable payments, often illegal, were made by large U.S. corporations to foreign governments, suppliers, agents, and customers. Examples cited were improper political contributions, improper overseas payments, and the establishment and use of off-balance-sheet slush funds.

The FCPA was passed specifically to deal with companies in this country. Part of it prohibits payments of bribes by U.S. companies, their officers, directors, shareholders, or agents. Another part deals with two areas that affect a public company's internal controls and recordkeeping. First, the company must "make and keep books, records and accounts" that detail transactions and dispositions of its assets, a statutory accounting requirement in addition to SEC accounting controls. The company must keep detailed records that accurately show and fairly depict any financial transaction involving the company's assets. Second, the company must "devise and maintain a system of internal accounting controls." An accounting control system must be implemented that assures an accurate tracking of all assets and their disposition.

It is important for the company's auditors to review the present system and recommend changes, if necessary, to make sure that the company is complying with the act.

Form 3

Form 3 is a relatively simple report that is filed with the SEC before a company's public offering becomes effective. It requires any officer or director holding 10 percent or more of the company's stock to file a statement of ownership with the commission as must any other holder of 10 percent or more.

Briefly, the report lists the numbers and types of securities held, the dates purchased, and the method of payment, such as cash or exchange of services, stock, or assets. It describes all stock owned by the individuals of record, beneficially (by family members of the immediate household), or otherwise.

It is also necessary in the event of the election of new directors or the appointment of new officers that a Form 3 be prepared and filed with the SEC within ten days of the event detailing the stock ownership of the new directors or officers.

Form 4

Form 4 is the continuing equivalent of Form 3. Any officer, director, or holder of 10 percent or more of the company's stock must file with the SEC if any change occurs in the securities owned. Any purchase or sale of the company's stock must be reported on Form 4, including the number of shares, the price, the resulting total ownership, and any other significant, related transactions. It applies to all classifications of stock—common, preferred, convertible holdings, rights, options, or warrants—and the conditions under which they were received or purchased. As with Form 3, the report must be filed within ten days after the end of the month in which the change occurred.

Insider Reporting and Trading Restrictions

An insider is anyone who obtains financial information about a company before the public can obtain it. Using that information specifically to buy or sell securities is considered a form of collusion or fraud by the SEC. Under SEC Rule 10b-5, insiders are those who come into possession of undisclosed material information in the course of their business activities and those who are "tippees" (persons or groups who receive such information from an insider or a third party), including officers, directors, employees, consultants, retained counsel, accountants, underwriters, broker-dealers, analysts, investment advisers, and those who are informed directly or indirectly by any of these people. Within the purview of Rule 10b-5, they are all insiders.

The Insider Trading Sanction Act of 1984 granted the SEC authority to obtain civil penalties up to three times the amount of profits gained or losses avoided. Liability extends to reporting persons, insiders, and tippees who trade on material nonpublic information.

Naturally, the whole area of insider trading is looked upon with great concern by the SEC. And because it is a complicated and constantly changing issue, it is imperative that management seek legal counsel any time any management team member, director, adviser, or employee wishes to buy or sell stock in the company.

Don't take chances. The SEC has made it very clear that it considers the elements necessary to establish liability for insider trading to be (1) that the information in question is material and nonpublic; (2) that the tippee who receives the information directly or indirectly knows or has reason to know that it was nonpublic and has been obtained improperly by selective revelation or otherwise; and (3) that the information be a factor in the decision to effect the transaction (in the securities of the company involved).

Under Rule 10b-5, liability could be found even in cases in which some-one innocently comes into possession of, and uses, information that he or she has reason to believe is intended to be confidential. Such persons can be held liable if, based on such information, they effect a transaction in the securities involved.

Short Selling

Section 16 of the Securities Exchange Act of 1934 deals with "short-swing" profits and applies to any "quick" profits on the company's securities that are realized during any six-month period, whether it's as a result of buy-ing long or selling short. Insiders who profit on those transactions are re-quired to turn over their profits to the company without any offset of losses that might occur. The company can sue the insider, as can any shareholder, on behalf of the company to recover the profits for the company.

The 1934 act also prohibits reporting persons (those filing Forms 3 and 4) as well as insiders from selling shares of stock they don't own—otherwise known as "short selling." "Sales against the box," which is selling "owned" shares but not delivering them within 20 days after the sale, are also prohib-ited under the 1934 Act.

It is very important for the CEO of an OTC-traded company to estab-lish strong controls to protect the confidentiality of inside information. One help would be to coordinate through a single source all press information, news releases, and contacts with brokers, analysts, and shareholders. Fur-thermore, all persons privy to inside information must be made aware of the need for confidentiality and the serious consequences that can come from trading on or tipping that information.

Schedules

Because of the nature of the Schedule 13s, the reports must be filed with the SEC and with the stock exchanges on which the company's stock is traded or, in the case of OTC-traded companies, with the NASD and the Nasdaq. The company must also keep complete files on these reports.

Schedule 13-G

This schedule discloses the names of each person or group that owns 5 percent or more of the company's stock. Within 45 days of the end of each calendar year, each must file a Schedule 13-G with the SEC. It is a relatively simple form, requiring information concerning share ownership with no intention on the part of the owner of changing or influencing the issuer's control.

Schedule 13-D

This is considered the takeover alert filing. Any shareholder or group of shareholders acting individually or together with the intention of making a tender offer, friendly or unfriendly, must file a Schedule 13-D. The schedule requires the following information:

- Identity of the buyer or buyers
- Number of shares owned or controlled by buyer(s)
- Dates of purchase
- Source and amounts of funds used to acquire shares
- The reason for the purchase

The number that warns of a possible takeover is 5 percent or more of the company's shares. If an individual or a group, for example, owns 4 percent of a company's stock and that position is increased to 5 percent or more, SEC regulations stipulate that the holder must file an amended Schedule 13-D, usually a clear signal that a takeover will be attempted. There are people in Washington, D.C., whose sole job for their company is to read all the Schedule 13-Ds that are filed to find out if takeovers will be friendly or unfriendly.

Schedule 13-E-3

This filing schedule is used by a company if management intends to take the company private or if it intends to reduce the number of shareholders to such a point that the company is no longer required to file periodic reports with the SEC.

Schedule 13-E-4

This filing schedule (called an Issuer Tender Offer Statement) is used by companies with securities registered under Section 12 of the 1934 act if they are making a tender offer for their own securities.

Other Forms and Schedules

The following forms and schedules are listed here simply because they will be required from time to time, and management should be aware of them:

Form 8-A. This form is used to register securities under the 1934 act. It must be filed immediately on completion of a public offering, usually in conjunction with an S-18 that calls for registration of securities not to exceed an aggregate offering price of $7.5 million. The form is occasionally used as an optional version of Form 10 under an S-1 filing (which is the basic registration form that can be used to register securities for which no other form is authorized or prescribed). Form 8-A is fast becoming obsolete, but it is noted here because the government has not yet eliminated it.

Form 10. This form is used to register securities with the SEC after a public offering is in effect. On filing it, the company becomes fully reporting, and all the information needed to complete it can be found in the offering prospectus. It calls for the following items as disclosures:

- Description of the business
- Financial information
- Description of properties
- Securities ownership of officers and directors
- Names of officers and directors
- Executive compensation
- Certain relationships and related transactions
- Legal proceedings
- Dividend information
- Recent sales of unregistered securities
- Description of securities to be registered
- Existing indemnification of officers and directors
- Financial statements and supplemental data
- Difference of opinion with accountants

Form 10-C. This form is used only by companies whose securities are quoted on the Nasdaq. It is used for reporting changes in the number of shares outstanding when the change exceeds 5 percent and is also used to report an issuer's name change.

Schedule 14-B. This form is used in the event of a proxy contest over the election or removal of a company director. Any person who instigates, or is a participant in, this type of contest is required to file a Schedule 14-B.

Schedule 14-D-1. This form is commonly used in takeover attempts by any person, other than the issuer, who is making a tender offer to purchase securities that would amount to over 5 percent of the company's ownership. It must be filed at the time of the offer.

Form 15. This form is used to officially notify the SEC of the suspension of the responsibility to make periodic filing reports, or it is filed by the company as notice of termination of a registration statement.

Form 20-F. This form is used only when there is a foreign company involvement.

This chapter does not cover all the forms and schedules and there will, no doubt, soon be more forms to file—as soon as the SEC can think of a reason for them.

FREQUENTLY ASKED QUESTIONS

Who normally keeps track of all these filings?

The company's securities counsel usually supplies top management with a list of what forms need to be filed and when. But bottom line, it's the company's responsibility.

Do the accountants become involved?

Both the legal and accounting departments play major roles in compiling many of the reports. Unless a company is large enough to have qualified in-house legal and accounting personnel, it's advisable to rely on outside help with all reporting.

What if someone forgets to file?

The SEC will let the company know. It usually grants a small grace period, but the fines could be substantial if total neglect is found.

Can directors be held liable for not filing?

Under most corporate charters, directors are shielded from this type of liability unless they are also executive officers, but directors are responsible for filing the forms related to their own stock purchases and sales as well as other insider trading reports.

29

SEC Rule 144

Rule 144 sets forth the criteria for the sale of restricted stock without registration. When a registration statement is filed for an initial public offering, the stocks that are sent out to new shareholders are newly issued shares of the company and are considered unrestricted or free-trading.

There are also existing stocks that are held by the officers, directors, and other inside shareholders, which were probably purchased in a private offering before the registration statement, and they are called "restricted," or "lettered" stock. These are stocks that have not been registered with the SEC and cannot be sold or freely traded in the new public market for a designated period of time. Some provisions, however, of SEC Rule 144 allow "leakage" (selling) of these securities.

One-Year Period and Two-Year Period

Generally speaking, the designated holding period on restricted securities is one year from the date they were purchased (a change from the long-standing two-year-long holding period that went into effect April 29, 1997). After one year, the shareholders who purchased the stock can proceed with filing Form 144, which allows them to sell (in any three-month period) formerly restricted securities. They may not, however, sell more than 1 percent of the total amount of shares outstanding of that particular class of stock during the three-month period. Or if they choose, they may sell up to 1 percent of the reported weekly trading volume on an exchange or the Nasdaq market during the four calendar weeks preceding their filing of Form 144. The most widely used approach is the 144 sales form based on the three-month period observed by the OTC as opposed to the weekly trading volume on the Nasdaq because it's too difficult and complicated to track the weekly volume. If the securities filed for sale under Rule 144 are not sold within the three-month period, an extension can be filed for an additional 30 days.

Restricted stock usually carries a legend, customarily stamped on the front or back of the certificate, that notes they are restricted securities:

> The shares represented by this certificate have not been registered under the Securities Act of 1933 ("the Act") and are "restricted securities" as that term is defined in rule 144 under the Act. The shares may not be offered for sale, sold or otherwise transferred except pursuant to an effective registration statement under the Act, or pursuant to an exemption from registration under the Act, the availability of which is to be established to the satisfaction of the company.

In addition to the legend noted on the stock certificate, the company's transfer agent, which keeps track of all stock certificates and sales of that particular stock, is automatically issued a "stop" on all restricted securities and will not initiate a transfer without first receiving notification that the transfer has been cleared by the company.

Two-year period. After a two-year holding period, a noncontrolling, or nonaffiliated, shareholder, who probably bought the stock in a private placement, becomes free of almost all the restrictions of sale. The paperwork amounts to just one simple letter (144-K), which prevents the company from blocking the sale.

144 (K) Letter

This letter refers to the "stop" and is actually a notification that comes in the form of a letter from the company's legal counsel telling the transfer agent that the company has assumed the responsibility and that the intended transfer conforms with SEC Rule 144 regulations.

The reason for the letter is that the SEC allows the sale of restricted stock only if adequate current information on the company is available to the public—mainly that the company is current in its filing of all 10-Qs, 10-Ks, and 8-Ks—which must be attested to by both the company and the restricted selling shareholders.

Affiliates

Broadly interpreted, an affiliate is a person who directly or indirectly through one or more intermediaries controls a block of the company's stock. Mr. Smith, for example, who is not part of the company in any way but who knows a director of the company, made a private purchase of a block of the company's stock before the company entertained the idea of going public. Now that the company's stock is publicly traded, Mr. Smith is still deemed an affiliate because he owns a block of the stock even though he has nothing to do with the company's operations. Should he purchase additional shares in the open market, the certificates will not be imprinted with the standard restrictive legend. Technically, though, Mr. Smith is considered an affiliate, which makes him a "control" person, so he can't freely trade his stock. He must therefore file special forms (Forms 3 and 4) to comply with Rule 144 if he wishes to sell his stock.

An affiliate can also be (1) any relative (child, cousin, aunt, uncle, and so forth) or spouse of the person who controls a block of the stock, any relative of the spouse (in-laws), or a person who lives in the same home of any of the above; (2) any trust in which the person owns 10 percent or more of the stock or serves as a trustee, executor, or in a similar capacity; and (3) any corporation or organization in which the person is the beneficial owner of 10 percent or more.

Other Considerations

Form 144 restricted stock can be sold only via a "broker transaction"—through a broker-dealer. The seller (who owns the stock) is prohibited from arranging for a buyer for his or her stock or from making any kind of arrangements between the potential buyer of the stock and the broker. The broker must do that independently. What's more, no payments are allowed except for normal broker commissions with exemptions for estates and nonaffiliates.

Although the selling shareholder is responsible for informing the broker at the first contact that the transaction is a 144 affiliate or nonaffiliate stock sale, brokers and their firms are still somewhat at risk in 144 transactions. They must justify their actions by keeping complete files and copies of all the documentation that goes with the Rule 144 transaction.

Many entrepreneurs have resigned themselves to looking upon their 144-restricted sales as a necessary break in the action before proceeding again because a certain amount of caution is required on the part of the sellers. Insiders, especially officers and directors, must consider the impact of timing on the sale of their 144 stock. Any insider buys or sells must be reported to the SEC, from which there seems to be a direct line to the financial press. The Street (Wall Street brokers) doesn't like to see management "bailing out," as they affectionately call it, even if the management team has spent four to five years building a successful and profitable company and justifiably believes it has a right to cash in on hard-earned gains.

It's legal to sell. The rules are there. Management knows it can't sell more than 1 percent of the market. Unfortunately, 144 sales are usually regarded suspiciously. Before insiders make their move, they must be cognizant of the trading volume. They don't want to sell in a down market as that could further depress the stock's price. Because, generally, the number of shares held by the public (public float) is thin (small in numbers compared to the total outstanding) on OTC stocks and the moves of management are public knowledge, management must be aware of the public mood at the time and take care that its trades don't jar the market or the price. An influx of management 144 sales could seriously impact the bid or selling price of the company's stock. To keep or not to keep, that is the dilemma.

FREQUENTLY ASKED QUESTIONS

Do these rules mean that anyone can sell 144-restricted stock after one year?

Yes, but as with lots of things there may be some restrictions. As an example; if you are an officer or a significant shareholder (i.e., 5 percent or more of a new IPO issue), your stock may have underwriter restrictions—that is, an underwriter can ask that a shareholder like you further agrees not to sell for a certain period after an IPO. Eighteen months is common.

Can I borrow money using restricted stocks as collateral?

Sure, if your bank or other lending institution will accept it as collateral. Many banks do but most discount the value considerably, as much as 50 to 60 percent.

Are the legal fees connected with securing a 144 (K) letter expensive?

Not really. Many companies will pay the cost as the letter is a pretty routine document. At most, the time charge should not be for more than an hour.

30

The Financial Press

Every day, every week, every month of the year, financial publications across the country pour out stories about the goings on in the financial world. Millions of facts, figures, and interesting bits of information about companies, mergers, tender offers, and stock prices, even local, national, and international news items with a financial slant are funneled through these publications. Those stories don't just appear out of the blue; somebody produces them. That somebody is usually a company's financial public relations person or firm, also referred to as investor relations.

To fully understand the relationship between financial public relations and the press, one must understand that it is literally impossible for today's financial press to accumulate all those pages of information by itself. The human factor as well as the cost to go around and dig up stories would be prohibitive. Much of the news that appears in financial publications is "fed" news—fed by financial public relations firms and by the companies who make the news.

Astute editors of financial publications welcome and rely on fed information to fill their pages. It is the most direct way they have of obtaining reports on items of interest to their readers. Of course, they have their own staffs of reporters, and they do check on the authenticity of a release, but they would be much less effective without the input from financial PR firms. This doesn't mean that financial publications will accept articles of no particular significance. Any story or release should be newsworthy and of interest to the publication's readers, and it should be simply presented. Editors recognize a printable item when they see one. Professional PR people know it is an insult to an editor's professional intelligence to send "tout pieces" or trivial releases.

Financial public relations, especially in the area of press relations, is an intangible commodity. It is often difficult to measure its effect, success, or failure. Because of this, many public company executives are tempted to handle their own public relations. That's a mistake! It takes a professional to do a professional job. Entrepreneurs should ask themselves, Am I a qualified expert in financial public relations? Do I really know the procedures? How well connected am I with the financial press? (See Chapter 12.)

When hiring a financial public relations firm, companies should choose one that has an intimate knowledge of, and a good working relationship with, the financial press. Financial publications are forever faced with tight deadlines. Their reporters, writers, and editors appreciate those who respect and understand how they work and the standards they must meet. Financial PR people must also be prepared to verify their sources to the press—to confirm the facts, figures, and content that create the news stories they are responsible for and to provide backup to the stories.

Another significant area of financial PR that companies should seriously consider is buying advertising space in the sections of the press generally titled "Corporate Reports." Almost all the OTC financial publications provide such sections, and they are also found in publications such as *Inc., Barron's, The Wall Street Journal, Fortune,* and others. These are sections where the company can place an ad to advertise itself. The ad could be in the form of a specific favorable report taken from its annual report. Or the company can use the space for a press release, a shareholders report, or a particular important corporate event, such as obtaining major financing or a valuable contract.

Having a good relationship with the financial press can pay off with big dividends. Listed below are some guidelines on dealing with business and financial editors.

- Be impartial—give the news to everyone at the same time.
- Don't pass an old story off as new.
- Don't ask to see a story before it is run.
- Don't expect to be notified if your story is used.
- Don't expect your story to be run as submitted—that's why editors were born.
- Don't be too commercial; if possible, mention your company name only once.
- Don't make exaggerated claims.

- Don't call it news if you ran it as an ad.
- Don't call a news conference if mail will do.
- Don't sit on a story; news is perishable.
- Write for the reader.

When dealing with the financial press, deal directly, honestly, and openly, and you will usually find that you will be treated fairly during good times as well as bad. Finally, it's worth mentioning again that every publication has a closing date. If, for whatever reason, the company doesn't get the release or ad in to the publication on time, it's sayonara.

FREQUENTLY ASKED QUESTIONS

What is the difference between financial PR and advertising?

Generally, advertising is paid for while PR is free unless, of course, you figure the cost of retaining a PR firm to help put together the PR releases.

Do I have to have a financial investor relations firm?

No, but this is a task that must have attention. If handled in-house, you'll need to maintain databases of individuals to contact as potential publishers of your press releases. This in itself can be a daunting task as the publishing industry is well known for frequent job shifts. There are a lot of other details involved with properly handling company financial PR and it's generally considered best to farm out this task for best results.

31

Shells and Pools

The best general definition for a *public shell* is an inactive public company. The best general definition for a *blind pool* is an artificial shell. The act of combining a privately held company with a shell, or pool, is called a *reverse merger.* These are backdoor ways of going public as the entities are, for all intents and purposes, nonoperating public companies. They also come with an existing shareholder base ranging from a few dozen to thousands of individuals.

Shells and blind pools are two other alternatives entrepreneurs can consider in their quest for a public company. They may very well save taking lots of aspirin for the headaches encountered in going through an IPO. They may also end up giving more headaches than one would receive from going through the regular process.

Public Shells

A public shell is a corporation that has marketable and tradable shares of its stock registered with the SEC and held by the general public. More than likely, it is not currently engaged in any active business operations, and its stock may or may not be currently trading. In addition, it may or may not be current in the required filings with the regulatory agencies, especially the SEC.

Shells are appealing for many reasons. One is the time and money saved from going through the tedious and costly process of taking a company public. Also, some companies are not glamorous enough to generate public acceptance if they go public, but the owners believe it would be to their advantage to become a public company. The reasons include making publicly held stock available for their employees or establishing a way to transfer ownership for an entrepreneur who wishes to retire. The easiest way for the owners to accomplish these goals is to acquire a shell company—a company that was once a public company but is no longer active—and merge their private company into the shell, thus automatically creating a public company.

There is an essential difference between going public via an IPO and going public with a shell. Characteristically, in an IPO the public pays a premium for participating in ownership, diluting its investment and increasing the net worth per share of the controlling shareholders. In the case of a shell with little or no assets, the original shareholders receive an increase in their per share net worth because the shares of the shell have little or no value.

If there are assets, there may also be offsetting liabilities, such as a mortgage against an office building. Or there may be debts that have accrued against the shell, maybe from lawyers or accountants, maybe rents, equipment rentals, or loans that haven't been paid. Very likely, there will be liabilities and no, or minimal, assets. These are the things that must be looked into when purchasing a public shell; and they're possible because public shells used to be operating, publicly traded companies. Many were probably started during some hot-market period by well-intended entrepreneurs with high hopes of heading a successful company.

Most shells are former IPOs that raised money, sometimes millions of dollars. The companies floundered and in some cases management disbanded operations, salvaging what it could by selling off assets and properties for cash. In other cases the companies kept operating until there was no cash left and management left, too. They also incurred debt that might still remain on the books.

The most desirable shells are those with few or no assets, minimal or no liabilities, and little or no negative net worth with a controlling shareholder base of only a few people. These people may have been the original founders who have gone on to other endeavors, hoping that one day someone would come along and offer them, if not a profitable buyout for their controlling stock, at least a face-saving solution for all investors.

More often than not, a shell is formed when a publicly traded company fails and the executives who operated it don't dissolve it. In any case, the major problem with all shells is past liabilities. Although those liabilities may still be on the record, in most cases they can be settled. The big question comes from potential ghosts in the closet: disgruntled shareholders who lie low until new management comes along with cash in the bank and then file suit for the old management's sins. It is extremely difficult to protect against this kind of action. The best hope is that investors can be convinced that the new company has great potential to make back the money invested plus more and leave well enough alone.

History

Shells have been around for as long as the public market has existed and have weathered good and bad reputations. In the late 1950s, the SEC prosecuted two notorious shell hustlers named Alexander Guterman and Lowell Burrell. According to reports, these two used shells to fleece investors and loot numerous companies. They manipulated stocks by spreading phony rumors to create grossly overvalued market prices and then unloaded their unregistered stock into the U.S. and foreign marketplace.

The same kind of operators are still around, but the SEC continues a careful surveillance, and the abuses are fewer. Today, going public via a shell is recognized as a very legitimate approach. In fact, many shareholders of public companies have no idea that their company was once a shell. There are many honest and dependable shell brokers who have been very helpful in bringing buyer and seller together. Even so, caution is advised.

Clean Shells

Some shells start out as clean shells. They are brand-new—the work mainly of attorneys, accountants, and other business people. A small interstate public company is formed with a few thousand dollars invested in an interest-bearing account. The shell has only a handful of shareholders, who hold on to their stock to "mature" it. The company doesn't have any operations, but just exists as a shell. The owners hold it for at least one year to comply with SEC Rule 144, which stipulates that restricted securities can't be sold before one year from the date they were purchased. At the end of the one year, the owners simply sell control to the new managers, who put their operating company into the shell. The original shareholders profit by selling the stock. They sell enough of it to the new management so that it can have control, but they hold the rest of the stock to sell into the market when the stock starts trading with new investor interest. If the company is successful, the promoters stand to reap a harvest. The advantage of this type of shell is that because it doesn't have any operations, the liability risk is negligible. The disadvantage is that the company lacks full registration, doesn't have any market makers, and has a very small shareholder base.

Advantages and Disadvantages of Shells

Every shell has its advantages and disadvantages. There's no perfect shell, but if it's workable, it fits. The entrepreneur should look into the shell carefully and ask a lot of questions. For example, how financially clean is the shell? What are its assets? If there's cash in the shell, it may become more attractive. The company may need the money to cover the cost of completing the final reports to get the company operating. The company, then, will "buy" the money but will probably have to pay a steep price for it—instead of getting 90 percent control of the company, the entrepreneur may have to settle for 70 percent control. Depending on the potential price of the stock, that could be an expensive exchange. Also, if there are tangible net assets, do they justify the increased cost of obtaining the shell? On the question of liabilities, the entrepreneur would want to know if the creditors would be willing to discount the debt or settle for stock. Net liabilities or technical bankruptcy don't make a shell unusable.

A shell that is in favor is one that has been around for long enough that the statutes of limitations have run out, thus limiting past liabilities. However, this type of shell can present other problems. Most dormant companies became delinquent in filing reports before they actually ceased doing business. Consequently, all missing reports, quarterly and annual, will have to be updated before they're relisted for trading. The reconstruction of these reports can be expensive and time consuming and in some cases will make the shell completely unacceptable.

Some shells are not fully reporting because they were filed under Reg A or an intrastate filing so that they didn't have to file quarterly, only annual, reports. A fully reporting company must file quarterly reports as well as an annual report. If the shell was not fully reporting, purchasing it may not be such a good move as the refiling process could be almost as extensive and costly as doing an IPO.

Control

The control of the shell must also be weighed carefully. Rather than buy the shell, a company may arrange to merge with it. The question is how to work out the postmerger percentage of control. Here's where the public float (shares held by the public) comes into play. Let's say that 60 percent of the company was restricted stock held by the original owners of the shell. The public float amounts to 30 percent as a result of the IPO. Private financing owns the 10 percent balance and the original owners can't decide whether to sell the new company 90 percent of their 60 percent or just 30 or 40 percent of it. They decide instead to issue more shares, which dilute the percentage of the public float and give them and the new company the lion's share of the outstanding stock. Now the public stock may be down to 5 to 10 percent of the total outstanding shares, which is too small a public float as far as brokerage firms are concerned because the inside shareholders have too much control. Should the inside shareholders decide to trade their stock one year later, when they can sell their 144 stock, the stock price could be driven down.

The actual percentage of control is the obvious number that the new management is concerned about. It will ultimately want majority control of the outstanding shares. Because many shells are acquired in multiple stages, a second acquisition could be conducted shortly after the first with additional shares issued to the principals, thereby giving them control. There are many ways to obtain and then retain control, including the issuance of different classes of common or preferred stock. These should be discussed with securities counsel and accountants to be sure that all areas involving the total shares publicly or privately held and the new management's holdings are covered. Many of these problems can be avoided by simply starting out in full control of the shell.

More Questions to Ask

Any entrepreneur considering a shell acquisition should answer the following additional questions:

- What was the company's product or service? Could use of the product result in liability lawsuits?
- What was the stock's trading history? Did it have wild price fluctuations that may have created disgruntled shareholders?
- What is the status of the founding second-round shareholders? Are they willing to sell out their original shares at a reasonable price or, at minimum, will they be cooperative in the timing of selling their shares back into the market?
- Were there any second-round or third-round original investors that need attention now to prevent future problems?
- Did the original company do any desperation, late-round financings that could carry forward added liabilities? (Late-round financings can take the form of preferred stock or subordinated debt.)

- Are there any outstanding options, rights offerings, or warrants? Are there any underwriter's warrants outstanding? (These usually extend for four or five years after the original effective date of an underwriting.)

An ideal shell could also be a currently operating company whose management wants to take it private. This is usually a no-asset, no-liability, currently reporting, very clean situation. If the shell in question is currently trading, questions to ask are as follows:

- Who are the market makers, and how many are there?
- What is the current stock price, and what was the last year's or last active trading period's history?
- Is there a current list of the brokers that maintain positions in the stock?
- What is the current status of all required SEC reports, including 10-Ks, 10-Qs, and 8-Ks?
- What is the status of state and local reports?

There are no questions here about carrying forward a tax loss because the government canceled that option in 1986. At best, only a small fraction is retainable.

Shareholders

Having a large number of shareholders on the books of a shell is a definite advantage as opposed to just a few, which there are in new shells. The popular consensus is that 300 to 1,000 is an ideal number of shareholders by showing a large enough base out there to get the market makers interested in trading the stock. Fewer than 300 may not indicate a sufficient public float. But more than 1,000 can create an excessive expense for a new company of contacting shareholders. All those shareholders must be communicated with when trading is reactivated: that comes to a lot of letters and reports to be sent out.

Compiling all the names of shareholders can also be a problem. A lot of stock today is held in street name through brokerage firms, which makes it difficult to get a firm handle on the number of shareholders and requiring direct contact with brokerage firms to determine the actual figure. Also, dormant companies usually have outdated lists, making it even more difficult to reestablish contact. But it is important to get to these shareholders.

Most reactivated shells have a base of shareholders who purchased the stock at substantially higher prices than the reactivated trading price. Consequently, they rarely sell out immediately. Instead, they wait until the stock has, at minimum, regained its purchase price. This is a great opportunity for management not only to keep these existing shareholders but to encourage them to make additional purchases and become faithful to their born-again company. The fact that the existing shareholders now own stock at higher prices could create new buying that may move a stock price up dramatically.

Finding a Shell

The OTC market and the National Association of Securities Dealers Pink Sheets are good places to start the hunt. Hunters look for stocks quoted at pennies, often with no bid, and with only one or two market makers. But these factors can also be misleading. It's possible that the company in question is just marginally profitable with thin market trading, and management has more interest in perpetuating salaries than producing shareholder returns.

A more fruitful method may be to watch ads in the financial press, contact broker-dealers, or make a direct contact with a shell broker. Most broker-dealers don't get involved in the purchase of shells directly, but they will refer inquiries to finders.

Finders, or shell brokers, make it their business to seek out shells or distressed companies that most likely will become shells. Their fees are negotiated and often include retention of stock. They can give a prospective purchaser a feel for current market pricing. Many shells are controlled by individuals who may or may not have a realistic value established for the worth of their holdings, and then the purchase price becomes a major bargaining point.

There is no set off-the-shelf price list for shells. Prices can range from $20,000 to $100,000 and up. Many variables come into play, including the amount of control, cleanliness of the shell, net assets, board control, number of shareholders, and reporting status.

Acquiring a Shell

There's more to acquiring a shell than meets the eye. A number of steps must be taken as seen in the following four:

1. The new management team purchases control of the shell by buying stock from the existing controlling shareholders.
2. They then set up a new, wholly owned subsidiary of the parent company, whose only asset is the parent company's stock.
3. The subsidiary acquires the private company in exchange for the parent company stock, thus increasing control by the new management group.

4. Because the parent company owns 100 percent of the subsidiary, it then votes an upstream merger with the subsidiary (takeover).

The result is that the parent company has merged with the private company without going to the shareholders for approval. At this point an information statement should be sent to shareholders, and ratification of the action is usually put on the agenda at the next shareholders meeting.

Although this has been a simplified approach to shell acquisitions, it wouldn't be wise to attempt acquiring a shell without the help of qualified legal counsel. One reason why Rule 144 came into existence was the abuses that occurred in shell combinations. Be aware that the SEC has tightened its requirements for proxies and other filings concerned with shells.

A point of interest about shells: they seem to run in cycles. When the number of IPOs go down, interest picks up in shells.

Spin-Off Shells

Spin-off shells are a fascinating animal. They have had an interesting history with the SEC, sometimes negative and at other times of little concern. Spin-offs occur when an existing publicly held company forms a new subsidiary and then grants or gifts stock in the subsidiary to its existing shareholders. The result is a new public company formed without the need for registration.

Sometimes a spin-off is formed by accident, such as when a subsidiary is formed to engage in a new enterprise that just doesn't work out or whose assets are sold to a different company with an empty subsidiary the result. In some cases the management of some publicly controlled companies form subsidiaries with the intention to sell them off as reverse merger candidates, generally specially constructed to be viable public shells.

In either case, spin-offs should be considered a possibility if the entrepreneur is seeking a shell. But, foremost, the entrepreneur is advised to deal with a reputable shell seller or broker and sincerely urged to bring in legal counsel to assist with the transaction. Both the SEC and state regulatory agencies have special rules dealing with shell transactions.

Blind Pools

Blind pools are similar to shells—only different. They have, at times, been considered the first phase of a shell. They are offerings in which participation money is raised, but the investors or company is not identified. Investors depend on the expertise and integrity of the blind pool founders to make the investment pay off.

Blind pools were first conceived in the oil and gas industry. As the story goes, a group of successful oil men wanted to prospect for oil but realized it would take more money than their finances would allow, so they approached investors to invest in them blindly without their even knowing themselves where they would drill or how they would spend the money. It was called a blind pool.

Blind pools have also been referred to as blank check companies and artificial shells. Many have been used as a means of bringing needed financing into existing operating companies that often turn to blind pools because underwriters didn't feel the companies presented a glamorous enough image and, therefore, didn't show interest in an underwriting. In essence, they are publicly traded, often not fully registered, shells with cash. Their corporate charters are written in broad language to allow the companies to engage in all lawful activities. Investors put their money into these companies, often without knowing who runs them or what they're going to do with the money.

Abuses

In the early 1980s, a lot of fast-buck operators abused the system, creating blind pool companies that violated securities regulations. These abuses included

- using undisclosed principals, major shareholders, and investors;
- setting up prearranged mergers;
- insufficiently disclosing conflicts of interest;
- issuing cheap stock to promoters;
- paying unjustified salaries to founders;
- giving bonuses to finders; and
- misusing proceeds.

As a result of abuses, the SEC stepped up surveillance of broker-dealers with attention to market manipulation, churning of customer accounts, investor suitability, trading spreads, and financial disclosure. The SEC along with many states also instigated new regulations, which, among other things, required all blind pools to escrow a large percentage of their proceeds until an acquisition was identified after which all shareholders were allowed to vote on the proposed acquisition.

Unit Offerings

As promoters became more sophisticated in assembling blind pools, they recognized they had to raise the ante, so they began to offer acquired companies more than just the money left after identifying a prospective merger candidate. They adopted the practice of offering blind pools as *unit offerings*. The blind pool stock is sold in units of common stock and warrants. As an example, a unit is priced at $1.00 and consists of one share of common stock and two warrants—an A warrant exercisable at $1.50 and a B warrant exercisable at $2.00. Most times, the warrants are "qualified." The A warrant is good for one year, and the B warrant is good for two years.

The concept behind the unit offerings is that if the company is successful, the price of its stock will increase and consequently the investors will exercise their warrants. Furthering our example, the initial offering would yield gross proceeds of $1 million, assuming the offering was for 1 million shares (units) at $1.00. A year later, if the company is successful and its stock is trading at $1.80 to $2.00 per share, the shareholders would exercise their warrants, bringing $1.5 million into the company (1 million A warrants at $1.50 each). The second year the process would be repeated with the B warrants, bringing in $2 million (1 million B warrants at $2.00). Thus, one blind pool underwriting could easily total $4.5 million in proceeds to the company over the two years.

Many variations to this approach have been put together, with some unit offerings having as many as four or five warrants.

Exercising Warrants

In theory, the concept of warrants being attached to a blind pool is a good idea. In practice, it has presented many problems. For instance, the original units are often issued in one of two ways. One is as an attached unit, in which the warrant stays attached to the common stock. The other offers a detachable warrant, in which the warrant is separated from the stock and trades by itself. The bookkeeping, or tracking, of the detached warrant holders can be a transfer agent's nightmare and very costly to the company.

In either instance, attached or detached, the responsibility to get the warrant exercised is the company's. Some companies prefer to contact warrant holders directly to remind them it's time to exercise their warrants. Others prefer that the lead underwriter handle the chore. Either way takes a lot of effort and precise tracking to obtain successful results.

What makes the task seem so thankless is that most original investors in blind pool units view the investment strictly as a gamble. Consequently, the dollar amount of their investment is usually small, maybe $500 to $2,000. Their hope is that the stock price will quickly increase 50 to 100 percent, and they can "turn out" for a quick profit. The bottom line is that the original investor is usually not interested in any further investment in the warrants.

Rules that apply to warrants include the following:

- A purchase warrant simply offers the holder a right to purchase a specific amount of stock at a specific price, exercisable at a specific time.
- The exercise price can be reduced but cannot be increased.
- The shares underlying the warrant must be registered, which requires the company to file a posteffective amendment. (This filing is equivalent to a full S-1.) The reason behind the SEC requirement for such an extensive update filing is that the whole nature of the company changes when a merger with a blind pool occurs. In effect, the company loses its privacy.

Costs

The cost of acquiring a blind pool is comparable to the cost of a shell. It can vary from $20,000 to $100,000 and up. The process usually requires the company to purchase control positions from the founding control shareholders. The deal often includes sizable options for additional shares for the founders.

Some blind pools are set up with differing classes of stock in order to ensure that management will control the voting rights. They would sell common stock with no voting rights to shareholders and preferred stock with voting rights to management to give it control. The original founders use these inside stock positions as bargaining points.

Hidden Costs

A major deterrent to becoming involved with a blind pool is the eventual total cost to complete the whole deal. Audited financial statements are a specific requirement. First, audited financial statements are required from the private company shortly after combining with the blind pool. Then, audited financial statements will also be required of the combined companies. Legal fees and filing fees must also be paid for the immediate and continuing reports.

The entrepreneur must realize up front that purchasing a blind pool does not relieve the company from the reporting requirements of a publicly traded company. A lot of blind pools will have met only minimal reporting requirements, so getting the new blind pool company up to full-reporting status may require just as much time and dollar expenditure as it takes to accomplish a new IPO. And that, of course, takes us all back to the beginning of this book.

FREQUENTLY ASKED QUESTIONS

Which is faster, doing an IPO or a shell–reverse merger?

Generally, doing a reverse merger. Under the right circumstances, a reverse merger can be accomplished in one to two months.

Which is less expensive?

The reverse merger route is less expensive than doing an IPO. But then again, a shell–reverse merger is a different animal than an IPO and usually the reasons for doing one or the other are thought through to justify the means, the means usually being different from the beginning.

Recognizing that they are all reverse mergers, which is best, shells, blind pools, or spin-offs?

Each has its advantages and disadvantages. After 20 years of working with all of them, I favor spin-offs but strongly qualify the process by emphasizing the need to have legal counsel involved.

A last word of caution. Any reverse merger, eventually if not sooner, has to have audited financial statements. Your company can't be publicly held without them. (Additional information can be obtained at the Venture Associates Web site: http://www.venturea.com/)

SIX

Internet Direct Public Offerings

32

Internet Direct Public Offerings

*N*ote. The World Wide Web and Internet are having a profound effect on our world and will continue to gain even more importance in our everyday lives. This is especially true in its impact on business and the way we conduct commerce. A significant example of this impact relates to this book. The fast-changing pace of Internet developments makes it difficult for authors to write and publishers to publish books with up-to-date, timely information. Consequently, I have chosen to establish and maintain a special Internet direct public offering (DPO) section on my corporate Web site. Throughout this section of this book, you will see references to the DPO Web site for additional or current information. This Web site's URL is http://www.venturea.com/dpo/.

Overview

I'm sure that the handful of stockbrokers who gathered under the buttonwood tree at 68 Wall Street in 1792 never in their most bullish imagination ever thought that sometime in the distant future companies and investors would be completing stock transactions all around the world—instantly. Remember, they didn't have telegraphs (invented in 1837), telephones (invented in 1877), TV (invented in the 1940s), or, much less, computers (digital ones invented in the 1940s) and the Internet (created in the 1970s and popularized in the 1990s).

That's 200 years from buttonwood brokers to the Internet. Two hundred years from talking face-to-face to today's e-mail, and 200 years of rules and regulations propagated in between. It's the rules and regulations that cause the Internet from being just as effective as the buttonwood brokers way back when. The SEC and state securities commissions don't know what to do about Internet direct public offerings (DPOs). They don't know for sure how to regulate them. They are confused by the nonregulation that surrounds the Internet—the biggest problem that Internet DPO entrepreneurs face today. However, the light shines bright at the end of the tunnel as the Internet train continues to gather momentum.

The governing bodies have just given lip service to the Internet DPO process; supposedly they have embraced the concept of electronic information transfer and processing. When push comes to shove, however, they haven't given us clear, defined guidelines under which to proceed, making implementation difficult to say the least.

In their defense, the governing bodies are moving to embrace electronic information transfer as fast as bureaucratically possible. In May 1996, the SEC completed implementation of the Electronic Data Gathering, Analysis, and Retrieval system, commonly known as EDGAR. EDGAR performs automated collection, validation, indexing, acceptance, and forwarding of submissions by companies and others who are required by law to file forms with the SEC. Its primary purpose is to increase the efficiency and fairness of the securities market for the benefit of investors, corporations, and the economy by accelerating the receipt, acceptance, dissemination, and analysis of time-sensitive corporate information filed with the SEC.

Publicly traded and reporting companies must file all their annual and quarterly, as well as some other, reports via EDGAR. Among the benefits is the fact that anyone with access to the Internet can go to the EDGAR site and view and download these reports. The implementation of EDGAR is a very positive endorsement by the SEC of its commitment to electronic information processing.

In October 1995, the SEC issued an extensive paper, the "Use of Electronic Media For Information Purposes," setting forth its views. Although it was an extensive 26-page document, which since has been further interpreted, the basic ruling that *whatever may be disseminated on paper may be disseminated electronically* was established. This determination is what has blessed and endorsed the concept of Internet DPOs.

Advantages of Internet DPOs

Internet direct public offerings (DPOs) offer certain opportunities and advantages over a traditional IPO. These include increased efficiency, decreased cost, and greater exposure.

Increased efficiency. The current process of advising the investing public of the availability of a company's IPO is cumbersome to say the least. It involves creating a tombstone ad, identifying and placing the ad in the appropriate media, collecting prospective investor information by phone or mail, and then the actual physical process of distributing a copy of the prospectus. All of theses steps can be conveniently accomplished via the Internet.

Decreased cost. The efficiency discussed above obviously relates to fewer costs for notification and distribution of offering documents. Considerable cost saving is realized in making amendments to an offering circular or in updating information. Online edits are a lot cheaper than reprinting. These cost savings pale in comparison with the savings in commissions. Assuming the company can raise all the money on its own without going through a broker, a DPO can save from 7 to 20 percent in commissions. This is significant money for companies raising less than $5 million.

Greater exposure. Traditionally, IPOs are reserved and sold to institutional investors or only a broker's top investors. With tens of millions of people currently accessing the Internet worldwide and millions more expected, the distribution process of DPO information is greatly enhanced. It is definitely faster and much less expensive. In short, the Internet brings the investment process back to the individual investor. It provides the DPO inexpensive, direct access to domestic and global investors. As many others have stated, it levels the playing field. It gives all investors, institutional and individual, an equal opportunity to participate in the growth possibilities of new publicly held companies.

With more DPOs, more advantages are expected. One big area where distinct advantages are expected is in aftermarket stock trading. When a true auction market is fully implemented, all investors will have equal access to timely information to both a company's news and its stock price.

Primary Differences with IPOs

Several primary differences exist between an IPO and a DPO. One is that with an IPO the selling process is under multiple regulatory scrutiny, whereas with a DPO no one is overseeing the selling process.

In a typical IPO, stockbrokers pitch a stock over the phone, making sure that how they pitch and how they sell remain within the boundaries of their individual brokerage firm's compliance department. In turn, compliance departments have established selling procedures to fit regulations of the NASD, the SEC, and the various exchanges or markets under which a particular security is sold. The whole selling process is under strict regulation (that's why when calling your broker, you are often cautioned that the conversation may be recorded and/or monitored).

A second difference is that an IPO is sold by an underwriter. Actually, the underwriter (brokerage firm) buys a part of the company's stock from the company and resells the shares to public shareholders, earning a commission for each sale. The lead underwriter frequently puts together a selling group or underwriting syndicate, which is comprised of other underwriter-brokerage firms that assist the lead underwriter in selling the stock. Consequently, the company seldom deals directly with purchasing shareholders as the underwriting stockbrokers actually sell the stock.

With a DPO, stock selling is officially done by the company, which in essence means an officer or director. The company takes responsibility for how the deal is pitched, a process dependent on the morals and wiles of the company's management. Desperate entrepreneurs may be selling the stock and are not necessarily bound by all the rules for selling stock, especially all the consequences and, most notably, the fines and disciplinary actions. They are, however, liable for fraud, which can mean fines and jail. But this does leave an awful lot of gray area open.

For a DPO, the company, or more properly the company's officers and directors, have a direct relationship with prospective shareholders. The officers and directors are involved in the whole selling process, from identifying prospects to evaluating them and then making and closing the sale as well as being sure the monies are received and stock certificates sent out to the new shareholders.

Companies that intend to do their own DPO without the assistance of an underwriter should consider carefully some important points, listed below in the form of questions:

- Where are the companies going to get a list of prospective share-holders?
- Do they have a built-in base of prospects because of the product or service the company provides? (Companies that sell products via mail order have a list of customers who are already purchasers of the products and have a natural affinity to the company.)
- Who in the company is going to be in charge of the process?
- How will the company get the word out that it is offering stock?
- Who will do the actual selling?
- Who will do the pre-DPO research?
- Who will structure the deal?
- How will fair valuation be determined?

These simple questions assume that the companies will comply with all the rules and regulations connected with putting together an offering. With an IPO, the underwriter assesses the deal and is then backed up by legal counsel and accountants.

Company Suitability for a DPO

Not every company should try a DPO. Companies still involved in doing research or trying to put together seed capital usually don't make good DPO candidates. The better candidates are companies that have an established on-going business that needs expansion capital. The more-established company has several natural affinity groups to cultivate for investment that include customers, vendors, and employees. It's easier to have these groups as a base from which to expand into family and friends, professional investors and angels, venture capital firms, and other more sophisticated investor groups.

In an IPO the underwriter will help the company with a lot of basic offering decisions. Pricing the stock is a key one. An underwriter will examine the historical and projected financials of the company, review the climate for public offerings, draw comparisons with the stock price of similar companies, and gauge the size of the issue and the impact of dilution. These and other factors help determine a price range for the stock. An underwriter will also advise the company about doing a firm-commitment offering (where the underwriter buys the company's stock) or a best-effort offering (where the underwriter uses its best effort to sell the stock) as well as advising about such issues as the determination of the value of a minimum/maximum offering or whether the offering should be issued as a units (stock and warrants).

For a DPO many other choices and decisions have to be made by the company's officers with input, it is hoped, from qualified legal, accounting, and DPO specialists. Properly researched and structured, a DPO can be accomplished well within legal limitations at significant cost savings.

FREQUENTLY ASKED QUESTIONS

Do you feel that Internet DPOs will become recognized as a legitimate and significant method of raising capital?

Legitimate is already happening. The SEC and state security commissions are working diligently to implement rules and regulations to accommodate this new form of raising capital. Significant is also happening. Assuming the regulatory bodies can contain abuses and entrepreneurs maintain high standards in their use of this vehicle, it promises to be a very viable method to gain funding.

What is an affinity group?

If you offer a product or service that has developed a strong, loyal customer base, that base is your affinity group. It is committed to what you offer and would be hard pressed to switch to a competitor. It's better yet if you deal with most members of the group on an individual basis. They are believers and are vested in seeing you succeed. Let them know via product advertising, general advertising, PR, phone, letters, and the Internet that you are raising money. They are ideal investor candidates. If, on the other hand, your company produces a product or service that has a small customer base, your task is to spread the word in other ways, such as through angel investors, your customers and suppliers, the Internet, and aggressive word-of-mouth.

Can I have a broker-dealer participate in my DPO?

Several broker-dealers in the United States are leading the way in Internet offerings. As the DPO proves its value, more will come aboard. If you have a local broker-dealer that you feel may be interested, ask. At a minimum, you may create some interest to attract broker-dealers as market makers when you complete your offering.

33

Introduction to the Regulation of DPOs

The SEC

The Securities and Exchange Commission (SEC), as discussed previously, was established to administer the laws, rules, and regulations enacted by Congress in the Securities Act of 1933 governing the offer and sale of securities and the Securities Exchange Act of 1934 governing trading in securities. Both of these acts have been extensively added to and modified since their inception and the process will continue as long as we have a government charged with protecting its constituency. The Securities Act of 1933 requires companies to make a full disclosure, and various parts of the act specify much of what comprises full disclosure.

Keep in mind that the SEC has no authority to evaluate the quality or validity of a business or its securities. Nor does it pass judgment on the merits of the company or the securities it's offering. Rather, the SEC is charged with rendering its opinion on whether submitted documents disclose sufficient and accurate information about the company, its business, how it conducts or intends to conduct its business, and the financial information that is furnished to investors. The SEC's primary responsibility under the securities laws is to protect investors and ensure that the capital markets (exchanges) operate in a fair and orderly manner.

Basic Registration of Securities

The SEC has a number of ways to register a public offering and it has also created exemptions to the registration process to assist companies in raising capital. There are registration forms for large and middle-size companies as well as for various smaller companies. The focus here is on smaller companies; in particular, the exemptions used to facilitate direct public offerings (DPOs) that incorporate the Internet in the offering process. First, however, I'll present a brief overview of the forms used for registration.

Form S-1

Form S-1 is the mother of registration forms. It is the registration document used for large companies and large underwritings. It involves full registration with a large amount of paperwork that must be assembled by a large number of attorneys, accountants, and other types of experts. Its disclosure requirements are extensive and its financial reporting requirements very stiff. The basic registration statement contains two parts. Part I is the prospectus (legal offering document), which must be furnished to all prospective purchasers of the securities. Part II contains additional information that is filed with the SEC and available to the public upon request (such items as articles of incorporation, bylaws, and many other exhibits).

Small-Business Forms

The SEC has created several junior forms under what is titled Regulation S-B (Small Business Issuers), not that this make things simple by any means, but it does make the filing process less onerous. To qualify, the issuer (company) must be a U.S. or Canadian firm with less than $25 million in revenues in its last fiscal year, and the total value of its securities in the hands of public shareholders must be below $25 million. These forms are alternatives to the full registration of a Form S-1.

Form SB-1

This is for small businesses offering up to $10 million worth of securities in a fiscal year. Although it is similar to a Reg A in terms of the disclosure, SB-1 requires audited financial statements, which must be prepared in accordance with detailed SEC regulations and must include three full years.

Form SB-2

This is the preferred public offering document for many smaller businesses. It allows an unlimited dollar amount of securities and can be used repeatedly providing the company falls under the definition of a small-business user—that is, less than $25 million in annual revenues. The disclosure requirements are less strict, especially in the areas of the business description and executive compensation, than those in an S-1. The financial disclosure calls for audited statements going back two years. The financial statements can be prepared in accordance with generally accepted accounting principles (GAAP) as opposed to the more stringent SX rules. The SEC allows filing both SB-1 and SB-2 offerings with its regional offices. The company files with the office that is nearest its principal business operations, which can be an advantage because regional office personnel are more likely to be familiar with local economic conditions and the financing environment, and the company's attorneys and accountants may know the reviewers personally.

The reasons for a registration statement are to provide the regulatory bodies with a document that ensures compliance with disclosure requirements. If any statement appears to be materially incomplete or inaccurate, the regulatory body will inform the company by letter and give it an opportunity to correct or add to the disclosure by filing clarifying amendments. The regulatory bodies can and do refuse or suspend the effectiveness of an offering if they find, in their opinion, that material representations are misleading, incomplete, or inaccurate.

Continual Reporting

Public companies that file as reporting companies (those filing under Forms S-1, SB-1, and SB-2) must continually disclose certain information. These filings come under a number of SEC rules and regulations, some at certain points (quarterly and annually) and others for various events. The reports require detailed disclosure on such subjects as company operations, financial conditions (audited), officers and directors (salary, benefits, and more), and competitive positions and plans.

In addition to the reporting requirements, most reporting companies also have to comply with precise proxy rules, which require the company to disclose all material facts concerning the items upon which they are being asked to vote. For annual reports when director elections are being held, rules require disclosure of the prospective directors and their personal history and qualifications.

As expected, there are certain exceptions to the rules dictating what companies need to report. Generally, they apply to the number of shareholders (fewer than 300) and financials (less than $5 million in assets). (See Chapters 23 and 28 for more information.)

Forms 1-A and 2-A

Form 1-A is a federal form of offering statement primarily used for Reg A offerings and consisting of three parts. Part I is the notification section of nine items including the names of and information about officers and directors, and a description of the securities being offered. Part II is the actual offering circular including financial statements with three types of disclosure models and is the disclosure document furnished to prospective investors. Part III, the exhibits, usually include advertising and promotional materials distributed to prospective investors.

Form 2-A is a complex Form 1-A. Filing a 2-A requires a company to meet periodic reporting requirements and file sales and use-of-proceeds information following the sale of its securities.

What the SEC Says

Regardless of the form chosen to file for a DPO, the offering company must comply with the preliminary guidelines set forth by the SEC. The following information is not complete but does offer initially determined basics. The DPO CEO is well advised to consult with the company's securities lawyer concerning the latest information as well as the inevitable continuing updates. Keep in mind that the semiofficial rule of the SEC is that whatever applies to a fully registered IPO also applies to a DPO.

Posting a Notice

Just as a tombstone ad is placed for a fully registered IPO, the DPO must post a notice that information is electronically available. A company can't just provide an offering circular without advising prospective investors that the final offering document is available both by e-mail and in printed form.

Equal Access

An offering available via the Internet must be updated just like a printed document. Further, the Internet investor must be able to download, retain, and print out the offering information, the electronic information must be kept updated, and continual access must be provided.

Substantiation of Delivery

Companies doing a DPO must provide evidence that they have met the delivery requirements established by the SEC. This is an extremely tricky area. It means that the company must obtain an investor's informed consent that the investor wishes to receive the document electronically and in fact has accessed the information and successfully received it. The mechanics of execution of this process is best handled by using Internet technicians to establish a confirmation process. The use of passwords, e-mail confirmation, and in some cases documentable evidence is needed to confirm that an investor has successfully accessed via a hyperlink.

Vehicle Choices

There are three distinct preferred choices for the types of filings commonly used for DPOs: Reg D-504, SCOR, and Reg A. Others could include Intrastate (Rule 147), Regs D-505 and 506, and other specific forms used by a few states (California has special requirements for a SCOR offering under Section 25113 (b)(2)).

Generally, Reg D-504 and SCOR are set out as one and the same. In reality, they differ in the amount of information presented in the documents themselves and in their acceptance by both investors and regulatory bodies. Reg A filings are becoming the most preferred form of DPO registration. The following shows briefly the primary differences between Reg D-504 and SCOR, and the next chapter explains the specifics.

	Reg D-504	**SCOR**	**Reg A**
Maximum Offering	$1 million	$1 million	$5 Million
Use Form U-7	Yes	Yes	Yes
Use Form 1-A	No	No	Yes
Use Form SB-2	No	No	Yes
Audited Financials	No	No	No—varies by state
Minimum Share Price	No	$5	No
"Test-the-Waters"	No	No	Yes
SEC Qualification	No	No	Yes
State Filing	Yes	Yes	Yes

FREQUENTLY ASKED QUESTIONS

I get really confused with all these different forms; can you help?

If your interest is in doing a DPO, it narrows down to Reg-D, SCOR, or Reg-A. If you want to raise over $1 million, use Reg-A. For less, choose between Reg-D and SCOR. SCOR is supposed to be the easiest.

There is no way that I will ever be able to get an audit of my books nor do I want to disclose detailed financial information. What do I do?

None of the three main exemptions (Reg-D, Reg-A, or SCOR) require audited financials. However, if you wish to obtain serious, qualified investors, or expect to have a viable trading market, you will have to get audits.

Can I use the higher level of offerings such as an SB-2?

You can. I expect that 1998 will see many traditional IPOs also offered over the Internet by some well-known brokerage firms, which will create additional creditability for DPOs.

34

Filing the DPO

The three preferred choices for the type of document used to file a DPO, as discussed in the preceding chapter, are Reg A, Reg D-504, and SCOR. This chapter reviews each, and sample copies of the documents can be located via the DPO Web site at: http://www.venturea.com/dpo.

Regulation A: A Quick Overview

Regulation A, more commonly referred to as Reg A, is a "conditional" exemption for certain public offerings—conditional from the standpoint that it allows a company to go public providing the offering meets with various conditions. In brief, the following are characteristics of Reg A offerings and will be discussed more fully below:

- Exempt from registration
- Raise up to $5 million
- Unaudited financials
- No minimum on share price
- No investor restrictions
- Freely tradable
- Easy Form U-7 (SCOR)

Reg A allows the company to sell and issue securities without SEC registration, but it does require the company to file an "offering statement" with the SEC that the SEC then "qualifies."

I stated earlier that Reg A is becoming the preferred method for doing a DPO for a privately held company. The above overview would suggest that it is a money-raising dream come true. Reg A has been around for a long time with some significant rule changes made in 1992. It has many advantages over Reg D and SCOR, but don't get too carried away until you have reviewed all the *fine print*.

Specifics of Reg A and Its *Fine Print*

Exemption from Registration

A Reg A offering is exempt from registration with the SEC within the reporting requirements of section 15(d) of the 1933 act. On the other hand, every state also deals with Reg A in its own distinct manner under its own blue-sky laws; and the SEC regulation requires that the company register with the state or states within which it intends to sell its stock. The *fine print* is that some states allow blue-sky registration by "coordination." This means that if the company has registered with the SEC, then its offering is also registered with the states that have adopted registration by coordination simply by filing those states' blue-sky forms. But be careful that you don't start selling before you are sure both your chosen states and the SEC have accepted your filings.

More *fine print:* in some states the registration is by "qualification." This means that the company files its documents with the states (or state) where it intends to sell its securities; and when those states have advised the company they have accepted its filing, the company then submits this information to the SEC. The SEC thus accepts the filing on the basis of the states' having qualified the offering—and thus considered accepted by qualification.

Still other states continue to use a process titled "registration by notification," which is a little easier to understand. The company files with both the states and the SEC at the same time, simply notifying both that it is going to sell securities. Then (even more *fine print*) there are some states that exempt Reg A offerings altogether. Check with securities counsel before moving your company to another state!

The obvious caution is that the company must check the requirements for each and every state in which it intends to offer its securities. If it is selling to an affinity group located in one or two states, the filing process is fairly simple, but if it is going to sell in multiple states, the filing process can get very time consuming with complications in determining and then remembering what can be done in which states.

Additional registration *fine print*. If the company has the opportunity to use an underwriter to assist or handle the sale of its stock, the company must also submit the "terms of the underwriting" to the NASD for its approval. Terms of the underwriting refer to the commissions, expenses, possible warrants, and other items denoted in the company's agreement regarding compensation to the underwriting firm(s).

And some final *fine print*. As with any type of securities offerings, all Reg A offerings are subject to the civil antifraud provisions in sections 12 and 17 of the 1933 act and section 10(b) and Rule 10b-5 under the 1934 act.

A company cannot use Reg A if it's an investment company, a currently reporting company (already public), involved in the sale of oil, gas, or mineral rights, or disqualified by "bad boy" provisions (known to have a record of security violations).

Raising up to $5 Million

A company can raise up to $5 million over a 12-month period including up to $1.5 million in a secondary offering from existing shareholders, with a *fine print* qualification: if the total money raised doesn't exceed $5 million in any 12-month period, *and* for selling shareholders if the company has had net income from operations in at least one of the last two fiscal years.

Unaudited Financials

The SEC rule for a Reg A declares that unaudited financials are acceptable. The rule does state that the financial statements must be prepared in accordance with GAAP and if the company prepares audited financials for other purposes, then audited statements must be furnished. Some states require only "reviewed" financial statements, which is a less expensive process than audited statements.

The *fine print* is that almost all states require audited financials and every exchange or market requires audited statements. Consequently, a company is advised to plan on obtaining audited financials 12 months, at a minimum, after the completion of its Reg A offering or by the end of the first fiscal year after an offering.

No Share Price Minimum

The SEC regulations for Reg A state that there is no minimum price for stock—that is, the stock can be sold for any price such as $.10 or $1 or $20 per share. The *fine print* is that many states and most exchanges have such minimum pricing requirements as $3 or $5 per share. Consequently, the company should consider the number of shares offered, the effects of dilution, and respective state rules before committing to a price per share.

No Investor Restrictions

Unlike some exemptions, such as Reg D Rules 505 and 506, Reg A offerings don't have any investor restrictions or qualifications. Any investor can invest regardless of his or her net worth or income, and there are no limitations on the number of investors. The *fine print:* some states have set investor restrictions.

Freely Tradable

Pretty simple idea. Any investor who buys stock in a Reg A offering can sell it to whomever whenever at whatever price. The securities, after they are issued, are freely tradable in an aftermarket. In reality, this doesn't work too well (see Chapter 35).

Easy Form U-7 (SCOR)

Every offering, whether it's a Reg D, Reg A, or SCOR, must include an "offering circular," sometimes referred to as an "offering memorandum" or an "offering statement." Supposedly, the SCOR document is the simplest to execute. Even though it is allowed for use in a Reg A, it really isn't very practical as the regulations limit a SCOR offering to $1 million. Most companies choose Reg A because they have an interest in raising up to the $5 million Reg A limit and consequently choose to file with a Form 1-A.

More *Fine Print*

Testing the Water

The idea behind testing the water is that a company can find out if prospective investors would be willing to invest in the company without the company's having to go through all the time, effort, and expense to compile all the needed documents. The company is allowed to publish factual information about its business and/or proposed business before gearing up for a full registration. Technically, no oral communication is permitted with prospective investors until after the test-the-waters information has been submitted to the SEC. This factual information can be in the form of a written document, a radio or television script, printed flyers, and Web site information. But (you knew the *fine print* was coming) no money can be accepted or even solicited until an offering statement has been qualified by the securities commissions and the prescribed offering materials have been delivered to potential investors; and no sales can be made until at least 20 days after the information has been submitted to the regulatory bodies.

After a company completes a Reg A offering, it must file a report with the SEC and most states where it sold its securities. After that, the SEC has no further periodic reporting requirements unless, *fine print* again, the company has more than $5 million in total assets and more than 500 shareholders.

Some companies cannot use Reg A. They include any companies that are already reporting public companies, "blank check" companies (i.e., those planning on doing the business of seeking unspecified businesses to invest in or buy), and investment companies registered or required to register under the Investment Company Act of 1940.

Reg A can be used by limited partnerships with a Form SB-2, but be sure to check with securities counsel before jumping in.

Filing steps for a Reg A are as follows:

1. Contact securities regulators for each state where the offering will be sold and obtain their specific requirements and forms. Also obtain SEC Form 1-A.
2. Fill out the forms. Use accountants for financials and have securities legal counsel review the total package.
3. File with the states and the SEC. Costs vary for each state; the SEC filing fee is $500 to be submitted with the initial filing.

SCOR: A Quick Overview

The Small Corporate Offering Registration (SCOR), frequently touted as the simplest filing, is composed of two parts. First is the filing of Form U-7 that must be filed in the states where the securities will be offered. The second part of the filing process is filing with the SEC a one-page document titled Form D. Keep in mind that not all states recognize SCOR and requirements differ in many states. (See California below; for the latest information about which states recognize SCOR, see the DPO Web site at: http://www. venturea.com/dpo.)

A brief summary of SCOR characteristics are as follows:

- The issuer qualifications are the same as for Regulation D, Rule 504 (see the next section and Chapter 19).
- The total amount of stock being offered is a maximum of $1 million.
- The company can sell to an unlimited number of either accredited or nonaccredited investors (see Chapter 19).
- The securities are not restricted, meaning that any resale is permitted and the stock can be freely traded in any secondary market (see Chapter 35).
- The company can advertise the offering and solicit investors with limited restrictions.

Background

Because the subject can get very confusing, here is some more background information on the SCOR program. In 1980 Congress enacted the Small Business Investment Incentive Act to promote a higher level of cooperation between the federal and states' securities rules and regulations and to lessen the burden of fundraising. The first result was Regulation D and its attendant Rules 504, 505, and 506. Reg D was designed as an exemption from federal securities registration if the offering followed state requirements and included a disclosure document.

Reg D was followed by an American Bar Association-designed uniform filing and disclosure form that the states could use. In 1989 the proposed form was further endorsed by the North American Securities Administrators Association (a prestigious group of state securities commissioners), which named it the Small Corporate Offering Registration (SCOR). To make it more confusing, they also called it Form U-7. To help clarify, consider SCOR as the process and Form U-7 as the form used in filing for the process. A full

SCOR document can be downloaded via the links portion of the DPO Web site at: http:www.venturea.com/dpo.

A large number of states (but not all) have adopted SCOR, although each state may have devised its own interpretation. The DPO entrepreneur will find that state securities departments are very helpful and will offer assistance in answering questions for completing the form. Generally speaking, the SCOR Form U-7 is provided as a question-and-answer type of form. It is supposed to be a simple method to provide uniform information to investors and make it possible for the entrepreneur to undertake the fundraising process without a great deal of legal and accounting expense, even though some users find it more cumbersome than the SEC prospectus format.

SCOR Form U-7 is called a disclosure document as opposed to an offering circular or prospectus. It is written with predetermined questions that the entrepreneur simply answers. Both the questions and answers rather than statements are presented in the document. Although it has been touted as a lawyer-free document, the entrepreneur is best advised to have legal counsel review the final version. One advantage is that many small-business attorneys are comfortable with this review, thus not necessarily requiring securities counsel. Ask the company's general counsel if he or she will review the form and render a legal opinion as to whether the shares are legally and validly issued, fully paid, nonassessable, and binding on the company.

Audited financial statements are not required by some states for the first $500,000 of securities offered. Some states allow "reviewed" financials, which are less costly than audited ones. The filing document can be used in multiple states and some states even furnish a computer disk to assist the process. Substantial printing costs are saved as the document can be processed on a computer and then simply copied.

Marketing the SCOR offering is a hands-on process by the company's officers and directors. The offering can be made through personal contact, advertising that includes direct mail, and the Internet. After a response to the offering is received, some preliminary information about prospective investors should be obtained, such as names and addresses. Then prospective investors can be furnished with a copy of the disclosure document and possibly other marketing materials. The final step is to receive share purchase forms from investors and their payment.

California SCOR requirements are worth noting and include the following:

- The company must use Form U-7.
- The maximum amount of the offering is $1 million.

- The offering price must be at least $5 per share.
- Only one class of common stock is permitted.
- Blind pools and oil/gas extractive/exploration is not permitted.
- Net proceeds must be used for the business.

Steps for Implementing a SCOR Registration

Step one: Obtaining materials

- Contact the security commission in each state where you intend to offer your stock.
- Request each state's specific requirements and filing procedures.
- Request Form U-7 and the state's or appropriate filing form.

Step two: Prepare filings

- Although SCOR is a uniform filing, some state regulators request additional information.
- Obtain audited financials if needed.
- Have a securities attorney review the completed filing documents.

Step three: Submit filings

- File the appropriate forms with each state. If multistate filings are being undertaken, submit all of them simultaneously. A number of states participate in regional reviews in which the comments of one state are recognized by the others. The DPO Web site offers a list of states that accommodate regional reviews: http://www.venturea.com/dpo.

Step four: SEC filing

- When a company has obtained the necessary state permits and starts the sale of its stock, it must notify the SEC by filing a one-page document titled Form D, which can be obtained from the SEC and most securities attorneys.

Regulation D - 504

Regulation D, including all its rules (501 through 506), are covered in detail in Chapter 19. The requirements and limitations for filing a Reg D-504 are as follows:

- *Issuer qualifications:* Any type of company may issue stock except investment, existing reporting, and blind pool companies.
- *Investors allowed:* No limitation is placed on the number or type (accredited or nonaccredited*) of investors.
- *Amount of offering:* An offering has a maximum of $1 million in any 12-month period.
- *Disclosure requirements:* If investors are accredited, no disclosure is required; if nonaccredited, they must be given an offering circular, which may be Form U-7. All investors must be allowed to ask questions and must be told that the securities will not be registered under the Securities Act of 1933.
- *Filing requirements:* Form D (one page) must be filed with the SEC in Washington within 15 days of the first sale and no later than 30 days after the last sale. Update filings are required every six months.
- *Restrictions on the securities:* The securities have no restrictions; they are freely tradable immediately.
- *Advertising and solicitations:* These are allowed, but caution is advised.
- *Financial statements:* These statements are not required.

* California allows only accredited investors to invest at least $2,500.

Reg D differs from SCOR by allowing the SCOR (U-7) question-and-answer document or a more complex document to be used or no document at all. The latter isn't advised and is prohibited by many states.

Intrastate—or Rule 147

Intrastate offerings are also covered in Chapter 19. Although this offering form could be used for an Internet DPO, it's not practical as it is designed for use by companies that intend to offer their securities only within the state of their principal business.

The offering amounts, time periods, and registration and disclosure requirements are all regulated by the individual states. To qualify for an intrastate offering exemption, the company must

- sell its securities *only* in its state of business,
- sell its securities *only* to residents of its state, and
- make sure its stock is not resold outside its state for nine months.

Closing Thoughts

Regardless of your choice of a Reg A, a Reg D-504, or a SCOR, the offering process requires attention to details. All DPO CEOs are advised to, at a minimum, have their attorney review their final documents before submitting them to the appropriate regulatory agencies. Most attorneys can make this review in several hours and will invariably find the need for some additions and corrections.

FREQUENTLY ASKED QUESTIONS

Is it true that the fine points can really trip up the entrepreneur?

True. The rules and regulations have many small nuances that need interpretation before the entrepreneur commits to a defined path. At a minimum, talk with someone who has been there. Best is to consult with legal counsel or an IPO/DPO professional.

How long does it take to put together the paperwork?

I've seen entrepreneurs do it in a week (they didn't raise any money). I've also seen entrepreneurs take as long as a year and never raise any money. If you have a good business plan—one that qualified people have told you is good—it should take four to six weeks to work up the official offering documents, including legal review.

How long does it take to raise the money?

Depends upon how well organized the company is. If it has a well-planned marketing strategy coupled with a quality offering, raising the money could be accomplished in as little time as a month. Most companies schedule 90 days with allowances for extensions.

35

Trading DPO Stocks

After a company has completed a DPO, it still has an additional hurdle. How and under what mechanism will its stock be traded? Companies that have completed DPOs under a SCOR, Reg D-504, or Reg A have issued freely trading stock, which means that anyone who owns the stock can sell it to anyone else.

In its simplest form, it means I can call you and ask if you would like to buy my 1,000 shares of *Ultimate Internet Brothers Enterprises, Inc.* You say, "Sure, how much?" I reply that I bought the stock at its DPO three months ago for $5.00 per share and just last week the brothers were joined by their sister, and now the company is really going to go places. I also heard from an uncle of theirs that they are getting a new contract from their father's company, and because of all this good news, their grandfather sold some of his stock to an aunt last month at the bargain price of $6.50 a share. So I figure a good price right now would be about $8.00 per share. In a stalling tactic, you say that since I've made $3.00 a share in three months, why would I want to sell. I reply I need the bucks for braces for my kid. You then reply that you'll buy half my stock for $7.50 a share and suggest I sell the rest to the kid's dentist. I say, "Done," whip out a stock certificate for 500 shares, sign it over to you, and take your check. Then I'm off to see the dentist.

Reality? Probably not but close to it. Private stock transactions take place every day. A buyer and seller come together and negotiate a deal. In the new world of DPOs, a lot of people are working on a solution for a valid trading market for DPO stocks. Some are already in place (see the Pacific Exchange below). At the time this section is being written, the best I can do is discuss what appears to be the top alternatives: order-matching services and the promise of electronic matching services.

First, a brief review of the complications in establishing viable trading markets. Security is the number one complication on the list. If I don't know you, how can I be sure that you either legitimately own the stock I want to buy or will make payment if I'm selling. Further, how do we find each other to begin with? The exchanges have taken care of that for larger-company stocks that have registered with the SEC and meet the financial exchanges' requirements. This trading function has a lot of secure activity going on behind the scenes. Transfer agents track and record who owns how many shares of which companies, and they guarantee these facts to the market makers, stockbrokers, and individual investors. The brokerage firms themselves assure transfer of monies and certificates to investors. These activities require large computers that work full-time and very efficiently, and the process is backed by several hundred years of established systems and procedures. Overseeing all this are the regulatory bodies that have established rules, regulations, and enforcement capability for all those involved in the selling and transfer process.

The great minds are befuddled, though, about what to do with smaller DPO issues. The survival risks of the smaller companies is high, the dollar volume of the trading is low, and the regulations are new or not yet fully in place. Large brokerage firms won't touch DPOs, which means that new ideas and new trading methods must be put in place.

Order-Matching Services

Order matching services are provided by brokerage firms, which assign a registered representative (stockbroker) to maintain a "book" on the DPO company. This book is comprised of the names of, and information for contacting, shareholders and the number of shares and price objective of each buyer or seller. When a match between buyer and seller appears, the broker asks them to open an account and then executes a trade. Transaction fees are charged to each side for each trade, ranging from $35 to $65. The broker will assist the parties in the transfer of the stock certificate and funds.

It is the DPO company's responsibility to establish an order-matching brokerage firm to represent its securities. Many brokerages perform a market-maker function for Nasdaq and Bulletin Board stocks. Frequently, the DPO company provides and refers names of shareholders to the brokerage. Most brokerages currently don't publish share prices or recent transactions. It is expected that more brokerage firms will instigate order matching as DPOs grow in popularity.

Electronic Matching Services

Electronic matching services are considered the future for DPO stock trading. Just as DPOs are sold via the Internet, Internet trading is also expected to become a standard. The intention of electronic matching is to enable buyer and seller to trade stocks without a broker as intermediary. Security issues remain to be solved, although the SEC reports that a number of suggestions have been submitted for review.

Current information on the status of order and electronic matching can be found at the DPO Web site at: http://www.venturea.com/dpo.

The Pacific Exchange

The Pacific Exchange (PCX), located in San Francisco and Los Angeles, has taken the lead in attempting to facilitate the trading of DPO stocks. It differs from other exchanges in that it has chosen to specialize in certain areas, such as the most active stocks, bonds, and options on the NYSE and AMEX and smaller companies that don't qualify for the larger exchanges. It is the third most active exchange in the United States and the third most active options exchange in the world.

The PCX is leading the way in establishing an exchange for secondary trading in SCOR and Reg A offerings. Secondary trading is defined as the trading that takes place after a company has completed its initial stock offering to the public; the PCX calls this the *SCOR Marketplace.* It believes that it provides a well-regulated, liquid environment to trade SCOR and Reg A securities, which consequently make them a more attractive capital-raising tool for emerging companies and interested investors.

PCX Listing Requirements

The PCX believes that it offers companies that qualify for trading substantial benefits over nontrading SCOR and Reg A companies. These benefits include increased visibility and recognition, a specialist for each company to oversee and maintain trading, and real-time quotes that can be accessed on terminals throughout the United States.

Just like the Nasdaq with its multiple levels of trading eligibility in Bulletin Board, small cap, and NMS stocks, the PCX also offers graduating tiers of tradability. These tiers are initial SCOR, Tier II, and Tier I. Their minimum quantitative listing requirements are summarized in Figure 35.1.

FIGURE 35.1

	SCOR	Tier II	Tier I
Net Tangible Assets	$500,000	$2 million	
Net Worth	$750,000		$4 million
Pretax Income			$750,000
After-Tax Income		$100,000	$400,000
Public Float (shares)	150,000	500,000	500,000
Market Value of Float	$750,000	$1.5 million	$3 million
Bid Price	$5	$3	$5
Number of Public Shareholders	250	500	800
Operating History			3 years
State Registration	Required	22 state blue-sky exemptions	45 state blue-sky exemptions

Maintenance Criteria

Once a company has gained a listing on the SCOR Marketplace, it must maintain the following minimum performance requirements:

- Total net tangible assets of $250,000
- Total net worth of $500,000
- Market value of float at $500,000
- Last sale price per share of $1
- Publicly held shares of at least 100,000
- Public shareholders numbering at least 200

In addition to the above minimum quantitative requirements, PCX also reviews the following qualitative areas:

- Financial condition of the company that includes its accounting practices, a nonqualified opinion on audited financials, and the company's ability to service its existing debt and expansion programs.

- Nature and scope of the company's operations that include a demonstrated ability to develop new products or services and a potential or proven market as well as plans for future expansion
- Management's experience in the company's industry, including management's reputation
- Competition and economic conditions within the company's industry
- Government polices on products or services
- Use of proceeds for expansion, marketing and licensing, working capital, and acquistions of complementary businesses
- Composition of assets, reserves, royalties, rights, and patents

Further, PCX will not list any company

- with a current "Going Concern" opinion in its audited financial statements;
- that is not expected to produce profits within a reasonable time period;
- in which business operations depend on the development of a product or system that will not be completed before listing; and
- that has been subject to law enforcement actions, including securities crime, fraud, state cease-and-desist orders, or injunctions in addition to a "bad boy" disqualifier as it pertains to officers, directors, large shareholders, promoters, and selling agents.

The quantitative requirements for a Nasdaq listing and PCX requirements are very similar, but the qualitative requirements of the PCX would seem at first blush to be stiffer than the Nasdaq's. Time will tell as more companies attempt to list and comply with the subjective, qualitative PCX requirements. Nonetheless, the PCX deserves praise for its efforts to provide a secondary trading market for SCOR and Reg A DPO offerings.

Listing Process

Because the SCOR Marketplace is a relatively new exchange, it's worth looking at the process a company must go through to obtain a listing. Following is a step-by step overview.

Step one: eligibility review. After a company has qualified at both the state and federal levels and raised at least $750,000, the company can request a listing eligibility review by submitting the following materials:

- Form U-7 (SCOR) or Form 1-A (Reg A)
- Audited financial statements

- $500 nonrefundable application processing fee
- Listing worksheet
- SCOR original listing application
- Legal opinion that the company complies with Corporate Governance Rules
- Additional information that the company considers beneficial to obtaining a listing (e.g., patents, distribution agreements, press clippings)

On receipt and after review to determine compliance, an Equity Listing Committee votes on the company's initial acceptance for listing.

Step two: SEC registration. Any company applying for a PCX listing must also register under section 12(b) of the Securities Exchange Act of 1934. This requires filing Form 10-SB or Form 8-A with the SEC; it's recommended that the company file these forms simultaneously with filing with the PCX.

Step three: final PCX submission. On endorsement of the PCX Equity Listing Committee, the company is required to submit the following materials:

- Listing agreement for common or preferred stocks
- Specimen stock certificate
- Balance of listing fee
- Board resolution authorizing listing on the PCX
- Legal opinion regarding legality of issue and issuer
- Copy of SEC Form 10-SB or Form 8-A
- Agreement with registrar/transfer agent
- Distribution schedule
- PCX's SCOR Marketplace supplemental form

Admission to Trading

Following the receipt of all materials and endorsement of the exchange's Equity Listing Committee, the exchange's board of governors must grant final approval. If a company is accepted for listing, the PCX notifies the SEC and sends the company a letter of approval. The stock can be officially traded after the SEC orders the 1934 act registration effective.

The PCX assigns the company a three-digit ticker symbol and the SCOR Marketplace stocks carry an "SC" suffix on their symbol. Congratulations! Isn't the SCOR Marketplace process much simpler than a full Nasdaq registration?

A final note regarding the Pacific Exchange's SCOR Marketplace. If your company is planning a DPO that you intend to have meet the PCX's SCOR Marketplace listing requirements, never, under any circumstances, imply that the PCX has endorsed your offering. In addition, even after a company is trading on the PCX, it risks delisting if it represents itself as exempt from state blue-sky regulations.

Additional and updated information can be found for the Pacific Exchange's Web site via the DPO links page at: http://www.venturea.com/dpo.

A Final Comment on DPO Trading

Just as all participants are struggling with the process, rules, and regulations of making DPO stock offerings, many people are trying to determine how to best trade them in the aftermarket. A zillion rules surround the selling and trading of securities because of the losses sustained by investors ever since stock trading began. Our society charges our regulatory bodies with protecting us from unscrupulous dealings and a small number of persons who are blatantly dishonest. The sudden explosion of the Internet and the fact that it is basically an unregulated media add to the difficulty of transferring the existing body of regulations to make them work effectively.

Many people with a large number of resources are working overtime to implement a truly viable way to integrate the Internet into our securities business. I have no doubt that by the year 2000, DPOs and Internet trading will be commonplace.

FREQUENTLY ASKED QUESTIONS

Is DPO stock trading really effective yet?

Yes and no. The PCX is obviously set up and doing business. Others are coming online fast and are worth watching carefully, even though the general public has yet to fully accept it, and the regulatory bodies continue to regulate and discover new areas for new rules. However, the die is cast: secure, reliable, and efficient trading is going to become commonplace.

Which is better, order matching or electronic matching?

Order matching is the most common at present because the system is in place to make it work and investors have faith in its security. Many experts feel that the electronic system is the trading system for the future and with the convenience of the Internet, it stands to reason that it will become the favorite. Internet trading will eliminate the broker, saving the investor fees and commissions.

Will a trading system be developed for lower-priced DPOs?

Offerings of companies with a net worth of less than a million dollars are currently hampered by a trading aftermarket vehicle. For the concept of DPOs to really succeed, some aftermarket exchange will have to be put in place. With the intensity of change surrounding the Internet, I would expect that to happen sometime around the year 2000.

IPO and DPO Investor Tips

If you "got the gold," this chapter is for you. You'll pick up some investing tips and read about some investing do's and don'ts. As a long-time participant in IPO investing, I have to admit to a certain bias. In fact, a great bias. I've reviewed literally thousands of IPOs and participated in hundreds. I've been around for the IPO company birth process and have a rather large collection of worthless stock certificates. I don't only have a great bias, I'm addicted. Addicted to the excitement of discovering new projects and meeting new entrepreneurs. Every day is like Christmas for me because I get to open some new business plan packages. Consequently, it's difficult for me to be negative about IPO or DPO investing. I admit, I do find the investigating and analyzing process fun and intriguing.

Risk

I believe there are some basics that every investor needs to recognize. The first big one is that the process of investing in IPO/DPOs is inherently risky. Risk is exciting; it stimulates vitality in the one taking the chance. The willingness to take a risk means you are willing to go beyond a familiar niche. Management consultant Peter Drucker has written, "To eliminate risk in business is futile, risk is inherent in the commitment of present resources to future expectations." For small companies the bottom line is only the summing-up of a dozen different kinds of risks on a daily basis. Entrepreneurs have a fundamentally different attitude toward risk. They don't treat it as a threat or undesirable event. To them it's simply an opportunity or problem to be met and conquered. They don't like risk but they understand it. Successful entrepreneurs know how to make risk work for them and instead of intimidating them, it energizes them.

If, as an investor, you are not comfortable with putting your money under the management of a team of people with that kind of attitude toward risk, *don't invest.* Stay on the sidelines.

Comfort

On the other hand, if you're comfortable with some level of risk, the second basic point for investors to recognize is their level of comfort—how much money can you afford to risk? Small-company investing is one thing, but IPO/DPO investing is riskier. With existing publicly held stocks, you can analyze their past track record and current standing. You can see if they have a past operational history that is profitable and you can compare individual companies. Many IPO/DPOs don't have a past history of profits and it may be only a short time since they started the business. Are you comfortable with that fact? Can you afford to lose your total investment?

Familiarity

If you are okay with risk and you can establish your financial level of comfort, from my experience the next basic area that has proven valuable for IPO/DPO investing is familiarity. I firmly believe that you need to be knowledgeable about the industry in which you intend to invest. Even more preferable is that you earn your living in some area aligned to the prospective IPO/DPO's industry. In this way you have an insight that is far superior to the nonindustry-involved investor. At a minimum, seek areas with which you are familiar. If you are a doctor, invest in medically related deals. If you are in manufacturing, seek companies that manufacture a product. If you are in a service business, look for companies that provide services as opposed to a product.

Your comment in response is: "But I want to invest in something new and exciting, and my business area is pretty dull." That's a valid comment and here's my best suggestion: research. Spend an abnormal amount of time researching and studying the industry area where you have an interest. Don't just get a copy of a company's offering document, although that's a must, but spend some time on the Internet learning about the industry, competitors, and trends. Pick up some industry trade magazines and read the editorial content, study the ads, and always look for new product/service releases. In our fast-paced business world, I guarantee you that some other company is developing or has a product/service that provides competition to your prospective investment.

Here's a personal hint. I review over 500 business plans a year and turn down at least twice that number via phone and e-mail. I've had the opportunity to invest in many first-time-ever projects—projects that are very common today like video rental stores, how-to-do-it videos, and brewpubs. Why didn't I get in on these firsts? My risk aversion and inability to choose. The first time I saw a brewpub proposal, I was excited. Ten days later I received my second proposal from another part of the country and a week later a third one from yet another location. When I see that many new projects from different sources in a short period of time, I simply pass on all of them. It's difficult to choose a good deal and much more difficult to pick a winner. Do I miss out? You bet. But that just makes me poor—not destitute.

Deal Flow

And this brings me to a final basic investment hint. *Increase your deal flow.* A number of surveys have shown, and successful investors will tell you, that a key to successful investing is to review a lot of projects. The way to see a lot of deals is to network. Tell your peers, friends, and relatives you're looking to invest. Let them know that you would like to see the deals they're looking at. Contact a number of brokerage houses and ask to speak to a broker. Any broker. Chances are that you will be directed to a new broker and she or he is looking for new clients. Tell the broker you are seeking IPOs and also private investment opportunities. You probably won't get invited into the next IPO but brokers will be happy to send you a prospectus. This is the way you gain a comfort factor with the strange prospectus language required by the SEC. Brokers are also one of the groups of people who know about the private financing done before IPOs. Look at those packages and even if you don't invest, you'll learn a lot about the process of corporate financing.

Here's another personal hint on getting deal exposure. There are about 150 venture capital clubs or groups across the United States and an increasing number internationally. (See the Venture Associates Web site for a listing at: http://www.venturea.com/links.) These groups, most of them nonprofit, conduct monthly meetings where entrepreneurs make presentations about their companies. You also have the opportunity to rub elbows with the professionals who surround entrepreneurs: accountants, attorneys, management consultants, and deal makers. Meetings are one of the best ways to get into a network that creates deal flow.

Investing Questions

When you get involved in IPO/DPO investing, you have to throw out a lot of the standard, time-proven investment truths. As an example, price-to-book value goes. That's the one where book value is the total of all assets less all debt and where one looks for an undervalued situation. New offerings are almost always upside down for this. An earnings track record also isn't common, especially in DPOs. But you might look for a decrease in losses. Was the last quarter's loss less then the previous quarter's or quarters'? Burrow into the details. Maybe the last quarter's loss was because of the extra expense in preparing for an offering. Check the operating loss areas. This will tell you what has been happening in the company's daily operations. Would the company be profitable if not for the offering expenses? Here are some points and questions that apply to new offerings.

Study

Study, really study, and think about the information presented in an offering document. Don't just read it. If you come up with questions or find areas that you don't understand, ask. Find someone to explain the nuances of SEC-speak.

Analyze the Business

Sure, you like the deal because it's in a hot, fast-moving industry. This is an example of when you really have to study. Ask yourself and confirm, is the market getting, or already, saturated? Does the company really have a market niche that is adequate for large sales numbers and is its product or service really unique or special? Apply some of the old 30-percent rules. Is what it sells 30 percent faster, 30 percent cheaper, save the user 30 percent in time or money? If not, it doesn't have a distinct customer advantage and may be just another me-too. On the other hand, is the product too leading-edge, too new to be readily accepted? Savvy investors are careful about this. They know how tough it is to educate a marketplace. Advertising is expensive and the response to it difficult to track.

Is the industry really on an upswing or is there just a little bump in current interest? Are a lot of other new companies surfacing? Is there room for all of them? Does your investment prospect seem to be a leader? Can you use, or do you know someone who does or will use, the product or service?

If you don't think the product or service is useful, I'd suggest you pass. Are you dealing with a solution with no real problem? The best deals are those in which everyone recognizes a problem exists and are ready to buy a solution. If the company has to spend a lot of time and consequently money educating potential users to the problem, forget it. You can afford to wait.

Be cautious about a one-product company, one that has invented or conceived of just one product or service. Sometimes such companies are all right if a second generation of the product is being developed and you can envision a third and forth application for the product. But normally, and there are exceptions, a one-product company is not going to be a successful long-term investment. If you can see that all it has to do (big challenge) is be "firstest with the mostest" and you're sure that a larger firm will snatch it right up as an acquisition, go for it. However, there are a lot of sad tales about a management getting caught up in its own hype and letting ego lose a sellout opportunity. Companies with a limited customer base must also be approached cautiously. The risk factor section of an offering circular will frequently disclose a limited customer base. If more then 50 percent of a company's sales are to one customer, pass—especially if it's the government.

Who's Selling and Who's Holding?

A section in every offering circular is titled "Dilution." It is comprised of two main parts and deserves special study. The first part discusses the company's "net tangible book value." Net tangible book value per share represents the total amount of tangible assets of the company *less* the total amount of liabilities divided by the number of shares of common stock outstanding. Simply, it's what the company owns less what the company owes divided by its shares. If a company has assets of $5 million and liabilities of $4 million, then it's book value is $1 million. If it has 2 million shares outstanding, the net tangible book value per share is 50¢ ($1 million divided by 2 million shares).

Say the company is doing an IPO/DPO of $6 million total or $5 million net after expenses and that it is offering its stock at $5 per share. This means that when the offering is completed, the company will have $10 in assets (the $5 million it had plus the $5 million net) and still have $4 million in liabilities, or now its book value is $6 million ($5 old plus $5 new less $4 old). The $6 million it raised by selling stock at $5 per share means there are 1.2 million new shares added to the 2 million old shares for a new total of 3.2 million shares outstanding. Now take the new book value of $6 million divided by the new 3.2 million shares and you come up with a new net tangible book value per share of $1.87 per share or an increase from the old per share value (50¢) of $1.37.

How does this affect you as an investor? How about the fact that every $5 you invested becomes $1.87, or you lose $3.13 just for putting $5 in. For the folks who owned the stock before the offering, remember that each share was worth 50¢. They like you because you just made them $1.37 per share. That's dilution. Almost without exception, every new issue means your investment decreases in per share book value when you make it.

The second part of the dilution presentation addresses several other points. It shows the number of shares outstanding before the offering and the number to be sold along with the total after all is said and done, and it's expressed in percentages (public float). In our example it looks like this.

	Number	Percent
Existing Shareholders	2,000,000	62.5
New Investors	1,200,000	37.5
Totals	3,200,000	100%

It's difficult to state what percentage of stock should be sold to the public. If the company has been around for a while, is profitable, and is seeking funds to finance its expansion, the percentage may be as little as 10 to 15 percent. With brand-new companies in which new investors are putting up most of the capital, the percentage could be in the 40 to 50 percent range. An existing company with some track record should be offering the public from 20 to 45 percent of its stock.

If a company has a negative net worth before an offering, and this is not unusual, the dilution can easily be in the 80 to 90 percent range. High dilution is common, so don't be alarmed. Just get educated and become a more sophisticated investor. This section of the circular may also discuss a lot of other little details like overallotments, warrants, ESOPs, stock options, and convertible securities just to mention a few. It's a great section to study details and gain insights on the nuances of public offerings.

Who Owns How Much?

Want to do some more snooping? Take a look at the offering section titled "Principal Shareholders," which shows each person or entity that owns 5 percent or more of the company, each officer and director, and the total for the whole group. Here are the folks who really have the say in what happens in the company. The tables show the number of shares each holds and the percent of his or her holdings before and after the offering. That's well and good but the better part may be in the footnotes. Study these to see if these same people have options for more stock. And while you're at it, take a look at the section titled "Certain Transactions," which goes into more detail about who bought what, how much, and when. Some of these are like mystery novels in that you will see that someone bought in and then got bought out or a director furnished some services and was paid in stock (check the price). Or, maybe the company owned a big boat or recreational property and the president had to buy it back, or there was a former president who had a golden parachute. You also might discover a few details about how the company has accomplished some of its financing: like a director who loaned the company several hundred thousand dollars, got paid back but also received some cheap stock for making the loan. Remember, this is all fair and the company is simply complying with SEC requirements for full disclosure. Of course, for some sophisticated investors these transactions are red flags for top management's way of doing business. You be the judge; it's your money.

A Quick Trip through a Prospectus

This chapter has referred to some of the subjects in an offering memorandum. Many other parts of this document are discussed in detail in the IPO chapters. What follows is a cover-to-cover discussion of what to look for in an offering memorandum from an investor's viewpoint.

Cover. Is there red print on the cover to indicate that you are reviewing a preliminary document (red herring), which usually states it is subject to completion and the date it was published? The important point for investors is to never make a final investment decision until you have reviewed the final document. There may be some significant changes recommended by the SEC before its acceptance of an underwriting. Even though it is the stockbrokers' responsibility to be sure you receive a copy of the final prospectus, experienced investors assume this responsibility themselves.

The cover always shows the name of the company and the number and type of securities being offered. The initial paragraph will go into greater detail about the securities. You will also note wording that is set in capital letters and bold print. This is standard wording required by the SEC and is usually oriented toward the high degree of risk involved. Another section will show you the price of the securities, the selling commissions, and the net proceeds to the offering company, usually followed by some subsections with numbers in parentheses that pertain to additional expenses or warrants regarding the offering. Check to be sure that the commissions don't exceed 10 percent and a 3 percent nonaccountable expense allowance. The bottom of the page will show who the underwriter(s) is/are offering the securities; in a DPO, this may be the company itself.

Inside front cover. This page is frequently devoted to pictures of the company's products or locations or other pictorial information about the company, giving the investor a quick look at the company's business.

Prospectus summary. This page or two will be a capsule of the company and its business as well as information on contacting the company. It will also include a further description of the securities being offered and summary financials. It is helpful to the investor to read these pages to get an initial feel for the company's business and financial status.

Risk factors. This is an important section that in most cases will be divided in two. One part will deal with risks associated with the company and its industry; the second will deal with risks associated with investment in the securities.

Company risks are the most important. The risks are too many and too varied to discuss in detail. As a prospective investor, you should read enough offering memorandums to learn to quickly determine which are important to your investment decisions about a particular offering. Some company and industry risks factors are as follows:

- New business and/or no operating history. This will tell you how long the company has been in existence, if the company has had any revenues, the extent of its losses, and the company's near-term prospects for sales and profits.
- Working capital deficit and/or going concern. This will note if the company has a current negative net worth and if the auditor's opinion indicates doubt about the company's ability to stay in business without the proposed financing. Neither of these is unusual, but they are significant risk factors.
- Need for additional financing and/or limited capital. This statement will tell you how long it will be before the company expects to be in business with the money being raised in the current offering; fre-

quently, the statement will say at least for the next 12 months. Other times it will state that the company anticipates it will need another round of financing before being successful. This happens with companies that are still in the development stage.

- Reliance on a single product; product acceptance not established; lack of commercial orders. All these types of risk factors pertain to the fact that the company has yet to establish a solid sales record and carry many warnings to investors to study the company's marketing plans in great detail.

- Reliance on key personnel. This is a pretty standard risk factor. It usually notes that the company is heavily dependent upon one or two of its founders. It will also note if the company carries life insurance on these individuals and if they are working under employment agreements. Sometimes you'll see that the company intends to hire other key people to carry out its plan of operations.

- Conflicts of interest and/or related transactions. This factor appears whenever an officer, director, or substantial shareholder is also involved in a business that competes with the company or a business that supplies anything to the company, or if the company rents, leases, or is provided with services by a person connected with the company. Frequently, it notes that the company believes it is obtaining or using these products or services at a price comparable to or less than, similar market prices.

- Dependence on suppliers and/or outside sources. This risk factor is common to product companies that purchase all or part of their products instead of manufacturing everything in-house.

- Additional product development and/or research and development. Many new companies have developed only one version of their product or service and will note that they intend to use some of the proceeds on additional or second-generation development. Frequently, this risk factor will note that the company uses outside firms to accomplish these tasks.

- Technology changes and/or possible obsolescence. This risk factor is common to high-tech companies. The wording will refer to rapid changes, alternative technologies, frequent upgrades, and unknown competition. It's a red flag to the investor to carefully consider the company's technology and its ability to gain and maintain its industry position.

- Lack of patents and/or proprietary protection. This is an important risk factor for high-tech and product companies. Patents, which are not always worth all that much, do indicate some value, however. Preferable is extensive proprietary knowledge. If a company has neither, it is much more vulnerable to competition.
- Competition. Almost every offering circular will list this risk factor. The investor's challenge is to determine how stiff the competition really is. Does the company have a true niche market? More than two paragraphs of risk factors alert one to more serious considerations.
- Regulation. This section applies to companies that are involved in any heavily regulated industry. Examples would include financial firms that must comply with SEC, state, or banking regulations. Other examples would be medical and food companies regulated by the Food and Drug Administration.

The second risk section pertains to risks relating to the company's securities. Most of these are boilerplate clauses such as the following:

- Determination of offering price
- Lack of a public market for the stock
- Lack or nonexistence of dividend payments
- Shares available for future sale
- Dilution
- Outstanding warrants

The risk section is helpful to the prospective investor as it brings out points to ponder. The SEC is the usual regulator of the contents of this section and has proven over a long period of time to be savvy in its requirements for including the appropriate factors. DPOs are not so well regulated and you are advised to create and think about them on your own. Familiarity with standard risk factor nomenclature is beneficial.

Use of proceeds. This section denotes how the company intends to spend your money. As an investor, the more details the better. Frequently, the most revealing parts of this section are the footnotes.

Dilution. This subject was discussed earlier. The dilution section sets out the figures in legalese, the most important figure noted as "Dilution per share to new investors." Footnotes will refer to total dilution when outstanding warrants are exercised, invariably making the dilution greater and sometimes obscene.

Capitalization. This presentation in table form shows the number, type, and dollar amount of the company's securities both before and after the current offering. It is simply a clarification table as the information is also contained in the company's financial statements.

Management's discussion and analysis of financial condition and results of operations. This long-titled section is applicable to existing public companies and is sometimes found in IPOs of companies that have been in business for a long time. It makes interesting reading to determine how a management team has conducted its business in the past and how it will use the proceeds of the new funding. This section is seldom found in circulars of new companies and most DPOs.

Plan of operation and/or business. This is the heart of an offering circular. It should logically and clearly explain what industry the company operates in, the company's history, how it does what it does, what its product or service consists of, its unique aspects, its markets, and how it produces and sells, or intends to sell, its products and services. It will also address competition, customers, suppliers, employees, facilities (current and planned), R&D, and regulation as applicable. Understanding what the company does is key to making smart investments. This section should evoke a lot of questions by the investor. The answer should be obtainable from your broker, from reviewing supplemental materials, or from direct contact with the company's management.

Management. This section names and denotes the titles of the management team, including directors. It will also indicate their qualifications and past business experience. It may provide information about significant employees, outside advisers, and consultants, including their compensation, certain perks, and benefits.

Certain transactions. This section was discussed above under "Who Owns How Much?" It discusses semidetails of how the company has funded itself since inception.

Principal shareholders. Here is where you find out the number of shares owned by the officers, directors, and significant shareholders (those holding more than 5 percent of the stock before the current offering). Read the footnotes for some interesting details.

Descriptions of securities. This extensive section is usually boiler-plate, describing the stock being offered and its relationship to the rest of the company's securities. As an investor, you shouldn't dismiss it until you are familiar with its contents and can safely scan it for abnormalities.

Underwriting. This is also a boilerplate section. Get familiar with the language used and always note the percentage amount of the commissions, nonaccountable expense allowance, and the number and price of the under-writer's warrants. After becoming used to the normal but high 10 percent commission, 3 percent unaccountable, and 10 percent of the new-issue stock in warrants at a 20 percent premium, you can then get a feel for the under-writer's confidence in its ability to sell out the offering and /or the company's ability to strike a good deal.

Legal matters, experts, and additional information. These sections are in every offering. Legal matters identify the securities counsel for the company and the underwriter (if appropriate). Experts indicate the ac-counting firm involved in the financial audit. Additional information states which regulatory bodies the offering has been filed with and where you as an investor can inspect the full registration information including all exhibits.

Financial statements. If the company has audited financials, this sec-tion will open with a copy of the auditor's opinion or report letter. As an in-vestor, look for language that states the auditor's concern for the company as an "ongoing business." This is called an auditor's *qualification* and will usu-ally state that in the auditor's opinion, the company is or will become "bust" if it doesn't get the proposed financing. A careful review of the following bal-ance sheets, statements of operations, equity, cash flow, and especially the attached notes will assist you in your determination of the company's viabil-ity. (Additional information about the items included in a registration state-ment can be found in Chapter 23.)

Wrap-Up

Initial Public Offerings

Initial public offerings have been part of the investment world since the buttonwood tree brokers started trading stocks. They are part of the world of venture capital, which is part of the larger world of investing. All investments have a degree of risk, but the risk level is higher with IPOs. The historical returns, however, are also higher. That is why traditional IPOs offered by large companies with a track record, as well as relatively new companies with a semiproven track record, have their offerings made by underwriters. Traditionally, these underwriters have used IPOs to reward their largest customers. Lone investors, trying to increase their return on a modest portfolio, seldom have the opportunity to invest in these larger offerings. When they do, the excitement level is usually so high that they seldom take the time to intelligently study the prospectus that is given with every new IPO.

The secret for investors is to study the process. Read a lot of offering circulars and become familiar with the terminology. Study the way a deal is put together and don't overlook the dilution section. And always watch the stock when it starts trading—not for just a few weeks but for a year. See if you can determine what makes a good offering by a solid company.

Direct Public Offering Investing

With the advent of the direct public offering, a lot of new excitement is building as investors have the opportunity to get involved on the ground level of emerging companies. The problem is twofold. First, for now and until the concept is proven, these are truly ground-level opportunities. Regulatory bodies will continue to develop the rules and regulations to make DPOs work. Underwriters will have to recognize and gear up to handle this type of securities transaction. Second, for now most of these offerings are for new companies, which for the most part are unproven in their viability.

Change is inevitable. The Internet is constantly changing and the pace is accelerating. Dataquest estimates that by the year 2001, 268 million computers will be connected to the Internet (81 million in 1997). Source-International Data Corp. predicts that ISDN lines (currently the fastest reasonably priced modem type) will be installed in 1.5 million residential homes, 1.4 million small businesses, and 1.5 million medium-size and large businesses by the year 2000. It seems that one hardly has the chance to sit back and digest. In fact, sitting back is not an option. You have to make decisions quickly and then make decisions how to make the technology work in your favor. You can't be afraid to make decisions just because conditions and technology are expected to change and make your current decision obsolete. You can't guard your turf as this is one of the most threatening elements in dealing with change. Surround yourself with people who embrace change and find it stimulating and nonthreatening. Ask questions and learn. The Internet has given the entrepreneur the opportunity to participate in a burgeoning global economy by selling more products to more customers at less cost. This applies to DPOs, exposing larger markets of investors to less-expensive stocks.

There are many interesting aspects to the Internet. One is that it is helping entrepreneurs create and expand a network, a network bound together via the Internet with entrepreneurs the core. This networking creates *value*. An example: The first fax machine cost "zillions" and when it was finished, it was worth zero. But the second one made the first one valuable. There was someone to fax to and a network was started. Pretty soon there were 20 in the network, then 200, then 2,000, and now millions. The fact that we are connected by fax machines made drastic changes in how business is conducted. Each additional fax, and now Internet connection, increases the value of the network. When a person signs on for an Internet connection, that person is not just buying a $20-a-month connection. That person is buying all the other connections tied into the network. The more plentiful the connections, the more valuable they become.

The Internet provides a collective interaction between entrepreneurs and their customers, between entrepreneurs and suppliers, and between entrepreneurs and investors. It allows entrepreneurs to post their investment proposals to an increasing number of investors and for these investors to react and provide feedback to the entrepreneur's proposal. Investors will communicate liking your deal or not liking your deal by the number who sign up to invest. Some investors will e-mail their comments, which gives the entrepreneur the opportunity for some one-on-one exchange. If the entrepreneur is on top of things, he or she will capture the investors' information and contact and recontact them. If an investor doesn't invest the first time around, sharp entrepreneurs will stay in touch via e-mail and keep the prospective investor aware of the progress in preparing for the second round of financing. It's called improving the value of the network.

I believe that Internet investing, including DPOs, has the potential of being the most significant change in the world of entrepreneurial financing— *ever*. With significant change, however, there are also challenges. The investor's DPO challenge is to learn about the process, study the differences from IPOs, assess the higher risks, and attempt to stay current with the practices. A large order for sure—but one that will pay handsome rewards to astute investors as we turn to the next century.

Glossary

accredited investor   A person or institution deemed capable of understanding, and able to afford, the financial risks associated with purchasing unregistered securities with a net worth exceeding $1 million or income over $200,000 annually in the past two years; other qualifications also apply.

acquisition   The term referring to one company's buying control of, if not all, the stock of another company.

active market   A securities market (Nasdaq, NYSE, AMEX) that has high levels of trading.

aftermarket   The stock market activity in which traders buy and sell shares in a public company after it has gone public.

allotment   The lead underwriter in a public offering will assemble other underwriters into a syndicate and "allot" each a certain number of shares to sell.

angels   Friends, family, or wealthy individuals who invest their money usually in start-up or early-stage companies.

ask (asking price)   The lowest price per share for which prospective sellers are willing to sell their stock.

auditor   The certified public accounting firm, which is not connected in anyway with a company, that reviews the company's financial records and renders an opinion according to specific auditing rules and regulations.

bad boys   Individuals who have violated securities laws. Reg A and SCOR regulations prohibit bad boys from participating in these offerings unless the Securities and Exchange Commission and state authorities consent.

balance sheet   The document that reflects a company's assets, liabilities, and capital at a specific point in time.

best-effort offering   A securities firm's sale of a company's stock to the public without guaranteeing the company any money. The securities firm uses its best effort to sell the stock without being contractually bound to sell it all. See firm commitment.

bid (bid price)   The highest price per share for which a prospective buyer is willing to pay to buy a stock.

blind pool   A public offering, also known as a "blank check" offering, wherein the company does not specifically state how it is going to invest the monies received from the offering. Most states have very strict regulations covering this type of offering.

blue-sky laws   State laws that regulate the issuance of a company's stock offerings. When a stock is "blue-skied" in a given state, it means that the company's stock offering is okayed to sell or trade in that state.

book value   Also known as net worth and denotes the value the company has placed on its assets less its liabilities to arrive at a shareholders equity figure.

broker (stockbroker–registered representative)   An individual who has registered with the SEC, the exchanges, the NASD, and appropriate states, and who has passed certain tests and requirements allowing her or him to be involved in the business of buying and selling securities.

broker-dealer   An individual or, more commonly, a group of individuals who have met certain standards and are licensed to buy and sell securities for others (broker) for their own accounts (dealer).

bulletin board stock (BBS)   An over-the-counter (OTC) stock for which bid and ask prices can be obtained from the OTC Bulletin Board operated by the NASD.

capitalization   A company's stock price multiplied by the total number of outstanding shares (e.g., 5 million shares outstanding times $5 per share equals a capitalization of $25 million).

closing   A meeting held between an underwriter and a company following a completed public offering in which the company delivers its stock certificates for transfer to individual investors and the underwriter delivers to the public company the money collected from its efforts in selling the company's stock to the investors.

common stock   Units representing ownership of a corporation. The owners (shareholders) typically are entitled to vote on the selection of directors and other company matters as well as receive dividends on their holdings. If the company is liquidated, the claims of its creditors and owners of bonds or preferred stock take precedence over the common stockholders; common stock usually has more potential for appreciation.

control person   An officer or director of a company or someone who owns 5 percent or more of the company's stock and is held liable for certain restrictions on buying and selling his or her stock and in passing on information about the company.

dealer   See broker-dealer.

deficiency letter   A letter that may be issued by the SEC or state authorities after reviewing a company's securities filing. The deficiency letter offers suggestions on what to do if the filing information is considered inadequate or insufficient. Although these are so-called suggestions, a company would be risking a possible "cease and desist" order, which prohibits it from selling its securities, if it does not comply with the suggestions for corrections.

dilution A term used to describe an increase or decrease in the amount of shareholders equity (net worth/book value) whenever new shares are issued by a company.

direct public offerings Offerings of new securities by a company made directly to the general public without the services of an underwriter or investment bank.

directors Individuals who are elected by the shareholders of a company to set policy and appoint the executive officers of the company.

dividends Payments made to shareholders disbursed from a portion of the company's earnings; usually paid in cash but may be paid in additional, newly issued shares.

due diligence The process of gathering and confirming information about a company and its business, management, and financial affairs.

earnings per share The portion of a company's net profit divided by the total number of shares outstanding. ($5 million in net profit divided by 1 million shares outstanding equals "earnings per share" of $5.)

EDGAR The SEC's Electronic Data Gathering, Analysis and Retrieval system by which a company files reports, copies of which the general public can obtain via computer.

effective date The date on which a company's registration statement becomes effective with the regulatory agencies (SEC and state agencies), allowing it to begin selling its securities.

equity The investment made in the company. When expressed as shareholders equity, it refers to the assets less liabilities plus or minus earnings or losses (i.e., net worth).

exchange The primary stock exchange on which an issue is listed (NYSE, AMEX, or regional exchanges).

exempt (securities) Securities, usually common stock, that are exempt from federal and state full registration laws.

filing date The date when a company files its registration statement with the SEC or state securities commissions.

firm commitment A public offering of a company's securities wherein the underwriter agrees to buy all of the shares. See best-effort offering.

float (public float) The number of shares owned by the public that doesn't include shares owned by officers, directors, or other inside shareholders, such as those who own 5 percent or more.

GAAP An acronym for generally accepted accounting principles that are observed by a company's auditors vis-à-vis a company's financial practices. Conforming to GAAP is a must for public companies.

going public The process wherein a privately held company sells additional shares to the general public via an initial public offering (IPO).

high The highest price at which a stock has traded for a specific time period (a day, week, month, quarter, or year).

initial public offering or IPO A private company's first public sale of a specific class of security, usually common stock.

insider   A person in a position to control what happens within a company and/or has access to nonpublic company information (commonly, executive officers, directors, and 5 percent or more shareholders).

institutional investors   Typically refers to pension funds, insurance companies, mutual funds, and endowments with large amounts of money managed by professional investors. The majority of the stock of large companies is held by institutional investors.

investment bank (banker)   A financial firm or individual, sometimes also a stock broker-dealer, who acts as an intermediary and whose principal functions are to identify companies that need financing and then provide them with advice on the corporate financing functions and methods to obtain both short-term and long-term financing. (The author's firm, Venture Associates, is an investment banking firm.)

issuer   An entity, usually a corporation, that has the ability to issue and distribute securities.

lead (head/managing) underwriter   The firm that takes primary responsibility for selling a company's securities and assembles and manages the other broker-dealers (syndicate members).

letter of intent   An agreement between an underwriter and a company about the terms and conditions under which the company's stock will be sold to the general public.

letter (restricted) stock   Stock that is purchased in a private offering and has certain restrictions on its sale or transfer.

listed stock   Stock of a company that is admitted for trading on the NYSE or the AMEX as opposed to trading over-the-counter (OTC).

low   The lowest price at which a stock has traded for a specific time period (a day, week, month, quarter, or year).

market capitalization   The total number of shares issued and outstanding multiplied by the market price of the shares. See capitalization.

market maker   A broker-dealer that quotes firm bid and ask prices in a given security and stands ready to buy or sell a stock at publicly quoted prices in the over-the-counter market in a minimum amount of 100 shares.

memorandum   A document similar to a prospectus, sometimes also referred to as an offering circular, which is the official document by which private placements are offered and sold.

minimum/maximum offering   Used in a stock offering where a minimum number of shares must be sold before the company receives the money and where a maximum number of shares are offered for sale. If the minimum amount is not received, the monies are returned to the investors.

NASD (National Association of Securities Dealers)   A self-regulating organization composed of broker/dealers which the SEC recognizes as a substitute for government regulation. Testing of individual brokers and operating requirements for broker/dealers are administered by the NASD.

Nasdaq (National Association of Securities Dealers Automated Quotations)   A computerized stock display information system, not a stock exchange, that furnishes bid and ask prices as well as certain trading statistics. Trading is usually accomplished via phone, fax, or computer.

NMS (National Market System)   The Nasdaq reporting system for trading larger, more highly qualified stocks.

net change   The difference between the most recent sale of a stock and its previous close.

new issue   The stock of a company that is now going, or has just gone, public.

offering circular   A disclosure and information document used to furnish information about a company and its stock offering to prospective investors; commonly used for exempt offerings and patterned after a prospectus.

offering expenses   Costs incurred by a company to make a public offering that include legal and accounting fees, management time and internal expenses directly attributed to the offering, underwriting commissions, and fees paid to regulatory bodies.

open   The first trade price of the day for a stock.

OTC   OTC stands for over-the-counter and is associated with OTC companies, their stocks, and the OTC market, where a broker-dealer quotes bid and ask prices at which he or she will buy and sell shares of stock.

OTC Bulletin Board   An electronic information system operated by the NASD that furnishes bid and ask prices of smaller capitalized OTC-traded stocks.

penny stocks (low-priced stocks)   Generally thought of as stocks with a trading price from a penny to $3.

Pink Sheets   A 300-page-plus "book" printed on pink paper and issued each trading day by the NASD that lists bid and ask prices and certain trading information on over 10,000 OTC stocks.

preferred shares   A separate class of a company's stock with certain preferential features over common stock that often include a right of its owners to be repaid before shareholders of common stock in the event of liquidation, rights to dividends before owners of common stock, and sometimes certain voting rights superior to those of common stock.

preliminary prospectus   A document by which public offerings are made after the filing of the registration statement but before the offering is declared effective. It is also known as a "red herring" because of the caveats printed in red on the cover warning the reader that the document does not contain all of the information about the issue and that some information may be changed before the final prospectus is issued.

previous close   The last price at which a stock was traded during the previous trading day

price-earnings (PE) ratio   The price of a stock divided by its earnings per share that is usually expressed on a historical or projected basis and is a common way to compare one company's stock with another.

private placement   An offering of securities exempt from full SEC registration requirements that is usually made directly by the issuing company but may also be made by an underwriter.

proceeds   The net amount of monies received by a company from a public offering; "use of proceeds" describes how a company intends to use the money.

projections   A company's financial estimates of its future operations.

prospectus   The official offering document that is part of the registration statement filed with the SEC in conjunction with a public offering of fully registered securities.

quiet period   A period of time beginning at the date when a company files its registration statement with the SEC and continuing for 90 days after the effective date of its offering. A company has to take special care in releasing information and discussions about its operations that are not disclosed in its offering prospectus during this period.

red herring   See preliminary prospectus.

registered representative   See broker.

registration statement   The official document that must be filed with the SEC, state securities departments, and trading market/exchanges before a company's securities can sold to the public. It includes the prospectus.

Regulations A and D, and SCOR   Exemptions made by the SEC from filing a full registration statement under the *Securities Act of 1933*.

restricted shares   Shares of stock usually obtained in a private placement or owned by an insider where their resale has certain restrictions.

road show   The process wherein an underwriter accompanies members of the management team of a company to present information about the company and its proposed public offering to prospective investors at various locations, sometimes internationally.

SCOR (Small Corporate Offering Registration)   An SEC-exempt offering for the sale of securities up to the amount of $1 million that must be qualified under state blue-sky laws. (Also known as ULOR.)

SEC   The U.S. Securities and Exchange Commission, which is charged with the administration and enforcement of federal securities laws.

secondary offering   A term generally applied to an offering made after an initial public offering.

secondary market   The trading market (aftermarket) for stocks after they have undergone an initial public offering.

securities   Broadly includes common or preferred stocks and bonds, but can also include other types of financing instruments such as debentures, warrants, and convertible offerings.

Securities Act of 1933   The federal law, including amendments, pertaining to the offering of securities administrated by the SEC.

Securities Exchange Act of 1934   The federal law, including amendments, pertaining to the trading of securities, stock exchanges, firms, and brokers administrated by the SEC.

shareholders   Individuals or entities who own the securities (shares/stocks) of a company.

shares outstanding   The total number of shares of stock held by all shareholders.

shell corporation   A company (corporation) with publicly owned shares but no active operations; typically, a company that has sold its operating assets or discontinued operations without dissolving the corporation as a legal entity. A private, operating company can be reverse-merged into a public shell that will result in the private company's becoming a public company.

specialist   A broker-dealer who maintains firm bid and offer prices in a given security by standing ready to buy or sell a minimum of 100 shares at publicly quoted prices on any exchange.

stickering (a prospectus)   The attachment of a paper to the cover of a prospectus (official offering circular/memorandum) that contains new information after an offering's effective date but before the conclusion of the offering.

stock market   The trading market for publicly held securities that includes the OTC (Nasdaq), the NYSE, the AMEX, and regional and foreign exchanges.

street name   A name used for stock certificates held by a nominee in behalf of the true owner. A securities firm usually owns a nominee firm that holds securities on behalf of individual investors to facilitate the quick transfer of stocks for trading.

tombstone (ad)   An ad or formal announcement that a public offering is being, or has been, made. It provides minimal information including the name of the company (issuer), the underwriter's name(s), the amount of the offering, and a statement that an official offering is made only by the prospectus.

transfer agent   Usually, a company that keeps records showing who owns, sells, and buys a publicly held company's stock.

ULOR (Uniform Limited Offering Registration)   Also known as SCOR, which is an offering exempt from SEC registration for offerings up to $1 million.

underwriter   A stock brokerage (securities) firm that sells the stock for a new public company.

underwriting   The process of doing an initial public offering.

underwriting syndicate   The group of broker-dealers (brokerage firms) that sell the stock of an initial public offering.

venture capital   The money invested to start and develop a company. Traditional venture capital firms that fund emerging growth companies are commonly funded themselves by institutional investors (pension funds, insurance companies, and investment trusts). On a broader basis, venture capital comes from founding company entrepreneurs, friends and family, angels, and other companies that may be strategic partners.

volume   The total number of shares traded for a specific time period, commonly per day.

warrant   A certificate giving its holder the right to purchase securities at a defined price within a specified time.

Index

A

Acceleration letter, 218
Accountability, 10–12
Accountants/accounting, 72–81
    accountability of, 80
    audits and, 75, 76–77
    due diligence and, 161–62
    evaluating, 76–77
    familiarity of, with company, 77–78
    fees, 30–31
    GAAP and, 78–79, 161
    selecting, 74–75
Accredited investors, 143–44
Acquisitions, 12–13, 193
Administration, 4
Administrative Procedures Act, 132
Advantages, of going public, 4–8
    for the company, 4–6
    to employees, 7
    for the founders, 6–7
Adverse change, 177
Advertising
    Regulation D and, 147, 148
    tombstones, 28, 41, 230
Advisers, 68–70
Advisory committee, 63
Affiliate, 278
Affinity group, 302
Aftermarket trading, 172, 249–58
    analysts, 255–58
    market makers, 252–55
    overallotment, 250–52
Agreement among the underwriters, 178.
    See also Underwriter(s)
All or none option, 167
American Bankers Association, 154
American Institute of Certified Public
    Accountants, 74
American Stock Exchange (AMEX), 8,
    237–38
Analysts, 255–58
    on-site visits by, 258
Annual reports, 10, 262–63, 265–68
    corporate message in, 266
    design of, 266–67
    mailing of, 268
    proxies, 267–68
Apple Computer, 118–19
Articles of incorporation, 110–16
    amendments to, 116, 117
    board of directors and, 114
    bylaws, 116
    conflicts of interest and, 114–15
    indemnification, 115
    shareholder meetings and votes, 115–16
Ash, Mary Kay, 52
As reported earnings, 126
Asset-based lending, 19, 22
Associates, identification of, 30
Association of Corporate Directors, 63
AT&T, 97

Attorneys, 82–88
    billings and fees, 85–87
    due diligence and, 157–59
    fees, 29–30
    integration and multistep financing
      plans and, 155
    interviewing prospective, 84–85, 88
    large vs. small law firms, 83–84, 88
    multiple counsel approach, 87–88
    responsibilities of, 87
    SEC regulations and, 133
Auction method, of trading, 237
Audit committee, 62
Audits, 30–31, 41, 75, 76–77
    change of auditing firm and, 262
    guidelines for, 76
Authorized common stock, 112

B

"Bad boy," 148, 153
Balloon payments, 20
Bankruptcy, 262
Bankruptcy Act, 131
Barron's, 281
Best-effort, 26, 167, 251
    closing, 232–33
Beta test, 141
Blind pools, 283, 290–94
    abuses of, 291
    costs, 293–94
    exercising warrants, 292–93
    unit offerings, 292
Block, Henry and Richard, 52
Blue-sky laws, 8, 41, 146, 177, 218–21
    fees, 33
    self-underwriting and, 185
Blue-sky lists, 220
Board meetings, 14
Board of advisers, 64
Board of directors, 57–64, 199
    in articles of incorporation, 114
    change of, 10
    committees of, 62–63
    common stock and, 112
    compensation of, 60
    disclosure of payments to, 10
    liability of, 34, 61
    preferred stock and, 112
    questionnaire, 64, 205, 207

SEC information requirements, 205,
    207
    state laws and, 110
British Companies Act, 135
Broker contacts, 100–101, 101–2
Broker-dealers, 243–44, 252–55
    direct public offerings and, 302
    restrictions on, 137
Bulletin board, OTC, 240, 320
Burrell, Lowell, 285
Business plan, 42–48, 140, 141, 337
    feedback on, 44
    follow-up on, 48
    as fundraising tool, 16
    oral presentation, 44
    preprivate financing, 47
    purposes of, 42
    special executive summary, 47–48
    stock price and, 125
    structure of, 45–47
    time estimate for, 40
    underwriters and, 174
    writing guidelines, 43–44
Bylaws, 116, 160–61

C

California SCOR requirements, 315–16
Capital
    defined, 4
    sources of. *See* Financing
Capitalization, 337
Capital stock, 111–13
Category listings, 126
Charitable organizations, 149
Chief executive officer, 34, 37, 51–53
    directors and, 58–59
Closing, of offering, 231–34
    best-effort, 232–33
    closing meeting, 231–32
    firm-commitment, 233–34
Combination, of financing, 24–25
"Comfort" letter, 30, 162
Commercial banks, and debt financing, 19
Commercial finance companies, and debt
    financing, 19–20
Commissions, 27–28
    Rule 504 and, 146–47
    underwriters and, 177
    warrants and, 123–24

Committee on Uniform Securities
    Identification Procedures (CUSIP), 243
Common stock, 112–13, 122–23
    nonvoting, 123
    warrants and, 123–24
Communication, 14, 94–95
Company, IPO advantages to, 4–6
Competition, 336
    competitive positions, disclosure of,
        10
    competitive profile, 46
    evaluating, 43–44
Compilations, 74
Conflict of interest
    in articles of incorporation, 114–15
    committee, 62
    as risk factor, 335
Consultants, 65–68
Continual reporting, 259–75
    annual report (Forms 10-K and
        10-KSB), 262–63, 265–68
    application of proceeds (Form SR),
        260–61
    current reports (Form 8-K), 261–62
    direct public offerings and, 305
    Foreign Corrupt Practices Act and,
        268–69
    Form 3 and, 269
    Form 4 and, 270
    insider reporting and trading
        restrictions, 270–71
    quarterly report (Forms 10-Q and
        10-QSB), 263–65
    schedules, 271–74
Convertibility
    clause, in subordinated debt, 18
    of preferred stock, 112
Convertible debenture, 124, 147
Convertible/subordinated debt, 23
Coordination review, 220
Coors Brewery, 123
Corporate bonds, 138
Corporate cleanup, 29–30, 157, 159–61
Corporate Directors Guidebook, 59
Corporate image, 5
Corporate message, 266
Corporation, formation of, 40
Cumulative voting, 113
Customer profile, 46

D

Deal flow, 329
Debt, retiring, 4
Debt financing, 17–18, 19–22
    commercial banks and, 19
    commercial finance companies and,
        19–20
    industrial revenue bonds and, 21
    leasing companies and, 20
    leveraged buyouts and, 22
    life insurance companies and pension
        funds and, 22
    savings and loan associations and, 20
    Small Business Administration and, 21
Debt-to-equity ratio, 126
Delaware
    incorporation in, 109
    indemnification allowability in, 115
Depository trust company, 268
Dilution, 120–21, 196, 331–32, 336
Directors. *See* Board of directors
Director's Monthly, 63
Direct public offerings, 186, 339. *See also*
    Investor tips
    company suitability for, 301–2
    continual reporting, 305
    intrastate, 317
    and IPOs compared, 300–301
    registration of securities, 303–6
    Regulation A, 152–54, 309–13
    Regulation D-504, 316–17
    SCOR, 297–302, 306, 314–16
    SEC and, 303, 306–7
    small-business forms, 304–5
    substantiation of delivery, 307
    trading, 319–26
        electronic matching services, 321,
            326
        order-matching services, 320–21, 326
        Pacific Exchange, 321–25
    vehicle choices, 307
    Web site, 321
Disadvantages, of going public, 9–15
    control or loss of control, 12–14, 15
    expenses, 14–15
Disclosure(s), 9–10
    finders' compensation and, 168
    quarterly reports and, 264

Disclosure(s) continued
    registration statement and, 203
    Securites Act of 1933 and, 136
    statements, 8
Discounting, 127, 249
Distribution plan, 44
Diversification, of portfolio, 6
Dividend policy, 196
Doing business in the state, defined, 151
Drucker, Peter, 327
Due diligence, 28–29, 41, 157–62
    accounting, 79, 161–62
    brokers' meetings, 226–30
    corporate cleanup, 157, 159–61
    legal responsibility, 157–59

E

Earnings ratios, 125
Economic conditions, and timing, 35
Economic trends, IPOs and, 13
EDGAR, 298
Educational organizations, 149
Efficiency ratios, 125
Electronic Data Gathering, Analysis, and
    Retrieval system (EDGAR), 298
Electronic matching services, 321, 326
Employee benefits, 160
    in IPOs, 7
    stock option plan (ESOP), 30, 193
Employee Retirement Income Security Act
    (ERISA), 161
Employment agreements, 159–60
Engineering, 55
Entrepreneurs, 52
Equipment
    industrial revenue bonds and, 21
    purchasing, 4
Equity capital structure, 47
"Equity kickers," 18
Estate tax, 6
Estate valuation, 12
Executive committee, 62–63
Executive officers, 199
Executive summary, of business plan, 45
Exempted securities, 149
Exempted transactions, 149–50
Expense, of going public, 14–15
    consultants, 67
    printing costs, 32, 89–92

professional costs, 29–31
promotion, 34
registration fees, 32–33
regulatory and related bodies, 33
underwriter costs, 27–29

F

Familiarization visit, 158
Family members, on management team, 56
Fee payments, 10
Filing, 41, 8–12, 222
    initial filing, 210–11
    prefiling conference, 208–9
    technicalities, 209–10
Financial Accounting Standards Board, 73
Financial management, 54
Financial press, 280–82
Financial printers, 89–92
    ancillary services, 91–92
    costs of, 90–91
    qualifying, 91
Financial projections, 44–45, 48
Financial public relations, 14, 93–102
    commitment to, 97–98
    financial press and, 281–82
    finding and evaluating a firm, 99–101
    functions of, 99–100
    mystique of, 93–94
    and nonfinancial PR compared, 95
    rewards of, 96–97
    steps to effective, 94–95
Financial ratings books, 33
Financial Reporting Releases, 192
Financial statements, 338
    registration statement and, 202–3
    SEC review of, 131
Financing
    business plan and, 16
    combination of, 24–25
    debt financing, 17–18, 19–22
    estimated time for, 40–41
    ongoing, 4
    preprivate financing, 47, 140–41
    private financing, 17, 141–42
    professional venture capital, 23
    research and development
        partnerships, 23
    Small Business Innovation Research
        grants (SBIR grants), 24

Small Business Investment Companies (SBICs), 23–24
  subordinated debt, 18–19
  time estimate for, 41
Finders, 168
Firm commitment, 26, 166–67
  closing, 233–34
Ford Motor Company, 119
Foreign Corrupt Practices Act (FCPA), 61, 73, 137, 161, 268–69
Forms, for periodic reporting, 136–37
Fortune, 281
Founders, IPO advantages to, 6–7
Fraud, Securities Act of 1933 and, 136
Funding sources, 44

G

GAAP, 78–79, 161
Gates, William, 6, 52
Going Public: The IPO Reporter, 171
Golden parachute provisions, 160
Government funding, 21
Government securities, 149
Grant programs, 24
"Green shoe," 167, 250
Growth, sustaining, 4
Guterman, Alexander, 285

H

Hewlett, William, 52
Hewlett-Packard, 52
Historic building renovation, 23
Hostile takeovers, 114, 160
Hot stocks, 37
Hughes Committee, 134

I

Inc., 281
Incentive stock option plan (ISOP), 30
Incorporation. *See* Public company, incorporation of
Indemnification, 110, 115, 181
Indications-of-interest book, 127–28
Industrial classification, of offerings, 166
Industrial revenue bonds, and debt financing, 21, 22

Industry
  dynamism, 70
  listings, 126
  movements, IPOs and, 13
  profile, 46
Initial public offering (IPO), 338–39. *See also* Investor tips
  advantages to company, 4–6
  advantages to employees, 7
  advantages to founders, 6–7
  and direct public offering compared, 300–301
  industry movements and, 13
Innovation, 125
Insider trading, 11, 137, 270–71
Insider Trading Sanction Act, 270
Insurance, liability, for directors and officers, 34
Integration, 146, 155
Interest costs, 18
Interest coverage, 125
Interim audit, 30
Internet direct public offerings, 297–300, 339–40. *See also* Direct public offerings
  advantages of, 299
Intrastate offerings, 150–52, 317
Intrastate shells, 152
Inventories, increasing, 4
Inventory
  asset-based lending and, 19
  financing and, 19
Inventory accounting, 78–79
Investment advisers, 138
Investment bankers. *See also* Underwriter(s)
  expense of, 31
Investment Company Act of 1940, The, 131, 138
Investment trusts, 193
Investor tips, 327–40
  analyze the business, 330–31
  deal flow, 329
  dilution and, 331–32
  direct public offering investing, 339–40
  initial public offerings, 338–40
  principal shareholders, determining, 332–33
  prospectus, analyzing, 333–38
  research, 328–29

Investor tips continued
  risk, 327–28
  study, 330
Issued common stock, 112
Issuer Tender Offer Statement, 272

J–K

Jobs, Steven, 6
Kansas, 218
Kroc, Ray, 52

L

Leaseback, 20
Leasing companies, and debt financing, 20
Legal counsel, 69, 82–88
  billings and fees, 85–87
  current reports and, 261–62
  due diligence and, 157–59
  fees, 29–30
  functions of, 55–56
  integration and multistep financing
    plans and, 155
  interviewing prospective, 84–85, 88
  large vs. small law firms, 83–84, 88
  multiple counsel approach, 87–88
  SEC regulations and, 133
Lettered stock, 276–77, 279
Letter of intent, 176–78
Leverage, 17
Leveraged buyouts, and debt financing, 22
Leverage ratios, 125
Liability insurance, 34, 73
Life insurance companies, and debt
  financing, 22
Limited partnerships, 313
Listings, 236–45
  American Stock Exchange, 237–38
  broker-dealers and wholesale market
    makers, 243–44
  New York Stock Exchange, 236–37
  over-the-counter market, 238–42
  public, 243
  regional exchanges, 238
Loan covenants, 17–18
Loan restructuring, 160
Long-term debt, 17
Low-priced issues, 128

M

Management
  consultants, 65–68
  presented in business plan, 44
  résumés, in business plan, 46
  team, 51–56
    administration and general
      management, 53–54
    analysts and, 256–57
    chief executive officer, 34, 37, 51–53
    chief financial officer, 56
    engineering and R&D, 55
    family members on, 56
    financial management, 54
    functions of, 53
    legal, 55–56
    marketing management, 54–55
    operations management, 54
    personnel, 55
  underwriters and, 173–74
  valuation and, 125
Managing underwriter, 163–64. *See also*
  Underwriter(s)
Margin requirements, SEC authority over,
  137
Market conditions, timing and, 35, 39
Marketing
  management, 54–55
  methods, disclosure of, 9–10
  strategy, 46
Market makers, 184–85, 243–44, 252–55,
  320
  purpose of, 253–54
  wholesale vs. retail, 252–53
Market share, increasing, 4
Mary Kay Cosmetics, 52
McDonald's Corporation, 52
*McGraw-Hill Guide to Writing a High-
  Impact Business Plan, The,* 45
Media exposure, 5
Mergers, 13, 193
Merit review, 219
Microsoft, 52, 244
Minority Enterprise Small Business
  Investment Companies, 24
Model Corporation Act, The, 110
Moody's, 33, 243
Mortgage loans, 19

N

Nasdaq. *See* National Association of
    Securities Dealers Automated Quotations
    (Nasdaq)
NASD review, 221–22
National Association of Securities Dealers
    Automated Quotations (Nasdaq), 8, 238,
    240–42, 320
        fees, 33
        market makers, 252
        SEC and, 131
National Association of Securities Dealers
    (NASD), 28, 41, 245
        fees, 33
National Market System (NMS), 242
National Securities Act, 135
Net capital, SEC authority over, 137
Networking, 329, 340
New York Stock Exchange (NYSE), 8,
    236–37
Nominating committee, 62
Nonaccountable expense allowance, 28–29
Non-arm's-length arrangements, 10
North American Securities Administrators
    Association, 154, 314
Notification review, 220

O

Obsolescence, as risk factor, 335
Offering circular/memorandum/statement,
    312
Officers
        disclosure of payments to, 10
        questionnaire, 64, 205, 207
        SEC information requirements, 205,
            207
Officers' liability insurance, 34
144(k) letter, 277
Ongoing financing, 4
Operating base, 125
Operating history, and valuation, 125
Operations, 4
        management, 54
        plan, 46
Order-matching services, 320–21, 326
OTC market. See Over-the-counter market
    (OTC)

Outstanding common stock, 113
Overallotment, 167, 250–52, 258
Over-the-counter market (OTC), 8, 236,
    238–42, 244
        analysts and, 257–58
        bulletin board, 240
        Nasdaq system, 240–42
        NMS market, 242
        pink sheets, 239–40
        SEC and, 137

P

Pacific Exchange, 321–25
        admission to trading, 324–25
        listing process, 323–24
        listing requirements, 321–22
        maintenance criteria, 322–23
Packard, David, 52
Patent/proprietary product position, 125
Patents, 10, 336
Pension funds, and debt financing, 22
PE ratio, 6
Performance comparison, 126
Performance ratios, 17–18
Periodic reporting forms, 136–37
Permanent equity capital, 17
Perpetual existence, 111
Personnel management, 55
Pink sheets, 239–40
Political prestige, 6
Portfolio diversification, 6
Postcompletion, 41
"Power Point" presentations, 229
Preemptive right, 113
Preferred stock, 112
        convertible debenture and, 124, 129
        with dividend provision, 124
Preincorporation agreement, 140–41
Preliminary prospectus (red herring), 41,
    89, 194, 215–16
Preprivate financing, 47, 140–41
Presubscription agreement, 140–41
Price-earnings ratio, 6, 126–27
Printing costs, 32
Private financing, 17, 141–42
        alternate methods of, 149–54
Private investment pools, 22
Private placement preparation, 40

Private sale exemption, 150
Proceeds, use of, 125
Product
    description, in business plan, 45
    development, 4, 24
    differentiation, 125
    quality, and underwriters, 174
    single, 335
Professional costs, 29–31
    accounting fees, 30–31
    investment bankers and consultants,
        31
    legal fees, 29–30
Professional venture capital, 23
Profit margins, 125
    disclosure of, 10
Projections, 44
Promotion, 34
Prospectus
    business information, 198–99
    description of securities, 201
    financial printers and, 89–90
    financial statements, 202–3
    management descriptions, 199–201
    overallotment or stabilization
        expectation, disclosure of, 250
    red herring, 41, 89, 194, 215–16, 333
    risk factors, 334–36
    stickers, 217, 251
    studying, 333–38
    underwriting, 201–2
Proxy, 12
    rules, 113
    solicitations, 137
Publications. See Financial press
Public attitude, analyzing, 94
Public company, incorporation of, 109–17
    articles of incorporation, 110–16
    state laws, 109–10
Public exposure, 5
Public float, 125
Public image, financial PR firms and, 95
Publicity
    allowed during registration, 225–26
    barred during registration, 224–25
    controlling, during quiet period, 234
Public listings, 243
Public relations. See Financial Public
    relations

Public relations firms, financial, 14
Public shells. See Shells
Public Utility Holding Company Act of
    1935, 131, 138
Pujo Committee, 134
Purchaser representative, 144

Q

Qualification review, 219
Quantum Computer, 118–19
Quarterly reports, 10, 263–65
Quiet period, 217, 223, 234

R

Reagan, Ronald, 139
Real estate
    companies, 193
    partnerships, 23
    projects, and industrial revenue bonds,
        21
Recapitalization, 4–5
Receivables, 4
Reciprocal indemnification, 177
Red herring, 41, 89, 194, 215–16, 333
Regional stock exchanges, 238
Registered office and agent, 113
Registration fees, 32–33
Registration Form U-7, 154
Registration period
    allowed publicity during, 225–26
    barred publicity during, 224–25
    quiet period, 223–26
Registration process, 38–39, 41
Registration statements, 29, 31, 32,
    189–207
    amendments, 213–15
    comment/deficiency letter, 211–12
    filing process, 192–93, 208–12
    in letter of intent, 176–77
    management and, 206–7
    misstatements in, 204
    officers' and directors' questionnaire,
        64, 205, 207
    prefiling conferences, 208–9
    preparing process, 205–6
    prospectus, 193–203, 215–16, 217
    public scrutiny of, 204

purpose of, 207
review of, 213, 219–22
SEC regulations and, 190–92
SEC review of, 130
Securities Act of 1933 and, 136, 139
stop order, 216–17
Regulation, of securities sales, 8
SEC. *See* Securities and Exchange
Commission
state regulations, 132
Regulation A offerings, 152–54, 309–10
exemption from registration, 310–11
limited partnerships and, 313
unaudited financials and, 311
Regulation C, 191–92
Regulation D, 17, 142–49, 314
commissions, 146–47
investors, number of, 147
Rule 501, 142–44
Rule 502, 144–45
Rule 503, 145
Rule 504, 145–47, 316–17
Rule 505, 147–48
Rule 506, 148–49
Regulation S-K, 190–91, 221
Regulation S-X, 161, 191
Regulatory agencies, timing and, 38
Religious organizations, 149
Repositioning, 128
Research, 4, 328–29
Research and development, 46, 55
partnerships, 23
Restricted stock, 276
Restrictive covenants, 21
Retail underwriters, 164–66. *See also*
Underwriter(s)
Return on equity, 17
Reverse merger, 283, 294
Reverse stock split, 128
Reviews, 74
Revolving lines of credit, 19
Reynolds, 97
Rights to purchase stock, 18
Risk, 327–28
Road shows, 226–30, 235
Roosevelt, Franklin, 134–35
Roosevelt, Theodore, 134
Royalty payments, 10
Rule 144, 150

S

Safe harbor, 263
Sales, disclosure of, 10
Savings and loan associations, and debt
financing, 20
SCOR, 147, 154, 245, 312, 314–16
SCOR Marketplace, 321–25
SEC News Digest, 132
Securities, description of, 338
Securities Act of 1933, 8, 130, 134–36
accountants and, 80, 161
exemptions to. *See* Regulation D
registration statements and, 136, 139,
189
Securities Acts Amendment of 1964, The,
138
Securities and Exchange Commission
(SEC), 130–33, 135
direct public offerings and, 303, 306–7
disclosure and, 9
divisions of, 130–31
fees, 33
investigation and enforcement, 131–32
management team and, 51
reference facilities of, 132
registration forms, 273
registration statements and, 189, 192
Regulation A and, 152–53
reporting requirements of, 126
Rule 144, 276–79
self-underwritings and, 185
shell companies and, 285
Small Business Investment Incentive
Act and, 140
timing, 39, 41
Web site, 138
Securities Exchange Act of 1934, 8, 73,
130, 134, 135, 136–37
Securities industry, rules pertaining to, 137
Securities Investor Protection Act of 1970,
138
Securities Investors Protection Corporation
(SIPC), 138
Securities legislation, federal, 134–38
changes in, 138
history, 134–35
regulations for portions of securities
industry, 137–38

Securities legislation continued
    Securities Act of 1933, 135–36
    Securities Exchange Act of 1934,
      136–37
Securities violations, SEC and, 131–32
Self-employed Americans, 52
Self-underwriting, 183–86
    blue-sky laws and, 185
    good candidates for, 186
    Internet and, 186
    market makers, 184–85
    pros and cons of, 185–86
Selling the issue, 223–35
    brokers' due diligence meetings, 226–30
    closing, 231–34
    escrow, 231
    publicity, during registration, 224–26
    tombstones, 230
Senate Committee on Banking and
    Currency Reforms, 135
Service Corps of Retired Executives
    (SCORE), 68
Shareholder(s), 332–33, 337
    approval, 12
    communications with, 14
    meetings and votes, 115–16
    sale of stock by, at IPO, 124–25
    in shells, 288–89
    voting history of, 120
Shells, 152, 283–90
    acquiring, 289–90
    advantages and disadvantages of,
      286–87
    shareholders in, 288–89
    spin-off, 290, 294
Short selling, 271
Short-term debt, 17
Small Business Administration, 68
    debt financing and, 21
Small Business Development Centers, 68
Small Business Informational Package, 191
Small Business Initiatives, 154
Small Business Innovation Research grants
    (SBIR grants), 24
Small Business Investment Companies
    (SBICs), 18, 23–24
Small Business Investment Incentive Act,
    140, 314

Small Corporate Offering Registration
    (SCOR), 147, 154, 245, 312, 314–16
    California requirements, 315–16
    Form U-7, 315
Smith, Adam, 139
Source-International Data Corp., 339
Special executive summary, 47–48
Special Study of Securities Markets, 138
Spin-offs, 290, 294
Spreadsheets, 25
Stabilization, 249–50
Staff Accounting Bulletins, 192
Standard Oil, 97–98
Standard & Poor's, 33
Standard & Poor's Index, 243
Start-up companies
    accounting fees and, 30
    exemption and, 155
    financing of, 140–42
    legal fees and, 29
Start-up operations, funding, 4
State incorporation laws, 109–10
Sterilized stock, 153
Stickers, 217, 251
Stock, 122–29
    capital, 111–13
    common, 112–13, 122–23
    determining type of, in IPO, 122–24
    dilution, 120–21
    discounting, 127
    low-priced issues, 128
    options, 7
    preferred, 112, 124
    pricing, 127–28, 129
    public float, 125
    repositioning, 128
    restricted or "lettered," 276–77
    sale of, by shareholders, 124–25
    sterilized, 153
    valuation and pricing compared,
      125–26
    value appreciation, 5
    voting stock, 12–14, 15, 118–21
    warrants, 18, 123–24, 174–75
Stockbroker, as underwriter source, 181
Stock exchanges, 7–8
    American Stock Exchange, 237–38
    New York Stock Exchange, 236–37

over-the-counter, 238–42
Pacific Exchange, 321–25
regional, 238
Stock market conditions, IPOs and, 13
Stub statement, 30
Subordinated debt, 18–19
Subsidiaries, 78

T

Telecommunications, 237
Tender offers, 137
Timing, 12–13, 35–41
    CEOs and, 37
    checklist, 36
    IPO process, 38–39
    planning and, 38
    pricing and, 127
    road shows, 228
    timetable, 39, 40–41
    underwriters and, 182
Tombstones, 28, 41, 230
Trailing earnings, 126
Transfer agent, 33
Treasury common stock, 113
Trust Indenture Act of 1939, The, 138
Truth in Securities Act, 135

U

U-7, 147, 154
ULOR, 154
Unaudited stub report, 197
Underwriter(s), 163–82. *See also* Self-
   underwriting
    best effort, 26, 167, 232–33, 234
    commissions, 27–28
    company evaluation by, 172–78
    costs, 27–29, 34
    finders and, 168
    firm commitment, 26, 166–67, 233–34
    industrial classification of, 166
    letter of intent with, 176–78
    negotiations and, 175–76
    nonaccountable expense allowance,
     28–29
    overallotment and, 250–51
    registration statement and, 201–2

shopping and, 169
    stabilization and, 250
    types of, 164–67
    underwriting agreement. *See*
     Underwriting agreement
    warrants, 174–75, 178
Underwriter's discount, 27
Underwriting agreement, 178–81
    cancellation, 181
    conditions, 180–81
    covenants, 180
    indemnification, 181
    introduction and definitions, 179
    representations and warranties, 179
    terms of the offering, 180
Uniform Limited Offering Registration,
   147
Uniform State Securities Act, 219
Unit investment trusts, 193
Unit offerings, 292
Utility companies, 138

V

Value, and pricing compared, 125–26
Venture Associates Ltd., 118
Venture capital clubs, 329
Venture capital firms, 18
Venture leasing companies, 18
Video presentations, 229
Virtual corporation, 56
Voting stock, control of, 12–14, 15, 118–21

W–Y

Wall Street Journal, The, 243, 281
Warrants, 18, 123–24, 174–75
    blind pools and, 292–93
    underwriter, 174–75, 178
Web sites
    DPO, 321
    SEC, 138
    Venture Associates, 329
Wholesale market makers, 243–44
Wholesale underwriters, 164. *See also*
   Underwriter(s)
Young, John E., 4, 5, 68–69

About the Author

James B. Arkebauer is the founder of Venture Associates, a Denver-based investment banking and consulting firm. He has been an entrepreneur for more than 25 years, and his experience in corporate finance includes all phases of this discipline. He has been involved in risk analysis and evaluation of many new technologies, assembled management teams, and structured and implemented equity and debt financing for private companies and more than 50 public companies. He is a cofounder and chairman of the Rockies Venture Club, one of the country's leading groups in the support of entrepreneurs; a frequent lecturer; and the author of six books, including *OTC Financial Public Relations, Ultrapreneuring, The McGraw-Hill Guide to Writing A High Impact Business Plan,* and *Golden Entrepreneuring.* More information on his firm can be obtained at his Web site: http://www.venturea.com.